PEASANTS AND GOVERNMENT IN THE RUSSIAN REVOLUTION

Peasants and Government in the Russian Revolution

Graeme J. Gill

Lecturer in Political Science
University of Tasmania

BARNES & NOBLE
BOOKS
10 East 53d St., New York 10022
(a division of Harper & Row Publishers, Inc.)

First published 1979 by
THE MACMILLAN PRESS LTD
London and Basingstoke

Published in the U.S.A. 1979 by
HARPER & ROW PUBLISHERS, INC.
BARNES & NOBLE IMPORT DIVISION

Printed in Great Britain

Library of Congress Cataloging in Publication Data

Gill, Graeme J
    Peasants and government in the Russian Revolution.

    Based in part on the author's thesis, London School
of Economics and Political Science.
    Bibliography: p.
    Includes index.
    1. Russia—History—Revolution, 1917–1921.
    2. Russia—Politics and government—1917–1936.
    3. Peasantry—Russia. I. Title.
DK265.G422 1979   947.084'1   78-25841
ISBN 0–06–492406–8

To Heather

Contents

Preface

Most western studies of the Russian revolution have concentrated their attention on events in the capital, documenting and explaining the shifting patterns of elite politics in Petrograd. This concentration is easily explained. The source materials available outside the Soviet archives are richer for Petrograd than for any other part of the country. But beside this purely mechanical factor is the quite natural disposition of those studying political science or history to focus their gaze on the point where the most important developments are occurring. In Russia this was the capital. It was here that the three-hundred-year-old Romanov dynasty was pushed from power in February and where, eight months later, the bolsheviks gave the Provisional Government the push that was needed to despatch it to Trotsky's 'rubbish bin of history'. The course of revolution in Russia in 1917 cannot be understood without studying the events in Petrograd. However, equally to ignore what was taking place outside the capital is to gain only a one-sided view of the Russian revolution. Not only is it one-sided by omitting two major frames of the triptych of the revolution (workers, soldiers and peasants) but, by implying that the capital remained autonomous of and unaffected by events in the rural areas in particular, it hinders our understanding of the mechanics of revolution in Petrograd. The focus of this study is the long-neglected rural areas.

The aim of this work is three-fold: to outline and explain the course of developments in the rural areas between February and October 1917, to analyse the achievements and failures of the Provisional Government in the field of rural affairs, and to suggest what effect developments in the countryside had on the situation in the capital and the creation of conditions favourable for Lenin and the bolsheviks to seize power. There are few dominating figures in this study, as there are in those which focus on the capital where personality was a major factor in elite politics. The focus is the broad sweep of the peasantry on the one hand and, on the other, governmental policy decisions. Background material on the political situation in Petrograd throughout the year has been kept to a minimum and introduced only when it was essential to illuminate the topic under discussion. This book does not aim to provide a comprehensive history of the Provisional Government. However it does present a detailed analysis of government legislation in the rural areas. The amount of detail is justified by the effect the government's decisions had in the countryside and because government action in this sphere of concern reflects in microcosm its general policy approach, and highlights the internal faults of the government which contributed so much to its fall. Of course this book is not the definitive work on the subject. That cannot be written until all the sources are available to us in an unedited form. That day is still a long way off. However if this book causes those scholars interested in the field to rethink some of their views, to ask more questions, and generally to enquire further into the revolution, it will have served its purpose.

This book is based in part on my Ph.D. thesis completed at the London School of Economics and Political Science between 1973 and 1975. In London I had the privilege of working with Professor Leonard Schapiro. His friendship, guidance, stimulus and encouragement played a major part in the production of this work, although it goes without saying that the shortcomings remain my own responsibility. Many people on both sides of the globe have contributed to this work, both knowingly and unknowingly. To these people I offer a collective thanks. However, one further person should be singled out for thanks, my wife Heather to whom this book is dedicated. She has had to live with the peasants for far too long, and were it not for her forbearance and support, in all forms, this work would never have been completed. I must also acknowledge the part played by those people working in the following libraries whose assistance greatly facilitated my task: the British Library of Political and Economic Science, the British Museum, the library at the School of Slavonic and East European Studies in the University of London, Bodleian Library, Bibliothèque de la Documentation Internationale Contemporaine, Australian National Library, and the Morris Miller Library in the University of Tasmania. To Jane and Kaye for handling a very messy early manuscript, and the girls in the Arts Faculty typing pool in the University of Tasmania for typing the final manuscript swiftly and accurately, my thanks. I would also like to thank the editors of the following journals for permission to reproduce material from my articles which appeared in the journals: *Soviet Studies*, Jan. 1978 (The Mainsprings of Peasant Action in 1917); *Slavic Review*, June 1978 (The Failure of Rural Policy in Russia, February–October 1917); and *Sbornik*, 2, 1976 (The Role of the Countryside in an Urban Revolution – A Short Note).

Dates are according to the Old Style calendar which, in the twentieth century, was 13 days behind that in the West. Russian names have been retained, anglicisation only being applied to names already widely familiar in the West. Geographically the study is restricted to European Russia in 1917 excluding areas occupied by the Germans, the Caucasus and Finland.

GRAEME J. GILL

Glossary

artel'	a peasant group organised for cooperative activity in production, consumption, or the sale of labour
barshchina	a form of obligation under serfdom whereby the peasant fulfilled his obligation by working on his master's estate
chinovnik	government functionary; bureaucrat (pl. *chinovniki*)
dessiatina	a measure of area equalling 2.7 acres (pl. *dessiatiny*)
duma	a body of municipal self-government (pl. *dumy*)
funt	a measure of weight equalling one pound (pl. *funti*)
guberniia	a province (pl. *gubernii*)
khutor	a farm established under the Stolypin legislation in which arable land was separated from that of the commune and the farmer's house was situated on his land (pl. *khutori*)
muzhik	peasant (pl. *muzhiki*)
oblast'	an administrative region, (pl. *oblasti*)
obrok	a form of obligation under serfdom whereby the peasant fulfilled his obligation to the master by payment in cash or kind
obshchina	peasant commune
otrub	a farm established under the Stolypin legislation in which arable land was separated from that of the commune but the farmer's house remained in the peasant village

pogrom	riot accompanied by killing and/or property destruction
PSR	Socialist Revolutionary Party
pud	a measure of weight equalling 36 pounds (pl. *pudi*)
RSFSR	Russian Soviet Federated Socialist Republic
skhod	traditional peasant village assembly (pl. *skhodi*)
stavka	General Army Headquarters
uezd	a county (pl. *uezdy*)
usad'ba	a kitchen garden around the peasant's home, held on a hereditary basis
verst	a measure of distance, slightly larger than a kilometre (pl. *versta*)
volost	a district or parish (pl. *volosti*)
zemliachestva	association for mutual support set up in the towns, consisting of people from the same areas of the country
zemskii nachal'nik	a land captain, an official appointed in 1889 with wide powers over the peasantry (pl. *zemskie nachal'niki*)
zemstvo	an organ of rural local government (pl. *zemstva*)

1 The Growth of Tension in the Countryside

During 1917 the political structure of Russia was changed fundamentally by a process of revolution stretching over eight months of
the year. In February, the apparent solid edifice of tsarism collapsed
as hunger, privation and war-weariness combined to undermine the
foundations of support upon which that regime rested. The fall of
the tsar was followed by a progressive radicalisation of the popular
mood in both the city and the countryside until that mood had left
far behind it the positions adopted by the succession of moderate
governments which held office until October. Lacking widespread
popular support in the countryside, at the front, and in the cities,
by October the government was vulnerable to attack by any
group which could marshal the force to push it from power. In
October the bolsheviks were able to master both the resolve and the
force to carry this out. The peasants played a major part in the
eight-month revolutionary process which culminated in bolshevik
victory. The roots of the peasants' actions lay in the character of
traditional peasant life.[1]

In Russia, as in all traditional societies, the life of the peasantry
revolved around the land. Living on the produce of small plots and
working long hours in the fields, most peasants lived in villages into
which the world of the industrialising towns and of intellectual and
cultural exchange entered only marginally, if at all. The peasants'
world view was focused almost entirely on questions of cultivation
and agriculture while their whole life style was shaped by the cycles
of labour in the fields, by the routine of farm-work. Throughout
much of the year, the peasants' waking hours were dominated by
the struggle to eke from their plots of land sufficient produce to
satisfy their own needs and to meet the multitude of demands made
upon them; a good crop resulted in sufficiency while a bad one
meant hunger, greater indebtedness, and possibly death. For many
peasants life was lived on the edge of catastrophe, with the

relationship to the land being the prime factor determining the good year from the bad. This relationship was measured in subtle balances between the number of 'eaters', the amount of available labour power, soil fertility and weather conditions. For the peasants, the key to the most satisfactory balance between these factors was greater access to land; it was believed that this would lead to increased production which would relieve the pressure of 'eaters' on resources, help overcome limited soil fertility, and limit the effects of bad weather. Land was regarded as the key to peasant well-being.

The physical contours of rural life within which the Russian peasantry lived and worked in the half century prior to the revolution stemmed from the legislation emancipating the serfs in the 1860s. It is not necessary to analyse the details of the incredibly complex legislation enacted at this time to deliver the serfs from bondage,[2] but its general features must be noted if the resentment festering in the villages at that time is to be understood. Although there were differences in detail in the legislation emancipating the serfs on private estates, serfs on land owned by members of the imperial family not in line for succession, state serfs, and those in the nine western *gubernii*, in essence the legislation was the same: it provided for the release of the peasant from his existing legal obligations along with the allocation to him of a plot of land. However the peasant did not receive this land free of charge. Within two years of the announcement of the legislation, during which time a 'land charter' was to be drawn up on all estates, the peasants were to enter a situation of 'temporary obligation' whereby the land-owner retained full ownership of his land, but ceded to the peasants part of his estate for use in perpetuity in exchange for rent and services. This situation could be ended only through redemption of the land by the peasant, a practice which became compulsory in 1881. The process of redemption was financed primarily by the state treasury. The land-owner was to relinquish his land in exchange for interest-bearing bonds and immediately-exchangeable credit notes issued by the treasury to the value of 80 per cent (in some cases 75 per cent) of the capital value of the land to be redeemed. The remainder was to be paid by the peasants direct to the land-owner through private agreement. The peasants were expected to re-imburse the treasury over a period of 49 years (44 years for former state serfs) by annual redemption payments. The peasants could escape the financial obligations involved in the redemption process by accepting a plot of land one-quarter the size of the maximum or statutory norm prevailing in that area, but few chose this 'beggarly allotment', which seemed to promise certain penury.

The terms of the emancipation engendered widespread frustration, disappointment and anger among the peasants, sentiments reflected in the outbreak of rural unrest in many areas during the early 1860s. Opposition to the imposition of redemption payments was widespread in the villages. The peasants' traditional belief that land should belong to those who worked it with their own hands[3] led them to view redemption payments as a means of making them pay for the long overdue transfer to them of their own property; they felt they were being made to pay for something that belonged to them by right. The affront to traditional peasant sensibilities posed by the concept of redemption payments was exacerbated by the level of redemption that was demanded; except in the western *gubernii*, the land the peasants were to redeem was greatly over-valued, with the result that the price they had to pay was higher than the market price of the land itself. It has been calculated that throughout European Russia, the original redemption loans which the government advanced to land-owners and then sought to recover from the peasants through the annual redemption payments exceeded the market value of the land under redemption by 218,800,000 roubles.[4] However not only did the peasants have to pay for the land they received at exorbitant prices, but also much land remained outside their control; private land-owners who did not work the land with their own labour were allowed to retain large expanses of their former holdings. The resentment that this caused was given a sharp cutting edge by peasant realisation that they were, in many instances, not being granted sufficient land on which to eke out a reasonable living.

In introducing the new legislation emancipating the peasants, the tsar had placed responsibility for the implementation of the new measures in the rural areas largely on the shoulders of the local land-owning nobility. However most of the nobility had greeted the legislation with trepidation, fearing that it represented a major threat to their economic position. Consequently they used the power granted to them under the legislation to protect their interests. The legislation specified maximum and minimum allotments per male soul throughout the country, with the exception of the south and southeast where a single statutory norm was established in each area. The maxima and minima, which were based on the average sizes of the pre-emancipation holdings per serf for each region, were to act as guidelines within which the land-owners and the peasants were to reach agreement on the size of the individual allotments. In the northern half of the country the soil was not conducive to the widespread cultivation of cereal grains. This is reflected in the practice of many land-owners passing large tracts of their estates over to their serfs and seeking the fulfilment of serfdom obligations through payment in cash or kind (*obrok*) rather than serf labour in their fields. In the southern black earth region the soil was very fertile and suitable for the cultivation of cereal grains on a commercial basis. As a result, under serfdom the land-owners tried to retain as much land as possible under their control, using tied serf labour to work that land (*barshchina*). The relative value of the soil in these two regions was reflected in the smaller size of serf allotments in the grain-producing south than in the grain-consuming north.[5] This, in turn, meant that the norms of allotment sizes to be gained at emancipation were smaller in the more productive region of the south than in the more barren north. This situation was exacerbated by the practice, common in the north, of land-owners using the emancipation legislation to rid themselves of what they considered to be unprofitable land, gaining large redemption payments in exchange. In the south, land-owners tried to maximise the land remaining under their control. The emancipation legislation gave the land-owners in the extreme south the right to retain 50 per cent of the non-waste land of their former holdings and in the black earth and forest zones 33 per cent, even if this meant reducing peasant holdings to the minimum size permitted and 'cutting off' areas of land from the holdings the peasants had worked under serfdom. Robinson reports that only in the sixteen *gubernii* of the western region (because the terms of the emancipation legislation were more favourable to the peasants there than in the rest of Russia) and the infertile areas of the extreme north, north-east and east was the peasants' allotment area increased as a result of emancipation. In all the other *gubernii* of European Russia the area held by the peasants was reduced as a result of the emancipation legislation; in that part of the black earth zone stretching from Poltava and Ekaterinoslav in the west to Kazan and Samara in the east, the reduction in most *gubernii* amounted to at least 25 per cent of the former allotments, while in Samara the figure was almost 42 per cent.[6] Furthermore not only did many peasants receive less land as a result of emancipation, but because of the powers given to the land-owners to determine what type of land the peasants would receive, frequently their post-emancipation holdings did not include meadows and pasture-land for the support of their livestock, or even ready access to water and forest-land. Thus the economic base of many peasant households in the half century before the revolution was very flimsy; not only did they possess an insufficient area of arable land to support themselves, but their failure to obtain other types of land as well made it impossible to achieve the balance necessary in such a finely-tuned economic situation.[7]

The emancipation legislation not only resulted in the peasants being left with insufficient land, but by reinforcing the traditional peasant commune as the dominant factor in the countryside, it also locked them into a formal structure which prevented the most efficient utilisation of the land at their disposal. In almost all instances the commune was made collectively responsible for the redemption of the allotments of its individual members; only if collective responsibility was assumed would the state provide the finance necessary for the beginning of the redemption process. The commune was also held collectively responsible for state taxes owed by its members. Under these circumstances communal control over its individual members was strengthened. Personal departure from the repartitional commune, both permanent and temporary, required the approval of the communal *skhod* and the head of the household, while the withdrawal of a land-holder required him to surrender his allotment to the commune, to pay off half the debt on his land, and to persuade the other members of the commune to assume responsibility for the remainder of the debt. If the peasant could not raise sufficient capital to meet his part of the debt or could not persuade the other members to take on the further financial obligations involved in accepting responsibility for the remainder of his debt, he could not leave the commune. In the hereditary commune the land-holder could renounce his membership and obligations only by paying off the debts on his land in their entirety or finding someone who was willing to take over his land with the debts included. Personal separation from both types of commune was thus in practice very difficult. The over-valuation of the land involved in the redemption payments made it difficult to find people willing to take over the allotment land of those wishing to renounce their commune membership, and therefore complete separations from the commune were not common.

In addition to restricting peasant mobility and the transfer of land in this way, the communal structure also hindered the efficient cultivation of the peasants' plots. There were two types of peasant commune, the repartitional and the hereditary, with the former weakest in the north-west, south-west and parts of the south-east.[8] In both types of commune the *usad'ba*, or kitchen garden situated around the peasant's house, was owned by the household on a hereditary basis, while meadows, pastures and forests remained undivided and in common usage for all member households of the commune. In the repartitional commune arable land periodically was redistributed among the constituent households, while arable land in the hereditary commune was assigned at emancipation by the commune to the individual households to be possessed in perpetuity. However the difference in tenure arrangements did not give any greater independence to the peasant in the hereditary commune when it came to cultivating his plots. Peasant agriculture throughout Russia was based on primitive technology and the three-field system, involving the annual rotation on a three-year cycle of spring crop, winter crop, and fallow. Individual peasant plots rarely were consolidated into single holdings, instead consisting of numerous strips of land scattered over the expanse of the commune's arable land. Even in the hereditary commune, consolidation of strips was rare.[9] In practice, consolidation was discouraged by the communal structure: in the repartitional commune the consolidation of an individual's holdings required the consent of two-thirds of the *skhod*, while in the hereditary commune the consent of all householders whose strips would be affected directly was required before consolidation could take place.[10] Both types of agreement were very difficult to obtain, thereby condemning most peasant land to remain fractured into small splinters spread across the countryside.

The division of peasant land into a multitude of small strips was a very inefficient basis for peasant agriculture. Many of the strips were so narrow that they were measured in terms of the width of a bast shoe, while frequently the strips were situated kilometres from one another and from the peasant's home. Furthermore there appears to have been little cooperation between peasant households when it came to the cultivation of their individual strips. This contradiction between communal tenure and individual cultivation, allied to the physical layout of peasant agriculture, undermined any prospect of the introduction of new, more efficient farming methods. Without greater cooperation between the peasants and the consolidation of their strips, substantial improvement in peasant agriculture was impossible. Under these conditions all were forced to adopt the same rotation patterns and work schedules, and initiative was squashed by the weight of mediocrity, ignorance and tradition. Even in the hereditary commune peasant land-owners could not please themselves what they did with their land; their work programmes were coordinated by the communal authorities, just like their counterparts in the repartitional commune.

The emancipation legislation made the peasants into an estate of their own, with the high wall of the commune restricting peasant escape from the land and acting as a buffer between the outside world and the narrow world of the rural cultivator. The tsarist administrative system was not firmly rooted in the countryside in the half century preceding the outbreak of the war. The reform of 1864, which established the basic structure of local government in operation at the time of the tsar's fall, gave the newly-established *zemstvo* wide powers over all aspects of local life, including education, health, agricultural development, stock breeding, trade, industry, maintenance of transport facilities, fire prevention, food supply, postal services and, indirectly, law enforcement.[11] However these bodies were based in the *guberniia* and *uezd* main towns, and were therefore to some extent isolated from many of the villages over which they were to exercise administrative control; direct contact between *zemstvo* administrators and the peasant villages often was limited. After the creation of the post of *zemskii nachal'nik* in 1889, the official administrative structure weighed more heavily on the peasants. The *zemskii nachal'nik*, a post which usually was filled by a member of the local nobility, had wide administrative and judicial power in the countryside, although this power was pruned in the wake of the agrarian disturbances of 1905–7. The basic responsibility of this official was to exercise supervision over the economic and moral well-being of the peasantry and, with the help of the police, the maintenance of discipline in the rural areas. With wide powers of review over the decisions of peasant assemblies, of discipline over individual peasants and, after 1893, limited power in the distribution of land, the *zemskii nachal'nik* had power to interfere widely in peasant life.

Within the bounds drawn by the state and personified by the *zemskii nachal'nik* (and these bounds were in practice often wider than a simple enumeration of the powers of the *zemskii nachal'nik* suggests) the peasants were self-governing through their own institutions. The principal organ of village or communal life[12] was the *skhod*, an assembly of the heads of the constituent households which decided questions facing the community by a process of wide-ranging discussion, usually followed by a vote. Such meetings rarely were the examples of direct democracy that socialists of the late nineteenth and early twentieth century often claimed; almost inevitably their proceedings were dominated by a few of the more active, powerful and wealthy peasants.[13] It was the *skhod* which, within the bounds outlined above, provided the guidance, direction and impetus for the peasants' lives. Within its competence was included the exercise of some judicial functions, control over the use and protection of land, organisation of some public services and amenities, collection and use of funds for common expenses, apportionment of land and taxation obligations, and punishment of arrears. The *skhod* normally elected an elder and other officials to carry out these functions. In addition, the communal *skhod* played a major part in the election of representatives to the *volost skhod*, a body similar to that in the communes or villages which together formed the *volost*. Thus peasant life in the wake of the emancipation was guided most immediately in all its aspects by these two peasant institutions; the *volost skhod* dealt with intra-commune matters. while the village or commune *skhod* dealt with intra-commune matters. These village-based institutions were to be of fundamental significance during 1917.

Emancipation had left the peasants bitter and disappointed. They had not received what they had hoped for—all the land without payment—but instead had gained what was widely considered to be insufficient land at exorbitant cost. Furthermore the traditional peasant commune had been strengthened and its role in the peasants' lives made even more dominant than it had been prior to 1861, with the unfortunate consequences for agricultural improvement mentioned above. In the wake of emancipation, peasant land hunger was rife. This position did not improve during the latter half of the nineteenth century.

In seeking to alleviate the land hunger prevalent throughout the countryside, a number of different courses of action were open to the peasants. The income of many households was supplemented by the labour of some of their members outside their plots. Large numbers of peasants migrated into the cities to seek employment in the expanding industrial sector of the economy. The links between these permanent migrants and their home villages remained strong, at least during the first generation; periodically they remitted part of their income back to their families remaining in the villages. Others sought seasonal work, either in the factories during the winter or on the remaining large estates during the busy times of the year. Many peasant households sought to supplement their income through the small-scale production of handicraft goods. Income from such pursuits seems to have been very low, and certainly lower than the cost of the labour involved. However, since it was done primarily at times of the year when agricultural work could not be pursued or by those whose labour was not required on the farm because of the chronic excess of peasant labour in the countryside, the value of this cottage industry lay purely in the addition to the household income which it made. No accurate figures are available to indicate the number of people engaged in these activities nor the extent of the contribution they made to the household income.[14]

The most important means of alleviating the pressure of needs on resources was to increase those resources by the acquisition of more land. This occurred on a large scale between 1861 and 1905 through the purchase and rental of the land of non-peasant land-owners and of some of those who migrated to the cities. The peasant purchase of land began almost immediately after emancipation, but it received an extra stimulus with the foundation of the Peasants' Land Bank in 1883, an institution designed to make finance more easily available to the village dwellers. Between 1877 and 1905 peasant purchases added 17,090,000 *dessiatiny* of non-allotment land to the peasants' land-holdings.[15] The practice of leasing land from private land-owners also was widespread during the latter half of the nineteenth century. However definitive statistics on the extent to which this occurred do not exist; estimates of the dimensions of peasant rental at the turn of the century have ranged from 19,800,000 to 49,800,000 *dessiatiny*.[16] If we accept the lower figure, it means that for every six *dessiatiny* of allotment land in the peasants' hands, they were renting one *dessiatina* of ploughland. Rental was in the form both of money and labour. Most of the land that was added to the peasants' holdings came from the former nobles; it has been estimated that between 1862 and the outbreak of the war, the nobles relinquished 53 per cent of their land.[17] However this enormous increase in the amount of land under the peasants' control brought about through purchase and rental, an increase that has been calculated at 30 per cent, did not keep pace with the rapid growth of the rural population, which increased by about 50 per cent during the latter half of the nineteenth century.[18] The enormous population growth, particularly in the black earth zone, created increased pressure from within the peasant community for the division of households' holdings and the establishment of new households. This resulted in a decline in the size of peasant plots. Although average figures without reference to regional variations and land quality can be misleading, they can also be useful by highlighting a particular situation in stark form. According to one observer, the size of the average plot per male peasant fell from 4.8 *dessiatiny* in 1860 to 2.6 in 1900.[19] Thus the widespread peasant acquisition of non-peasant land during the half century after emancipation did not result in a substantial increase in the amount of land at the disposal of peasant households.

However the declining sizes of their plots was not the only problem that confronted the peasants at this time; the demands that they had to meet from the produce of their plots were becoming increasingly onerous. In this respect the extension of peasant landholding was a mixed blessing. Where the purchase or rental of land occurred it increased peasant production of food per household, but, as Robinson argued,[20] the increased production usually did not cover the rental or the repayments, and therefore it placed the peasants even further in debt. In addition, the widespread purchase of non-peasant land drove the price of that land up, thereby undermining the peasants' future prospects as purchasers; according to one source, the average price in the 45 *gubernii* of European Russia on the eve of emancipation was 12.69 roubles per *dessiatina*, but by the end of the century this had risen to 66.92. In the Ukraine the price rise was sharper, from 17.76 to 119.80, and in the southern steppes from 11.34 to 123.97.[21] Although lacking the precision we would like, these figures do indicate the way in which land prices soared. These rapidly-rising prices forced the peasants either to forgo the extra land or to go even further into debt. Furthermore the peasants had to meet a whole range of pressing obligations from the produce of their plots: the expanding population had to be fed, until their abolition in the wake of the 1905 agrarian disturbances redemption payments had to be made, taxes had to be paid to the state, *zemstvo* and commune, and in many instances loans incurred in acquiring extra land had to be repaid. Indirect taxation on goods purchased by the peasants also was high. The weight of these obligations bore down heavily on the peasants, most of whom fell increasingly behind in their payments the longer the period wore on; by 1900 the peasants were in arrears on their redemption payments for an amount greater than that which they owed for that year.[22] A police report of 1905 succinctly stated the problem:

> Very often the peasants do not have enough allotment land, and during the year cannot feed themselves, clothe themselves, heat their homes, keep their tools and livestock, secure seed for sowing and, lastly, discharge all their taxes and obligations to the state, the *zemstvo* and the commune.[23]

Thus the half century after emancipation witnessed the exacerbation of widespread peasant land hunger as the weight of their obligations increased while the size of the plots from which they had to meet those obligations shrank. The only solution to this problem in the peasants' eyes was to increase the area of land under their control.

Peasant frustration and resentment at the continuing land hunger welled up in 1905 into an attempt, lasting with interruptions until 1907, to increase the amount of land in the peasants' hands by seizing the land of non-peasant land-owners. However this effort collapsed, along with the rest of the revolutionary upsurge, before the peasants could gain substantial amelioration of their position. Nevertheless it did prompt the government to take some action in the agrarian sphere. However the government's response did not please the vast majority of the peasants but served instead to increase the resentment and land hunger characteristic of most rural dwellers. The central plank of the government's action was Stolypin's 'wager on the sturdy and the strong', an attempt to undermine the authority of the commune (which in the government's eyes had proved itself too revolutionary in 1905) by making it easier for people to withdraw from that body and establish enclosed holdings. The aim of creating a sturdy class of yeoman farmers dedicated to the principle of private property also had the added advantage of creating an environment more favourable for the introduction of new and improved farming techniques which would have been impossible to implement under the strip system characteristic of the commune. The core of the Stolypin legislation is contained in six statutes: on 3 November 1905 redemption debts were cancelled; on 4 March 1906 Land Organisation Commissions were established to supervise the process of land consolidation in the various areas; on 5 October 1906 communal authorities were stripped of some of the power they had exercised over commune members, including the power to prevent a person from leaving the commune by refusing to issue him with a passport; and on 9 November 1906 a decision was taken dealing with land tenure and the reallocation of allotment lands. This was extended and amplified by decisions on 14 June 1910 and 29 May 1911.[24] In communes with hereditary tenure, individual householders could bring about the consolidation of their own land only by gaining the consent of all land-owners whose land would be displaced in the process. This was not changed in the new legislation. However the former provision that a consolidation of all plots could take place only with the consent of all householders was changed in 1906 to require a two-thirds majority, and in 1910 a simple majority. The import of this legislation for the repartitional commune was more wide-ranging. According to the new legislation, individual sep-aration of tenure, and therefore the establishment of an hereditary holding, could be carried out at the will of the householder. Any householder could demand the consolidation of his holdings at any time (the 1906 decision had specified that such a claim could be made only at the time of a general redistribution, unless the householder had previously gained a separation of title, in which case he could make the claim at any time, but this was changed in 1910), and the commune was obliged to implement this, provided that the local Land Organisation Commission was satisfied that it would involve no 'special difficulties'. If 'special difficulties' were encountered, the commune had to offer a money indemnity in place of the land, the size of the indemnity being determined by the Commission. Thus the repartitional commune, in which the majority of peasants lived, lost all power to oppose the demands of one of its members for the consolidation of his land and the separation of title. Consolidation of all allotments remained at the will of a two-thirds majority. After 1910 in communes where there had been no repartition since the original land endowment the land-holders automatically became proprietors of the land in their hands.

The Stolypin legislation appeared, on paper, to strike a telling blow at the commune. Indeed in theory this was the case: the liberation of the individual householder from the commune's power over the land undermined the basis of the commune's dominating position. However in the years between the adoption of these decisions and the fall of the tsar, the commune was not substantially weakened. Although inadequacies in the available statistics prevent accurate calculation of the number of peasant households leaving the commune, more than 80 per cent of member households seem to have remained within the traditional institution.[25] Many of the newly-consolidated holdings retained strong links with the commune. The separators often preferred to retain their home and *usad'ba* in the traditional village, travelling daily to their consolidated landholding to work (*otrub*) rather than to separate themselves physically from the village by moving their house onto their newly-enclosed land (*khutor*). Even when the separators established *khutori*, usually they retained usage rights in the undivided land, the pastures, meadows and forests.

In one sense the departure of the separators from the commune strengthened the traditional structure, thereby producing the opposite result to that desired by Stolypin. The new-found strength of the commune stemmed from the attitude toward the separators adopted by those who remained within the traditional institution. Those remaining in the commune were opposed to the enclosure movement. The consolidation of geographically-diverse strips into a single holding could not be achieved in any one instance without the at least partial readjustment of the other strips. Frequently such a readjustment involved a decline in the overall quality of the land held by particular individuals who retained their land within the commune. This caused resentment, particularly since it may have been forced on the commune against the wishes of the majority. Moreover by taking advantage of loans through the Peasants' Land Bank, loans which could be sustained more easily because of the better economic prospects offered by consolidated holdings than by scattered strip cultivation, many separators were able to enlarge the size of their farms through the purchase and rental of state land, privately-owned land, and the land of peasants leaving the villages for the city. The increase in the size of enclosed holdings in this way was resented by those remaining in the commune because they felt that this denied to them the use of much land which otherwise they may have been able to use: communal land, and therefore land to which they would have had access in a future redistribution, was shrinking because of enclosure and the acquisition by separators of the land of those going to the city, while much non-communal land which they may have wished to acquire in the future was being removed from the market by the separators' actions. Already hungry for land, the peasants in the commune perceived their future prospects of acquiring more land to be threatened by enclosures. In their opposition to the enclosure movement, as personified by the separators, the commune-based peasants fell back on the commune as their chief support. The only means of protecting their economic interests against the threat posed by enclosures was the restoration of communal norms. The implications of the Stolypin reform thus served to reinforce the sense of communal membership among the peasants remaining within the traditional structure.

With the seizure of privately-owned estates temporarily closed as an avenue to increased peasant land-holding after 1907, the peasants turned once again to legal channels to gain control of more land. Between 1906 and the outbreak of the war, the peasants of European Russia embarked on the rental and purchase of land on a wide scale; according to one source, 9.5 million *dessiatiny* of non-allotment land were bought by the peasants (and cossacks) in 47 *gubernii* of European Russia in this period.[26] However this practice was once again leading the peasants into massive debt because of their inability to purchase land without financial assistance. Nevertheless it was expanding peasant control over the land, with the result that, according to Robinson, by 1914 they owned 40 per cent of the land in European Russia, although the proportion of exploitable land in their hands was undoubtedly higher than this.[27]

The war had a major impact on Russian agriculture. The first area to be affected by the opening of hostilities was that of labour power on the farms. The army grew from a pre-war size of 1,370,000 to somewhere between 15 and 16 million in mid-1917, with 80 per cent of those called to the colours being peasants. This constituted 40–50 per cent of the able-bodied male village population.[28] The effects of this were far-reaching. It led to a severe shortage of workers on those farms, including the remaining large privately-owned estates, which used hired labour; peasants employed in this way returned to their family plots to take the place of relatives called to the front, if they were not thus called themselves. Many peasants also left agricultural work for the high wages in the factories to replace the urban workers who entered the army. Even the use of prisoners-of-war and refugees in field-work could not compensate the larger estates for this loss of the regular work-force.[29] Nor could this loss be overcome by increased use of machinery because most industrial production was turned to the war effort and traditional foreign sources of such goods were cut off by the war.[30] Unable to work their land, many land-owners sought to profit from it through rental to the peasants. An accurate assessment of the extent of this practice cannot be made, but the desire of the land-owners to lease out their land is reflected in the decline in rental prices during the early years of the war; according to one source, the price (for what area of land is not specified) fell as follows: 1912–14 14.68R, 1915 9.95R, 1916 4.32R.[31] By the eve of the fall of the tsar the peasants had more than 75 per cent of all the agriculturally-exploitable land in European Russia in their hands.[32] This must have been very close to the maximum which the peasants could work under the war-time conditions, since much privately-owned land remained unworked during the war years; the sown area in European Russia decreased by about 10 per cent between 1914 and 1917.[33] Most of this decrease occurred in non-peasant agriculture; private land-owners in Kherson, Taurida, Saratov, Samara, Ufa, Orenburg and Astrakhan experienced decreases in area as high as 50 per cent.[34]

The labour shortage which afflicted the larger farms did not at first affect peasant plots, most of which did not use hired labour. The mobilisation of men siphoned from the rural economy some of that enormous pool of under-employed which bedevilled a land-hungry peasantry; it has been estimated that between 50 and 80 per cent of a peasant family's working power was unnecessary.[35] The places of those called to the war could be filled by the reserve army of the under-employed, by those working under hire agreements elsewhere, or even by those members of the household normally exempt from field-work, the very young and the very old. In addition, attention could be turned from some handicraft pursuits, factory-work and, as a last resort, land rented from land-owners, to the family plot to ensure that the family did not starve. Such reserves of human labour also helped to compensate, at least initially, for the loss of livestock as a result of the war; both working horses and working cattle decreased in number by about 40 per cent in European Russia during the war.[36] Furthermore the peasants benefited from a new prosperity flowing into the countryside. The closure of foreign markets, high grain prices (which were of benefit only to the peasant producers, not to the consumers), *zemstvo* allowances for the families of mobilised men, government compensation for requisitioned livestock, and the inability to buy liquor (traditionally a large item in the peasant budget) because of prohibition, ensured that during the early part of the war many peasants had more to eat and more money in their pockets than at any time before.[37]

However such apparent signs of outward prosperity were not

soundly based. Private land-owner farming was openly in disarray and, the longer the war dragged on, the greater were the difficulties experienced by peasant agriculture. The tools and equipment used by the peasants were deteriorating and with industrial energies turned primarily towards the war effort and imports restricted, there was no means of replacing them or of gaining the metal parts needed to carry out repairs. The front continued to drain the villages of their manpower, straining the labour resources of peasant households to their utmost.[38] The continued decline in the number of livestock on the farms exacerbated this labour situation and created shortages of natural fertiliser which, in the absence of imported mineral fertiliser, was essential to gain the high yields required. In addition, the stocks of capital which the peasant had accumulated during the early part of the war were being eaten away by increased exactions for the war effort and by rapidly-growing inflation.[39] The introduction of government regulation of the grain trade late in 1916 exacerbated this situation for the producers by placing limits on their main money-earner while leaving their main items of expenditure unregulated. As 1917 opened, many peasants were in a difficult situation: their economic base was deteriorating rapidly and yet there was little they could do about it. In this situation of uncertainty, the peasants' gaze again turned to the traditionally-perceived panacea, the land currently in non-peasant hands.

The fifty-six years between the beginning of emancipation in 1861 and the fall of the tsar in February 1917 thus witnessed the growth of widespread peasant frustration, anger and resentment. Their hopes and expectations were crushed by the provisions of the emancipation legislation, and their search for economic security was condemned to failure by the combination of rapid population growth and primitive agricultural technology. In this situation of economic difficulty, the peasants looked with an increasingly hungry gaze at the expanses of land still in the hands of non-peasant owners, the land which they felt rightfully belonged to them and which they had been unjustly denied at emancipation. Their resentment was given a sharp focus by the common practice of renting land from these non-peasant land-owners; they felt they were being forced to pay for something that was their own property by people whose interest in the land seemed not to be related to a desire to put it to productive use, but simply to drain profits from it. This sense of injustice was fuelled by the naive belief that possession of the land not currently in their hands would solve their current economic difficulties; land remained the panacea in the peasant vision. Developments during this period thus brought a vivid contrast to the forefront of peasant consciousness: while the acquisition of more land was perceived to be the means to the solution of their difficult economic position, there were wide expanses of exploitable land which they did not possess and which the owners did not wish to work productively themselves. The non-peasant land-owner appeared to stand between continued economic difficulties and salvation. The injustice of this situation was clear and the tensions it created were volatile. All it needed was a trigger to make these tensions explode, and that was provided by the collapse of the tsarist autocracy.

2 The Spring Honeymoon

In the early months of 1917 it was not only the rural areas that were experiencing hard times as a result of the war. The inhabitants of the cities too were finding living in the war-time situation increasingly difficult. Recent substantial price rises had made food very expensive for the ordinary working man of the city, while deficiencies in the transport and distribution systems led to food shortages in the capital and the need to queue for long periods in order to obtain the necessary supplies. Furthermore in a winter in which both Petrograd and Moscow experienced exceptionally low temperatures, city dwellers also suffered from a shortage of coal. With both food and a major source of heating in short supply, dissatisfaction and frustration grew.

This pervasive sense of frustration and dissatisfaction, expressed intermittently throughout January and early February by strike activity, was given a sharper focus toward the end of the latter month. On 22 February the management of the giant Putilov works attempted to end a strike over higher wages and the reinstatement of some dismissed workers by closing the doors of the plant in a lock-out, thereby throwing thousands of their employees onto the streets. On the following day, the socialist holiday International Women's Day, female textile workers in some plants went on strike and called for support from workers in other industries. The response was so great that by 25 February the strikers numbered over 200,000 and the strike was general; no newspaper appeared, tram-cars stopped running and many businesses were forced to close. But what made this strike successful in political terms while workers' unrest in 1905 had failed was the changed attitude of the soldiers. In 1905 the troops had refused to give widespread support to the popular unrest, but in February 1917, after initial hesitation, they threw in their lot with the workers against the remaining bastion of tsarist power in the capital, the police. Against this alliance the police were powerless with the result that by the end of the month tsarist rule in the city had evaporated. This was formalised by the abdication of

Nicholas on 2 March and his brother's refusal to accept the throne the following day. The power vacuum that this created at the apex of Russian society was filled by two bodies, one formed from below and the other from above, which existed in uneasy partnership until the bolshevik coup in October.

The first of these bodies was the Soviet of Workers' and Soldiers' Deputies. This body, formed as the Soviet of Workers' Deputies on 27 February and transformed into the Soviet of Workers' and Soldiers' Deputies on 1 March, was an organisation of the lower classes modelled on the celebrated Soviet of 1905. The leading role in the organisation of the Soviet was played by intellectuals from the major socialist groups, and it was these people who played a prominent part in the executive committee of the Soviet. There was a clear division between the moderate socialist intellectuals on the executive committee and the rank and file delegates of the workers and soldiers who formed the body of the organisation. This division was to have political ramifications of major importance within the Soviet later in the year. However in the first flush of revolution this split was of little practical significance. It was overshadowed by the dominant position in Petrograd that popular allegiance gave to the Soviet; the general strike ended only when the Soviet called on the workers to return to work, only after the Soviet's decision could newspapers begin to be published again, and it was the Soviet which was able to obtain employer agreement to the eight-hour working day. In the situation of dual power which prevailed, the potential for power possessed by the Soviet was enormous. However it did not realise this potential to the full; although it acted as the revolutionary conscience of the government on a range of issues, on others it played no significant part at all. One of those areas outside the scope of the Soviet's activities was that concerning the peasants. As a result, the role of the Soviet of Workers' and Soldiers' Deputies is not of central concern to this study.

The second body, the Provisional Government, was formed on 2 March by an informal Temporary Committee of the State Duma. The first Provisional Government, which ruled Russia until early May, superficially appeared more united than those which succeeded it. Headed by the non-party liberal Prince G. E. Lvov, it consisted primarily of representatives of parties of the right: of the other ten Ministers, four were Kadets (Miliukov, Manuilov, Shingarev and Nekrasov), three were Octobrists (Guchkov, Godnev and V. N. Lvov) and one was from the Progressive Party

(Konovalov, who joined the Kadets in June), while the other two positions were filled by the formally unaffiliated Kievan sugar magnate Tereshchenko and the nominal S. R. Kerensky. The two ministries of most relevance to peasant affairs were interior and agriculture, held respectively by G. E. Lvov and Shingarev. Kerensky was the only member of the government whose views could be classed as in any way left-wing, and then only moderately so, while the remainder were rooted solidly to the right in the political spectrum. The political complexion of the government was clearly at variance with that of the Soviet and was one which had little sympathy for the popular aspirations unleashed by the fall of the tsar. By late April these contradictions had come to the surface on the issue of Russian war aims and, as a consequence, relations with the Soviet. The result was the recomposition of the government on a new and wider basis.

The toppling of the tsar caught the country by surprise. Even the most optimistic revolutionary had not dared to hope that the tsarist edifice could be felled so easily and no-one had expected it to fall at that time of national danger. News of the collapse of the monarchy was spread unevenly throughout the country; the news reached Pskov 300 *versta* south of the capital, two weeks later than it reached Nikolaev 8000 *versta* away on the shore of the Black Sea; people in parts of Mogilev and Kazan did not hear of the tsar's fall until late March–early April.[1] The patchy distribution of the news resulted in large part from deficiencies in the official communications network, from its low level of technical development and its uneven coverage of the Russian land mass; the first to hear of the February events were usually the industrial centres linked to the capital by rail. Furthermore the effectiveness of the government's moves against the political parties during the war years meant that the underground grapevine which normally would have sped the news to many areas untouched by the official communications network was in a state of total disarray. Many of the major party functionaries were in exile in Siberia or abroad while many of the ordinary rank-and-file who had formed the backbone of the parties in the pre-war years had dropped out of political life altogether. Thus neither the official nor the unofficial communications network was capable of spreading the news of the tsar's fall efficiently throughout the country. This position was exacerbated in some areas (Mogilev and Kazan in particular) by the active suppression of the news on the part of the local authorities. Afraid of the popular reaction to the news and politically opposed to the events in Petrograd themselves, some local government officials tried to keep the population in ignorance of developments in the capital.

However the population could not be kept in ignorance of the change in regime and the news gradually filtered into the villages. By means of rumour, hearsay and half-understood stories, often spread by deserters from the front, delegates of factory workers' organisations, soldiers from the Petrograd garrison who had been given short leave to spread the news of the revolution to the villages, and even workers returning home to the villages to celebrate Easter, the peasants learnt of the changes at the pinnacle of society. Confusion was frequently the reaction in the villages. Many peasants refused to believe that the tsar had been overthrown and drove from the villages those bringing the news. However, in many instances the news was accepted immediately and joyfully, one official report speaking of 'universal joy' at the tsar's fall.[2] Acceptance of the fact was soon widespread in the villages, only Bessarabia and the southern *uezdy* of Chernigov and Mogilev experiencing the widespread expression of pro-monarchist sentiments. But even in these areas the peasants soon accommodated themselves to the new situation.

Initially the peasants greeted the new government with widespread support, although such support rarely was unqualified. The overthrow of the tsar was interpreted in the villages as symbolic of the collapse of the old, unjust property structure in the countryside, the end of the period when they would be denied their rights to the land currently held in non-peasant hands. However although the fall of the tsar produced opportunities for the satisfaction of their long-cherished demands, at least in their own eyes,[3] the peasants were at first quite willing to proceed to the satisfaction of those demands through the new government. The following peasant resolutions, dated respectively 6 March and 30 March, are typical of peasant views as a whole in the sentiments they express:[4]

We, the labouring peasant population of the village of Ust' Izhor, Petrograd *uezd*, greet the new government and the Soviet of workers' and soldiers' deputies and will support it with all of our strength until the convocation of the Constituent Assembly . . .

The Kineshma *uezd* Soviet of Peasants' Deputies in Kostroma decided:

To support the Provisional Government, so long as it does not breach the declaration of freedom and goes unwaveringly along the path toward the quickest convocation of the Constituent Assembly on the basis of universal, direct, equal and secret ballot.

The sentiments expressed in these resolutions are characteristic of the general peasant attitude to the government: they offered their support to the government as long as they believed that it would act in their interests.

The initial approach to the land question in the villages is indicative of peasant support for the government. In discussing the question of the land being placed in the hands of the working people, a congress of peasants' delegates in Samara in late March made the following points:

Aiming for the best provision of grain for the motherland and the retention of civil peace in the country, immediately, prior to the solution of questions in a legal form, everything possible must be done for the increase of the sown area, for the best use of pastures and meadows, and for the temporary solution of the land question, especially in those localities where the peasants are placed in a difficult land position. If land-owners do not themselves sow and do not wish to sow, (their) equipment will be transferred to organisations of *volost* committees of people's power.[5]

The resolution then continued on means of widening the sown area. Concern with the sowing of unsown lands, with the production of increased harvests, was an important characteristic of the outlook of most peasants during the early part of the year, a concern summarized by the generally recognised need to 'save the Russian land from famine'.[6] Although this desire was doubtless partly a result of the traditional peasant concern to maximise production under all circumstances, it also stemmed from a patriotic upsurge in the villages. Such renewed enthusiasm for the motherland was manifested by a rise in support both for the war and for the government. This was shown in concrete terms by a surge of grain deliveries to the cities and to the front as peasants throughout the country made extra efforts to supply grain to these areas of need.[7] Through such actions the peasants showed their support for the government in the most concrete and effective way, by helping the government to come to grips with the food shortage in the cities which had been the trigger for the downfall of the old regime.

The cooperation given by many peasants to local government organs and their initial willingness to proceed in local affairs through those organs is a further indication of peasant support for the government. A striking example of this is provided by the decision of a village in Penza in March. The villagers claimed that for decades they had been cheated and oppressed by a local land-owner, Bakulin, and that now, because of his political views, 'it would be dangerous to allow him to remain at large.' However, the peasants did not take arbitrary action against Bakulin, dragging him before the *skhod* to be found guilty and punished, as they would have done a few months later. Instead they asked the government commissar to arrest Bakulin and bring him to trial.[8] There could be few clearer examples than this of the peasants rejecting arbitrary action and putting their faith in the new government institutions to bring about the realisation of their desires. Even disputes over land frequently were taken before government bodies.[9] Such faith in the government, albeit conditional on the government acting in the peasants' interests, was an important factor in the early part of the year.

However the peasants' faith in the government did not last. The initial wave of support soon foundered and popular enthusiasm turned into disillusionment as the government continually failed to implement the measures demanded by the peasants. The broad outlines of government policy went no way toward satisfying the peasants' demands. Disillusionment began to set in soon after the government came to power, initially as a result of its moves in the sphere of local administration.

THE GOVERNMENT PROGRAMME: LOCAL ADMINISTRATION

In the sphere of government administration the Provisional Government's position was outlined in its first declaration, dated 7 March:

> While taking measures to defend the country against the foreign enemy, the government will, at the same time, consider it to be its primary duty to make possible the expression of the popular will as regards the form of government, and will convoke the

Constituent Assembly within the shortest time possible, on the basis of universal, direct, equal and secret ballot, also guaranteeing participation in the elections to the gallant defenders of our native land, who are shedding their blood on the fields of battle.[10]

Although this statement concerning the Constituent Assembly appears to be simple and straight-forward, in the conditions of 1917 it reflected a government position that was ambiguous. The requirements outlined for the election to the Constituent Assembly, 'universal, direct, equal and secret ballot', demanded conditions that could not be realised throughout the country in the short term. The mechanical task of registering voters and drawing up electoral rolls would have been daunting enough in a stable country at peace; in a country like Russia in 1917, in the midst of revolution and fighting a war on its western border, this task was even greater. Furthermore the requirement that all the soldiers should participate increased the problem. Participation of those at the front could only take place in the regularised fashion demanded by the government if hostilities were ended, at least temporarily. In addition the government exacerbated these organisational problems by a tardiness in implementing the necessary preliminary measures; the formation of a Special Council to draft a statute for elections to the Assembly was announced on 25 March, but it did not meet until 25 May.[11] The prolonged delay in the convening of the Assembly meant that major problems continually were pushed to the side with no attempt made to remedy them.

The declaration of 7 March continued:

The Provisional Government deems it necessary, at once, before the convocation of the Constituent Assembly, to provide the country with laws for the safeguarding of civic liberty and equality, in order to enable all citizens freely to apply their spiritual forces to creative work for the benefit of the country. The government also will undertake the enactment of legal provisions to assure to all citizens, on the basis of universal suffrage, an equal share in the election of local governments.

The government thus pledged itself to establish a legal order safeguarding the rights of all citizens and a governmental structure throughout the country based on popular election by the people. However, even before this declaration was made, its spirit had been violated by the abolition on 5 March of the imperial posts of Guberniia Governor and Vice-Governor and the creation in their stead of the posts of *guberniia* and *uezd* commissars; these positions were assigned temporarily to the chairmen of the *zemstvo* boards.[12] The function of these officers was, in part, to establish an efficient administrative network in their regions. In this respect they were instructed by the government:

> That it is desirable to retain, wherever possible, the entire existing administrative mechanism, with the aim of upholding the normal course of life in the country.[13]

On 20 March *guberniia* commissars were instructed to establish, through the intermediary of *uezd* commissars, *volost* committees where this seemed necessary. These bodies were to be the basic level units of the administrative structure in the countryside and were to perform the functions of the traditional *volost* administration until the formation of the *volost zemstvo*. Their specific duties were to include the preservation of supply to the army, the maintenance of social order, and the protection and retention of the buildings and files of the *volost* administration. The commissars were directed to turn to food committees, cooperative organisations, bodies performing social work and *volost* committees that were already in existence for assistance in forming the new *volost* committees. However in peasant eyes the tenor of the government initiative was set by the following part of the instruction:

> It is recommended also to draw into the work of these committees local land-owners and all the intellectual forces of the countryside.[14]

It was from among these people that the chairmen of the committees were to be drawn.

Thus in its early moves to establish an administrative framework throughout the country, the government went counter to the undertaking given in its initial declaration to have that administration popularly elected; the new local government posts were appointed. In the chaotic months of early 1917 the government had little alternative except to try to establish a national administration from the top. With its priority on holding the country together and keeping it in the war, it had to take quick action to establish its control in the countryside. Under these circumstances there was little alternative to appointment from above; it could not await the lengthy procedure of elections, particularly since this was meant to be a purely stop-gap administration. However it was unfortunate for the government that so early in its life it could be seen to be taking a course that was counter to its publicly-declared position. Furthermore this was exacerbated by the fact that, as indicated below, the people upon whom the government relied were anathema to the broad mass of the peasant population.

An integral part of the establishment of an administrative framework in the rural areas was the necessity on the part of the government to face up to the emerging problem of rural unrest.[15] The outbreak of rural unrest caught the new government off-balance, a position from which it never recovered. The government was reluctant to use force to bring rural disorders to an end. Memories of tsarist oppression, feelings of popular sovereignty and the belief that government should be based on trust and cooperation with the people were important in this. The emergence of unrest led to a conflict of principles within the government. On the one hand, the government believed that armed force should not be used against the sovereign Russian people. On the other, it knew that rural unrest could lead to the loss of everything that had been gained in the revolution, everything for which it stood. This conflict led to the government adopting an anomalous and self-contradictory stance toward rural unrest. This was evident from the start of the government's rule. An outbreak of disturbances in Kazan in early March led to a government decision on 9 March which, while affirming the inadmissibility of the use of armed force for the suppression of agrarian disorders 'at the present time', confirmed that 'plunderers' had to be prosecuted for criminal action.[16] However the two parts of this decision were, in practice, irreconcilable because the large numbers involved in the unrest made the bringing of 'plunderers' to justice impossible without the use of armed force. The government position was thus, effectively, a reluctant and ambiguous sanctioning of the use of armed force to put down rural disorder.

The government's position became clearer during late March and April. On 22 March in a circular from the Ministry of the Interior to commissars regarding the formation of a temporary militia in the rural areas to replace the disbanded tsarist law enforcement agencies, commissars were told:

In case of the aggravation of disorders and the impossibility of stopping them by means of persuasion, the summoning of troops and the destruction of liquor stores is permitted.[17]

This position was reaffirmed in early April in the government's reply to a question from the General Staff on the conditions under which local commanders could send troops into an area to help suppress agrarian unrest. The government response was to assert that the *guberniia* commissars and public committees were responsible for the suppression by 'all legal means' of infringements of rights in the agrarian sphere. Commissars had the responsibility directly to contact the local military authorities if they deemed this necessary to maintain order and the normal course of rural life.[18]

During late April the government also established two organisations designed specifically to deal with rural unrest. On 20 April the government announced the formation of a permanent militia in the rural areas to replace the temporary militia established a month earlier.[19] The establishment of this body, nominally under local control, gave local authorities the means, in theory at least, to enforce their decisions and maintain order. The second organisation was the mediation and conciliation chamber. This was to be an organ attached to all *guberniia* and *uezd* land committees, and its function was to adjudicate on all questions of land relations until the land question was resolved by the Constituent Assembly.[20] Cases were to be brought before these chambers on the agreement of both parties to the dispute, the decision reached by the chamber being binding on both protagonists. This was a major weakness of the chambers—both parties had to agree before a dispute was brought to adjudication. Those who violated legal rights were unlikely to accede to the demand of the victim to submit the matter to arbitration. Furthermore, even when cases were brought before the chambers, these bodies had no power of their own to enforce their decisions. Their ability to resolve land disputes rested primarily upon their persuasive power or on the capacity of the local militia to enforce their decisions; their utility in combating rural unrest was limited.

Thus by the time of the fall of the first Provisional Government in early May, the broad outlines of local government had been sketched. The government had decreed the establishment of commissars at the *guberniia* and *uezd* levels, a militia which was to be based in the major towns, and *volost* committees where these were deemed necessary. In addition, discussions were taking place in the government regarding the future establishment of the *volost zemstvo*, the institution envisaged as the permanent form of local government to which reference was made in the government's initial declaration on 7 March. However a basic weakness in the emerging administrative structure was already clear. Responsibility for dealing with rural unrest was shared broadly between four bodies—commissars, the militia, *volost* committees, and mediation and conciliation chambers, but no clear demarcation of function or responsibility was made. Administrative ambiguity was the result. Such institutional diversification could only hamper the government's attempts to deal with unrest in the rural areas.

THE PEASANT RESPONSE

The government's early moves in the sphere of local administration provoked disappointment and disillusionment in the countryside. The peasants interpreted the fall of the tsar as signifying an end to the traditional rule of the land-owners and the *chinovniki* sympathetic to them, and the establishment of an administrative structure responsive to those over whom it ruled.[21] There was to be no room in the new era for these remnants of the past; the traditional exploiters in the peasants' eyes should be banished forever. But it was precisely to these traditional power-holders in the countryside that the government was turning, to the *zemstvo* chairmen, the local land-owners, and the 'existing administrative mechanism'. The peasants' attitude was clearly expressed in the resolution of a peasant meeting in Kostroma on 15 March:

> The immediate reformation of the local administration is necessary on the basis of universal, direct, equal and secret ballot; prior to the publication of a corresponding act by the central government, a meeting of representatives of individual *volosti* will democratise the local administration, including *guberniia* and *uezd zemstva*. All administrative police authority will be concentrated in revolutionary *guberniia*, *uezd* and *volost* committees; the transfer of this power to the chairmen of the *zemstvo* boards is inadmissible and would represent the loss by the revolutionary people of their most important gains: the circular of Prince Lvov on the appointment of chairmen of the boards must officially be revoked at once.[22]

In the peasants' eyes it seemed that nothing had changed; they were to be ruled over by land-owners and former appointed officials, just as they had been prior to the tsar's fall, while the main purpose of the local power structure remained the defence of the established order in the countryside, the maintenance of the power of the land-owners. Continued calls by the government for the peasants to refrain from land seizures and the occasional use of armed force to quell rural unrest confirmed the land-owner orientation of the local administration in the peasants' minds. From Tver *guberniia* in April came a typical sentiment:

> The land is being consolidated under the old laws. . . The people are losing all faith in the new government . . .[23]

The government appeared to be doing little more than renaming the old oppressive power structure while retaining it intact. Such a situation made it impossible for the new government commissars and committees to enjoy the 'confidence and authority among the wide ranks of the population,'[24] which the government hoped would enable them to maintain order in the rural areas.

The widespread peasant rejection of the emerging administrative structure was linked with the strength throughout the countryside of traditionally-based peasant organisations rooted in the fabric of village society. The initial reaction of the peasants on hearing of the tsar's fall was to meet together in their village assemblies to discuss the situation. Although the precise timetable differed from village to village, sooner or later, and in the majority of cases it was sooner, the peasants in all villages embarked on the same broad path, that of rejecting the authority of the formal administration and of establishing an authority of their own. Throughout the country the peasants turned on local functionaries of the old regime, especially the *zemskie nachal'niki*, placed them under arrest and drove them from the villages. The old administrative order became paralysed and irrelevant to the current situation. It soon disintegrated. In place of this old administrative framework the peasants established their own committees to run their affairs. In the words of the decision of a meeting of representatives from 27 villages in Arkhangel *guberniia* on 16 March:

> A committee would be selected for the organisation of the militia and the leadership of affairs of the *volost*.[25]

Peasant committees were elected throughout the country at both the village and *volost* levels, either by general meetings of peasants or by the respective *skhodi*. These committees assumed numerous different names throughout Russia: *volost* committees, village committees, revolutionary committees, committees of peoples' power, committees of public security, peoples' committees, land committees, food committees and many more. However despite the different names that these committees assumed, they were all essentially the same institutions: low level bodies responsible to the peasants and responsive to their desires.

Early elections for these bodies fell far short of the stringent requirements established in the resolutions of peasant bodies for the conduct of elections. Peasant resolutions almost invariably called for universal suffrage, direct and equal vote, and secret ballot.[26] However, peasant tradition and illiteracy combined to frustrate this ideal. Traditional norms of peasant life and the chores of the household kept the women away from the assemblies, while voting was often done by a show of hands or by voice. The results of elections often were widely disputed, and new elections frequently were called within the space of a few weeks.[27] Initially throughout the countryside there was no general pattern of membership of the new committees; membership differed from village to village and from *volost* to *volost*. The composition of individual committees appears in the first instance to have been determined by the relative strength of three conflicting impulses which characterised peasant life in all areas. The changing relationship between these impulses was a determining factor in the course of development of peasant organisation in 1917.

The first of these impulses was a tendency among the peasants to look upwards for guidance and direction. Traditional reluctance to act without some sort of guidance from above was reinforced in early 1917 by the speed with which unforeseen events occurred in Petrograd. In the ever-changing situation, the peasants were particularly anxious to learn of the new events because of the effect those events could have on their own life situations. Virtually from the time they learnt of the fall of the tsar, peasants throughout Russia sent delegations to the capital to try to determine what was happening and the meaning of those events, and to request assistance in carrying out the revolution in their own region. In the words of an instructor from the provincial section of the Moscow Soviet of Workers' Deputies:

The peasantry say frankly that they are waiting for people, like the spring sun, who would explain to them what to do, how to act.[28]

This expectancy of direction from above was so strongly entrenched within the peasants' minds that it was not easily eradicated. In the middle of the year it could still be said:

All the peasantry still do not understand what has happened and think that someone gives an order to them from above which they must obey, and on explanation they say 'This is Antichrist'.[29]

The peasants' search for guidance began by looking to the cities, to the newly emerging mass organisations which were springing up in the factories and the suburbs.

However the peasants' search for guidance from above was profoundly influenced by their low level of political sophistication. This is well illustrated by an official report:

The peasant understands only when he speaks and puts questions himself, but not when he listens to what is said without direct address to himself – to Ivan, to Petr to Sidor.[30]

Possessing only very limited capacity to think and generalise in the abstract, the ability of the peasant delegate sent to the capital to comprehend all that he heard and saw was severely circumscribed. The problems of his own particular village and its immediate concerns tended to get lost in the broad sweep of the revolution, which was the prime concern of those in the cities. They were concerned with generalised social forces, with 'the peasantry', 'the proletariat' and 'the bourgeoisie' rather than with the more immediate and specific focus of the peasant delegate, his own village. Swept up in a whirl of party and faction politics and impromptu and frequently badly-organised meetings, many peasant delegates were unable to grasp the meaning of the events surrounding them. Bombarded with opinions of widely differing hues, peasant delegates usually left the cities in a state of greater confusion and uncertainty than when they arrived.[31]

The lack of sophistication was clear in the villages where the vast multitude of peasants were either wholly illiterate or only semi-literate. This induced in the peasants what amounted almost to veneration of the written word. Decisions and resolutions of peasant bodies frequently were accepted as compulsory and binding, and no distinction was made between projected legislation and that which was actually on the statute books. Even newspaper reports were accepted as law on many occasions.[32]

The general confusion plus the low level of peasant political sophistication created conditions conducive to the exercise of influence by agitators coming into the countryside. Although peasant reaction to agitators was coloured by early patriotic anti-deserter feeling, by growing hostility to the towns, and by traditional wariness of strangers, on the whole the villages were receptive to these outside influences. Most agitators brought with them the certainty of ideological conviction, or at least they possessed an ideological framework through which they could interpret the changing political situation. From this basis they could give the peasants the guidance they were seeking, portraying the vast spectrum of hues that was the Russian political scene in 1917 in stark black and white terms. Peasant confusion and uncertainty could thus, superficially at least, be cleared up by a vast process of over-simplification on the part of the agitators. However, unfortunately for the government, the definitions of the situation offered by the agitators often involved the portrayal of the government in very stark and negative terms; in the black–white scenario painted by most agitators, there was no room for the grey of the government position. Agitators contributed to the radicalisation of the peasant mood. In the words of an official report:

> As regards the mood of the countryside at first it was quiet but from the time of the appearance of soldiers in rural work, the mood sharply changed. There were cases of seizures of land-owners' land.[33]

Peasant violence and destruction often was inspired and encouraged by agitators; soldiers were involved in the first instance of violence against a landed estate mentioned in the militia reports.[34]

As well as defining and interpreting the political situation for the peasants, agitators frequently played a major role in peasant organisations at the village and *volost* levels. The presence of these 'outsiders' possessing an apparent understanding of the situation and frequently some organisational experience, was in many cases all that was needed to prompt the peasants to form their own organisations. They offered guidance in the form such organisations should take, in the desired membership, and in the conduct of elections for these bodies. On many occasions they also became members of the peasant committees, often exercising substantial influence within those organisations. Frequently the only literate member of the committee, the agitator played a major role in the crystallisation and formulation of peasant views. Such views were expressed formally in resolutions and decisions of peasant meetings, these resolutions and decisions being drafted by the literate member of the group, the agitator. The influence of the agitators is evident in the form many of these resolutions and decisions took. Often they were framed in terms of the revolutionary rhetoric of Petrograd, the use of standard party phraseology compressing the diverse peasant opinions and demands into the more familiar channels of inter-party debate in the capital.[35] This transposition of peasant views into the language of the urban political parties forced peasant desires and demands into a strait-jacket of intellectual concepts that was foreign to the demands of the countryside. This urban tyranny of concepts served not only to blur the distinctions between the aspirations of the rural and urban dwellers, but also it helped to hide the true situation in the villages from those like the bolsheviks who lacked the ability to test their ideological preconceptions against widespread first-hand knowledge of peasant life.

In the early part of the year the second impulse characteristic of peasant life at this time was particularly significant in the contours adopted by peasant organisations. This was the struggle by traditional peasant leaders to retain their positions of leadership in the new situation in the village and *volost*. As the peasants moved toward the establishment of new revolutionary organs, many local traditional leaders, the elders of the *skhod* and other officials, successfully maintained their old positions of influence. From the village of Ust' Izhor, Petrograd *guberniia*, in early March came the following report of a peasant meeting:

> The meeting was opened by the *volost* elder Dobroradov. On his proposal to elect a chairman of the present committee *volost* elder Dobroradov was elected unanimously.[36]

From Smolensk came the report in early April:

> We have organized a *volost* committee of twelve men from the

citizenry, from the richest *muzhiki*, and they gather in meetings attended by the elder, the secretary and the village elders, all servants of the old regime. . . .[37]

One observer has noted, probably with some exaggeration, that *volost* elders became chairmen of *volost* committees in a majority of cases.[38] Such people often were very popular in the villages and therefore it was natural that they should attain influential positions within the new organisations. Others benefited from a combination of popular inertia and habit, while in other instances former elders retained their positions because they had the experience and the ability to control peasant meetings. Many retained their positions despite challenges from the younger members of the village, particularly those who had returned home radicalised by life in the cities or at the front. Many unpopular elders fled from the villages with the fall of the tsar, often having remained in power prior to the revolution only through the support of the land-owners. Thus the formation of peasant committees was directly influenced by the state of the local traditional leadership and the ability of the local leaders to retain themselves in power under the changed circumstances.

The third impulse affecting the formation of local committees was the peasant desire to govern themselves. A tradition of some local autonomy combined with distrust of land-owner administration led to a desire to handle their own affairs in the new circumstances:

Our affairs must be handled only by ourselves.[39]

This feeling was stimulated by the government's action in appointing former administrators and land-owners to positions of administrative importance early in the year. Distrust of those outside the traditional framework of peasant life led to the widespread rejection of those whose roots were not immediately found in the villages. Always an important consideration, this impulse became more significant the longer the year progressed, eventually becoming the most important factor of the three in determining the composition of the lower level committees.[40] This was a significant part of the process of introversion by the traditional community which was a major feature of rural life in Russia in 1917.

The working out of these three impulses in practice is evident from the membership of many of the early committees, the composition of which reflects the operation of these conflicting pressures on the peasants. In a *volost* in Smolensk the membership of a newly-elected committee included

> Two ardent monarchists, the local psalm-reader, one person encouraging the peasants to commit arson and seizure, and a dissipated nobleman . . .[41]

Local teachers, priests and shopkeepers were elected to these committees on many occasions, while local land-owners, including in at least one instance a prince, also occasionally gained election. However in most cases peasants appear to have been elected to the majority of positions on the committees, although it was not unusual for members of the local intelligentsia, mainly teachers, to be elected to the more prominent positions of leadership. Peasants who had established consolidated farms under the aegis of the Stolypin reforms and women rarely were elected.

However the composition of these committees did not remain static. These bodies were subject to frequent elections as peasant dissatisfaction with the existing membership developed. If the peasants felt that the local committee was not serving their interests, they dismissed it and held a new election; in Podolsk a village committee was dissolved and a new election was held because the committee had tried to restrain the peasants from the seizure of property. Indicative of the prevailing sentiment was the peasant retort:

> We elected you, and if you do not go in concert with us, we will throw you out.[42]

When new elections were held for the low level peasant bodies, they almost invariably involved the expulsion of all non-peasant elements from the committees. Particularly noticeable was the removal from their leading positions of school teachers and other 'intellectual forces', with the result that the committees' capacity for organisation and administration declined sharply; during the summer and autumn in many committees there was no literate person who could write the protocols of the meeting. By eliminating the non-peasant members of the committees, the peasants made those bodies more responsive to the desires and moods of the peasants as a whole. Largely unencumbered by representatives of the non-peasant rural population, the committees were accurate reflections of the changing moods in the villages. On those occasions when non-peasants did retain membership of the committees, it was at the price of losing all independent influence over the committees; they had to accede to peasant desires or lose their places. Thus as the mood in the villages became more radical over the course of the year, the low level peasant committees moved with that change, both fuelling and reflecting the change in attitude.

There were no standard procedures for electing the village committee. It was formed either at a general meeting of all inhabitants of the village or, more usually, at a meeting of the village *skhod*. Many of the committees thus formed were quite large, with the result that on some occasions a smaller executive committee was formed also. The village committee's authority theoretically was confined to management of all aspects of life in the village: village administration, village police, the food question, the refugee problem, the care of families of those summoned to the war, and the aged were all considered to be within the scope of the village committee's authority.[43] However in practice the authority of the village committee ranged beyond the immediate bounds of the village to take in all of the surrounding farm land, including the farms of separators and eventually the privately-owned large landed estates seized by the peasants. Demarcation disputes between village committees were not uncommon in many parts of the country.

The *volost* committee was envisaged by the government as the lowest level of administration until the establishment of the *volost zemstvo*. It was to be broadly based on the whole rural population; the right to vote was not restricted to peasants but, formally, was extended to land-owners, priests and urban dwellers also. It was to perform basically the same functions as the older *volost* administration, although its powers tended in practice to be wider and more ill-defined. The *volost* committee was expected to concern itself with the management of all administrative and economic work in the *volost*, including the food question. It was also meant to ensure the regularity and legality of the acts of the village committees. However in practice the *volost* committee was far removed from the government's expectations. Instead of acting as a government organ, it became wholly dominated by and responsive to the peasants. It consisted of representatives from all the villages in the *volost*, elected either directly by each individual village, or indirectly by the *volost skhod* or by a general *volost* assembly consisting of delegates from each village.[44] Non-peasants rarely played a prominent part in *volost* committees, particularly in the summer and autumn. This peasant domination is reflected in the fact that *volost* committees tended to become instruments of peasant unrest rather than of government administration. This is ably illustrated by a letter from a Saratov land-owner in mid-April:

> . . . from many places news is received that recently formed *volost* and village committees are composing illegal resolutions on the basis of which the peasants wilfully seize farmers' and separators' land which has been prepared for spring sowing.[45]

No accurate figures can be obtained for the number of village and *volost* committees formed throughout Russia. The absence of figures for committees at the village level is not surprising since many of these institutions were *ad hoc* in the extreme, sometimes being little more than a cabal of the more radical peasants in the village. Furthermore it was at this level that illiteracy was most widespread, with the result that reports of meetings of these bodies were likely to be noted down more haphazardly and less frequently than at higher levels. Despite the lack of solid evidence, it is clear that during the year the vast majority, and probably all, peasant villages did have some form of peasant committee, albeit somewhat shadowy and ill-distinct from the traditional *skhod*. At the *volost* level too accurate figures are rare. However those figures that do exist indicate the development of *volost* committees on a wide scale: for example, in Elatomsk uezd Tambov *guberniia volost* committees had been formed in nineteen of the twenty-six *volosti* by 21 March, while by June committees existed in all *volosti* of Viatka and by August in 220 of the 253 *volosti* in Nizhegorod.[46]

Although village and *volost* committees developed widely throughout European Russia between the February and October revolutions, the traditional *skhod* did not disappear as a major factor in the peasants' lives. The *skhod* was frequently the mother of the new village and *volost* committees, and as such the new organisations often tended in practice to be little more than executive organs of the older assembly. This was more often the case at the village level, where the *skhod* could be called at very short notice, than it was at the *volost* level. When new elections were held for the peasant committees, it was often the *skhod* that initiated the election and carried it out. When the peasants of a village or a *volost* decided to take some action against the local land-owners or the local administration, that decision frequently was made in the *skhod*. There was, of course, substantial overlap between the *skhod* and the newer organisations; a common membership and a coincidence of interests and aims ensured that the two worked in harmony. The line between the two types of institution remained indistinct right up to the time of the bolshevik coup, with the result that it is impossible to assign the bulk of initiative in revolutionary action to one type of body or the other. They were interacting entities, both firmly rooted in the peasant consciousness. It is a matter for little surprise that the institutions at the *volost*, and particularly the village, levels were the main organisational vehicles for peasant unrest during 1917.

Peasant unrest was not coordinated on any large scale. The scene of rural disturbances was primarily local, the peasants acting at the village or, at most, the *volost* level, rarely venturing outside their immediate geographical area. Neighbouring villages did not always coordinate their actions and often came into conflict over land, forest and crop seizure. Nevertheless despite this absence of formal overall coordination, a broad similarity of physical situation and of aims brought about a general coincidence of action on the part of the peasants in all areas; over the eight month period between the two revolutions, Russia-wide peasant unrest was characterised both by different types of actions and by varying levels of intensity at different times. Regional variations in these patterns did occur, but the nation-wide patterns of action remain clear. However the broad national patterns should not obscure the highly segmented nature of rural unrest at the local level. Individual villages were not in a continual state of ferment from February to October: the peasants did not carry out revolutionary actions every day of every week. Their actions were disjointed, bursts of revolutionary activity being interspersed with periods of relative quiescence when the normal routine of rural life again established its ascendancy. The timing and nature of these bursts of revolutionary activity were determined by a combination of local factors and the similarity of physical situation and of aims referred to above. To the extent that local factors differed from one village to the next, each village situation was unique. This uniqueness of the constituent parts should be borne in mind when looking at the national pattern of unrest as a whole.

Acceptance of the news of the tsar's fall created great excitement among the peasants. They realised that the collapse of the old structure held the promise of major benefits if only they could capitalise on it. Hence they left their villages with staff, axe handle and gun in hand and turned on the local land-owners. In March the dominating strand of rural unrest was destructive; according to the reports received by the Chief Department of the Militia,[47] more than half the instances of rural unrest in March involved the physical destruction of private property. Estates and manor houses were pillaged and burnt on a wide scale. According to one land-owner in Menzelinsk uezd, *Ufa guberniia*:

> My estate . . . was destroyed by citizens of the surrounding villages on the seventeenth of March; grain, edible stocks, seed, thoroughbred horses, cattle, pigs, birds, machines, tools, all property was taken and the buildings burnt. Losses were enormous. I only just escaped myself.[48]

Peasant destruction swept over wide areas of the country; not only the large privately-owned estates but the farms of smaller land-holders, grain stores, stocks and equipment and even a local post office were objects of peasant depredations. Privately-owned and state-owned forests were felled in a feverish wave of timber-cutting. Such timber was either taken back to the village to be divided between the peasants or was left where it fell under the protection of specially appointed guards. Grain was seized on a wide scale. Inevitably peasant ire also was turned against former administrators, land-owners and their defenders, many of whom were arrested, physically assaulted and even killed. With this sudden burst of destructive activity, rural unrest appeared to many in the countryside to be a form of apocalypse which, unless halted, would violently drown the old rural social structure based on land relationships in a sea of wildly rampant peasants.

However this primarily destructive form of unrest did not last past the end of the month as the form which set the tone of unrest as a whole. As the level of rural unrest climbed to a peak in mid-summer, the destructive element dwindled in significance to become, by July, the smallest strand of unrest as a whole. It was overtaken in the spring and early summer by types of unrest which, in March, had been of minor importance compared with the rash of destructive activity.

The most important aspect of unrest during April, and indeed right through until the end of August, was the seizure of land, both privately-owned and state-owned. Throughout the country peasants began ignoring legal formalities about ownership and moved on to the land, beginning to cultivate the arable land and graze their cattle on private and state meadows. The boundary-markers separating *obshchina* land from privately-owned land were abolished and tracts of land outside traditional peasant control were integrated into the traditional holdings. In some instances owners or their workers were driven from an area as the peasants moved in to take over the land; on other occasions they simply occupied land that was currently unused by the owner. The seizure of land was not always accompanied by attempts on the part of the peasants to cultivate the areas they seized. In many instances the land was left unworked, although its physical control had in fact shifted from the manor house to the village. However in many instances the peasants threw themselves into the cultivation of newly-seized lands with such vigour that they neglected to cultivate their traditional holdings. The reason for this was simple: fearing that the land-owners might return to retake their land, the peasants wanted to get the maximum benefit from that land while they could.

As well as the direct seizure of land by occupation, many peasant land seizures were implemented by what has been termed 'surreptitous' or 'semi-legal' methods.[49] The peasants used two means of bringing such seizures about. The first involved the arbitrary establishment of land rent levels by peasant bodies. Such rentals were established both on land that was already held by the peasants on short-term leases, in which case the level of the rent was drastically reduced, and on land which the peasants did not currently work. In the latter case the peasants were taking into compulsory rental land that previously had not been available for rent: in the words of the executive committee of social organisations in Ranenburg *uezd* Riazan *guberniia*:

> The land of large land-owners is to be surrendered for rental. The size of the rental is fixed at ten roubles for an unploughed *dessiatina* and thirty roubles for a ploughed *dessiatina*:[50]

The decisions of peasant organisations were not as all-embracing as this in every instance; early in the year many committees were content to take only that land which the peasants believed they needed, thereby leaving some land in the hands of the legal owners.

Superficially the establishment of rental levels by the peasants does not appear to constitute a form of land seizure; the peasants would gain use of the land while in return the legal owners would be paid rental. However this apparently simple exchange was not as simple as it appeared. Rental rates frequently remained a fiction; peasants often refused to pay any rent at all, and when they did often this was directed to the peasant committees rather than to the land-owner. The legal owner of the land was not deprived of rental in this way in every instance, but as the months passed and the peasants increasingly rejected all notion of land-owners' rights, this became more common and developed into simply another mode of open land seizure. The fiction of paying rent and having legal obligations toward a private land-owner disappeared during 1917.

The second tactic of 'surreptitious seizure' utilised by the peasants consisted of disrupting the functioning of the land-owners' estates. The peasants' thinking behind such action was two-fold. Firstly, if the normal operation of the estate could be sufficiently disrupted, the owner might be induced either to abandon the estate altogether or to pass it over in rental to the peasants. Secondly, by a decision of 11 April the Provisional Government decreed that land unused by owners was to be taken over by local food committees. These committees had to bring that land into production, either through their own efforts or through the rental of that land to those willing to work it. In the light of this legislation if the peasants could ensure that large areas of estates remained unworked by the owners and if they could secure control of the local food committees, which usually they had no difficulty in doing, they could bend the law and claim some semblance of a legal right to take that land over.

The most direct means of disrupting work on the estates adopted by the peasants was openly to prohibit the land-owner from ploughing, sowing or harvesting his fields or from mowing his meadows. In the words of a peasant meeting in Kudriav *volost*, Dankov *uezd*, Riazan *guberniia*:

All land-owners must immediately proceed to sow their land, and must finish in ten working days. The unsown area will be taken over by the local *volost* committee.[51]

The approach adopted by peasant bodies throughout Russia was not uniform. In many instances the peasants permitted the land-owners to retain and work only that amount of land which they and their families could work effectively without the aid of hired labour or prisoners-of-war. Other peasant bodies took the approach of Kudriav *volost* outlined above: land-owners were given advance notice of the takeover of any land which remained unworked. In this early period the practice of leaving some land in the hands of the legal owners was characteristic of many peasant land seizures. Certainly there were instances of the immediate seizure of all the land belonging to particular land-owners, but this does not appear to have become the norm until the late spring – early summer. In April the peasants usually contented themselves with seizing that land which the legal owners were not working.

Another tactic the peasants used to disrupt the working of the estates was the removal from those estates of the source of labour power on which the land-owner relied. This took a number of forms. The managers and employees of estates were arrested or expelled and prisoners-of-war were driven from the land in all regions where such labour was used. This was usually accompanied by the expulsion from the estates of all hired labourers. On those occasions when no outright prohibition was placed on the use of hired labour, the use of labour from outside the district was prohibited. This prohibition was rigidly enforced in relation to Asian workers introduced in the early years of the war to ameliorate the rural labour shortage; racial prejudice gave a sharp cutting edge to peasant economic frustration and hatred of the land-owners. Where the use of hired labour from the district was permitted, the peasants established new, and often exorbitant labour rates. Peasants in Simbirsk demanded four roubles for a male and two for a female while those in Voronezh demanded five and 3.50 respectively for an eight-hour working day; one observer noted that peasants were demanding up to twenty roubles per day.[52] Most land-owners were unable to pay such steep increases in labour costs, with the result that the hiring of labour was no longer a feasible means of working their estates for many owners.

The working capacity of the estates also was reduced through peasant confiscation of farm implements, machinery and livestock. Like the peasant approach to land outlined above, early in the year the peasants did not always leave the land-owner completely without the capacity to work some of his land: small numbers of working beasts and equipment were left in the land-owners' hands on many occasions. However the productivity of the estate was drained further by the imposition on the land-owners of arbitrarily-established taxes and fines, such funds usually being used to finance the local peasant organisations. Under these conditions many land-owners were totally incapable of working their estates adequately. According to Kazan land-owner K. V. Molostvov:

> To carry out any kind of work on the farms is impossible since the peasantry remove workers, seize seed, in many areas carry away all property from the farmsteads, threatening the owners with death and violence, they do not allow the chopping of firewood and they drive away state procurement officers.[53]

The effect of such disruptive activities was exacerbated by a broad peasant embargo on the land-owners selling their land, equipment, livestock or crops. Thus not only were the land-owners unable to work their estates, but they were also unable to dispose of those estates and their accoutrements. In consequence, many land-owners ceased even trying to farm their land.

Another major strand of peasant unrest during the spring was the establishment of peasant control over forests and wooded areas. Such control was established in two ways. The most spectacular means of doing this was by the peasants going into the forest and felling the timber themselves, either for use at home or for speculative sales to the fuel-hungry towns. In the words of a Novgorod land-owner:

> The *muzhiki* immediately and openly set about the felling of our timber, twice and three times a week carting it to the town market.[54]

Although such felling usually was regulated by the local peasant bodies, to the legal owners of the timber it seemed arbitrary and unregulated. No more justified in the eyes of the owners was the other means through which the peasants established their control over the wooded areas. Local peasant bodies placed either a blanket prohibition on the owner's use and exploitation of his timber for any purposes whatsoever, or allowed access to it only for his own personal and familial needs. Defence requirements, commercial contracts, and city and railway needs for fuel usually were rejected by the peasants when they imposed such bans.

Thus the tone of peasant actions changed from March to April. The month immediately following the fall of the tsar was marked by a high level of anarchic violence and destruction in the rural areas. Estates were destroyed and their occupants and employees sometimes killed. In April the destructive element was replaced as the major form of unrest by the seizure of land, the widespread disruption of estates, and the seizure of timber and forest land. The anarchic and violent strain, so marked in March, was substantially subdued in April. However this does not mean that rural unrest was less significant or dangerous in April than in March; the level of unrest was higher and its distribution throughout the country wider in April than in the earlier month.

The changing contours of rural unrest were determined by a complex of factors. Initial peasant acceptance of the collapse of the old system was the first step in their search for the satisfaction of the land hunger with which they were afflicted, a search which was to end with the revolutionising of land relations in the countryside. In the words of one land-owner, the news of the tsar's overthrow

. . .caused strong excitement among the peasants[55]

while another claimed that the peasants worked on the maxim

. . .now we have no tsar we have no-one to whom we can answer.[56]

The rush of passions in the countryside conjured up by these two land-owners was manifested in most striking terms by the rash of destruction and violence in March. Years of pent-up resentment, suffering and misery could be vented on the old structure which now appeared incapable of defending itself. The fall of the tsar acted as a trip-wire for the release of the peasants' suppressed frustrations and emotions. However the immediate force of these suppressed feelings was soon moderated. This is reflected in the decline in the destructive element in the post-March period. The peasants' realisation of their own best interests was instrumental in this: peasant hunger for land and all the accoutrements that went with it (buildings, machinery, crops and stock) could only be frustrated by the destruction of those things. Thus after initially venting their pent-up frustrations in a most destructive manner, the peasants moved to different methods, less destructive of that which they hoped to possess.

A major determinant of the course of rural unrest was the pattern of agricultural life which the peasants led.[57] March and April, when the level of unrest was lower than it was to become in the succeeding months, was a period of intensive work in the villages. During the spring months the crops planted during the previous autumn and beginning to sprout had to be tended, the soil made ready for the spring sowing, and the spring crop sown. Moreover in those areas suffering from spring floods as a result of the thaw of the winter snows, repair work around the villages was a time-consuming activity. The need to turn their attention to the routine tasks of rural life severely restricted the time available to the peasants to engage in disruptive activities.

The agricultural cycle of life also deeply influenced the types of actions undertaken by the peasants. Peasant concentration on their crops during this period was reflected in the fact that most of the productive land that was seized during these months was arable land; only in May with the beginning of hay-mowing was pasture land seized in large quantities. The peasant concern to gain fresh food supplies at the end of the long winter was an important element in the high level of crop seizure in March compared with later months. The extraordinarily high level of tree felling and timber seizure too was related to the rural pattern of life: the extreme cold of the Russian winter focused the peasants' attention on the need for firewood, and they knew from past experience that the cold weather could continue past Easter. The monthly decline into summer in the significance of the seizure of timber highlights the way in which the peasant attitude to timber was conditioned by such considerations. The demands of repair work around the villages also placed a premium on timber at this time.

Although field work remained a major demand on the peasants' time during April, the level of unrest inexorably continued to rise during that month from its modest beginnings in March. In part this was a natural and purely mechanical development: as news of the tsar's fall spread to all parts of Russia, increasing numbers of peasants became aware of the implications of this development. In addition, in those areas where knowledge of the tsar's fall was widespread soon after the event, the government's failure to stem the upsurge of unrest stimulated further unrest. However a more significant stimulant to unrest during April was the beginning of the crumbling of the fragile peasant faith in the government. Some aspects of rural unrest during the early spring reflect the existence of this faith. Initial land seizures seem to have been aimed at ameliorating the peasants' immediate economic position rather than at completely overturning the established land relations in the countryside;[58] they expected this to be done by the government in the near future. The seizure of parts of estates rather than entire estates and in many cases of land not being used, instead of land currently under cultivation, reflects a desire to disrupt production as little as possible and a confidence that the more substantial changes they desired would be implemented by the government. In addition, the widespread use of 'surreptitious' methods of seizure indicates a concern with legal forms and a desire to avoid an open challenge to the government at that point. However as spring wore on the peasants' faith in the government evaporated. No precise date can be established as the point at which widespread disillusionment set in; the peasants' loss of faith in the government was a process rather than a single cataclysmic event, and this process proceeded at different speeds in different areas of the country. Peasant faith in the government had been shallowly rooted right from the outset; the peasants had been disappointed too many times before by different governments naively to place their whole trust in the Provisional Government. Because their faith in the government was not deeply rooted, it did not take much to shake that faith. In the space of a few months the government succeeded in alienating a large segment of the peasantry.

The basis of the growth of peasant disillusionment with the government was disappointment with, and opposition to, government policies and actions in the three spheres which most affected the peasants: local administration, land and food. The government's moves in the sphere of local administration and the peasants' reaction to them have already been noted. Although the main thrust of peasant unrest directed against the government's food and land policies did not emerge until the first coalition government was in power, the basis for this was laid by the policies introduced by the first Provisional Government.

THE FOOD QUESTION

The most pressing question the Provisional Government had to face on coming to power was that of food supply. On 2 March the Temporary Committee of the State Duma, in agreement with the Soviet of Workers' and Soldiers' Deputies, established a food commission for the broad direction of food matters in the state. Three days later the new commission called on the population to send increased quantities of grain into the government store-houses. At the same time it instructed *guberniia zemstvo* boards to requisition grain from all land-holders (tenants as well as owners) having no less than 50 *dessiatiny* of land, and from commercial enterprises and banks.[59] The instruction went on to grant *guberniia zemstvo* boards the right to form *guberniia* food committees to handle food matters in the *guberniia*. These committees in turn, were authorized to organise local, *uezd*, *volost*, minor regional and city committees 'on wide democratic principles'. This early venture into the morass which was eventually to sap the strength and power of the government had little practical effect on the food situation since before it had time to become established, it was submerged by a flood of government legislation relating to this problem. Nevertheless this initial move was important because it established, at least in outline form, two of the basic principles upon which the government's food policy was to rest: the requisition of grain and a hierarchy of organised committees through which food affairs could be administered.

On 6 March responsibility for matters concerned with food and forage was transferred from the Ministry of the Interior to the Ministry of Agriculture, headed by the Kadet A. I. Shingarev. This shift of responsibility was institutionalised three days later by the formation of a State Food Committee under the chairmanship of the Minister of Agriculture.[60] Membership of the Committee was to consist of four representatives from the Executive Committee of the State Duma, five from the Soviet of Workers' and Soldiers' Deputies, five from the Soviet of Peasants' Deputies, four from both the All-Russian Unions of Towns and of Zemstva, six from the cooperatives (two each from producers', consumers' and credit cooperatives), three from the Central War Industry Committee, three from the Council of the Trade and Industry Congress, two from the Chamber of Agriculture, and one from the Executive Committee of the Congress of Statisticians. Representatives of government departments were to have only a consultative vote.[61] The Committee was to prepare a state food plan and to draft broad guiding principles and general measures on the food question. The Minister of Agriculture was to act 'in agreement' with the Committee. The new body thus constituted the central administrative agency for the management of food affairs on the part of the new government. As such, it replaced the food commission established a week earlier by the Temporary Committee of the State Duma and the Soviet.

The State Food Committee was an improvement on the earlier food commission which it replaced. It was rooted firmly in the institutional structure of government in Petrograd, thereby directly involving all the resources of the government in the struggle for food in a way which the legislation establishing the commission had not done. However the new Committee as established on 9 March was deficient in that no provision was made for membership of it by people who were closely in touch with the production of food or with conditions in the villages. The Committee was a capital-oriented organisation, the membership coming from the central organs of the various bodies rather than the branches scattered throughout the country. The composition of the Committee clearly reflected the gulf that existed between city and countryside during 1917. Within government circles it had been hoped that the urban nature of the Committee would not matter since its actions and decisions would be based on information and advice received from local bodies established, in part, to fulfil that function. Although such bodies formally were established a little over a fortnight later, they did little to overcome the isolation of the decision-makers in Petrograd from the actual producers of food in the villages.

Discussion had been taking place for some time within the government about the state monopoly on grain established by the former government. On 10 March the government issued a statement announcing its support for a state monopoly on the grain trade with some increase in the fixed price. The precise details remained to be worked out by the Minister of Agriculture. In addition the government acknowledged the need for a more efficient distribution to the producers of such articles of prime necessity as leather, iron, kerosene and wheels because of the great shortage of such items being experienced in the countryside at that time.[62] This statement was important not only because it foreshadowed the future grain monopoly, but also because it showed government recognition of the need to balance the grain monopoly by an adequate distribution of other goods to the peasants. The government recognised that the payment of increased prices for grain compulsorily purchased from the producers was likely to be of little incentive to the peasants to produce more grain if they were unable to purchase their requirements. Extra cash was of no use to the peasants; they needed fuel, tools and spare parts, not roubles.

On 25 March the government adopted the piece of legislation that was to form the crux of its food programme in 1917: the 'Law on the Transfer of Grain into the Direction of the State.' A 'temporary statute' dealing with food organs also was introduced.[63] The establishment of the grain monopoly was announced publicly in the official press five days after the decision was made, along with the following explanatory announcement:

> The difficult situation regarding food and the need to provide grain for the army and the population as soon as possible forces the Provisional Government to resort to the most urgent measures in the region of food. Henceforth all surplus grain reserves must be turned over to the state. This difficult task is entrusted to local organs which are being organised for assistance to state authorities. In accepting grain at new fixed prices in order to achieve a uniform and equitable distribution of food, the government at the same time considers that its first duty is to proceed at once to the establishment of fixed prices on articles of prime necessity (iron, textiles, kerosene, leather, etc) and to make these available to the population at the lowest possible prices. Thus the government believes that the new law which is being put into effect constitutes the first serious step on the road to bringing order into the economic life of the country which has been disrupted during the war and by the bad government of the old regime.

The decision of 25 March set out to implement two of the three main points contained in this announcement: a state monopoly on grain with fixed prices and a framework of food committees. However little attempt was made to fix the prices of articles of prime necessity.

The crux of the law on the passing of grain into the direction of the state was simple: all food and fodder grains except that deemed to be necessary for the owner were to go to the state through the medium of local food committees. Excluded from the compulsory alienation was to be that amount of grain necessary for the sowing of the fields for the maintenance of production, for the needs of the family and those employed on the farm, and also for such economic necessities as food for birds and livestock. In addition, an extra 10 per cent above estimated needs was to be retained on the farm for use in case of unforeseen circumstances. The precise amount of grain deemed necessary for each category was to be determined by the *guberniia* food committee in accordance with principles laid down in the legislation. The surplus was to be delivered by the owners to the local food committee at the date and place appointed by that body and at the price established by the government.[64] Failure to deliver the grain to the station or wharf where the food committee would receive it for further shipment meant that the food committee itself would collect the grain and deduct the cost from the amount due to the owner in payment for his produce. Refusal on the part of the owner to surrender his grain made it subject to requisition, and the hoarding of grain was declared illegal, as was the pledging of grain as surety. Until the grain was delivered into the hands of the food committee, the owner was responsible for its retention and protection, although the local food committee could relieve him of this responsibility if it considered this necessary. Local committees were also given the right to take over an owner's tools if he was deemed to be unable to utilise them to their fullest extent and therefore was not processing all the grain which his farm produced.[65] Provision was also made for the drawing of cooperatives, public organisations and private commercial-industrial enterprises into the task of grain procurement. Once the grain had been collected, the sale price was to be fixed by local organisations on the basis of purchase price plus overhead. Such prices were subject to ministerial approval.

In its attempt to increase the flow of grain from the countryside into the cities through this legislation, the government tried to deal with only one aspect of the problem. Despite repeated recognition of the need to balance the grain monopoly by improvement of the distribution of articles of prime necessity and the fixing of the prices of those articles, in practice the government virtually ignored this question. The powers granted to food committees in this sphere discussed below remained little more than a deferential nod in the direction of a vitally important problem. Although a Commission to Investigate the Supply of Articles of Prime Necessity to the Population was established on 23 April,[66] it was not until early June that responsibility for this was placed in the hands of the government department administering the grain monopoly, the newly-formed Ministry of Food.[67] Few practical moves were made to increase the production, improve the distribution and limit the price rises of these goods. This was a serious omission in the government's legislation of 25 March. It trapped the grain-producers in a vice composed on the one hand of fixed grain prices and, on the other, of rising prices of other necessities. The rampant inflation, the decreased production of articles of prime necessity due to industry's concentration on the needs of the war effort, and the chaotic distribution system meant that grain-producers had to pay ever-increasing amounts for the goods they needed. However with the price of grain pegged, and frequently at a level that was below the cost of production,[68] many could not afford to buy the goods they needed. As a result producers widely held their grain back from the government. As early as April a report from Nizhegorod asserted:

> There is grain in the *guberniia* but the peasants refuse to surrender it at the fixed price while there are no fixed statutory prices for the articles of prime peasant need.[69]

The government's decision of 25 March was generically incapable of solving the food problem even if an efficient distribution system could have been devised because it gave no encouragement to the producers to surrender their grain to the government.

The establishment of the grain monopoly also stimulated price rises. The government had hoped that by increasing the price of grain by 60 per cent over that prevailing before 25 March, producers would be encouraged to send their grain to the collection points in far greater quantities than they had hitherto done. However this steep rise in the price added fuel to the fire of inflation. The townspeople and those peasants dependent on the market for their supplies of grain now found their food bill substantially increased as a result of the government action. Furthermore, the effect this substantial price rise had on increasing the devaluation of the currency helped to offset to some extent the effect of the 60 per cent increase in price as far as the producers were concerned. The extra money meant virtually nothing because the prices of the goods they needed rose at a similar rate or faster. Thus the increase in the level of the fixed price for grain exacerbated the already difficult position of the grain consumers and, by increasing the rate of inflation and therefore of the effective devaluation of the currency, it did not substantially improve the position of the producers. They needed articles of prime necessity more than they needed money.

The government grain monopoly failed also because the comprehensive survey of grain, land-holdings and the local economic situation necessary for it to be implemented correctly was never completed. As a result, attempts by the committees to secure grain usually were conducted either under the old imperial formula or according to standards arbitrarily established by the committees themselves. The grain monopoly thus provided a cloak under which the illegal seizure of grain could be carried out.

The law transferring grain to the state was only part of the government's attack on the food question at this time. This decision was accompanied by the establishment of a structure of food organs throughout the country. The task of the newly-established food committees was more than simply the implementation of the grain monopoly, which essentially would have involved making an inventory of local grain stocks and requirements and the actual procurement and distribution of the surplus grain. The new food committees were also to involve themselves in 'the organisation of agricultural production'; they were to play a role in the actual process of farming itself, in the production of grain. This projected wide role of the food committees reflects Ministry of Agriculture views on the needs of farming outlined below. It also represents, at least on paper, a far greater degree of government involvement in the sphere than is implied by the law establishing the grain monopoly.

In the government's view the most important food committee was to be at the *guberniia* level. The *guberniia* committee was to head a hierarchy of committees established at the *uezd*, municipal and *volost* levels. If the *guberniia* committee considered it necessary, it had the power to establish regional committees along with, or in place of, *uezd* or *volost* committees, while the latter (plus municipal committees) were authorised to form smaller committees within the boundaries of their territories if the need arose. The functions of the *guberniia* committees as outlined in the 25 March legislation consisted of the general direction of food matters in the *guberniia*, the execution of orders of the Minister of Agriculture concerning the satisfaction of the food needs of the army and population and the provision to the population of articles of prime necessity, the supply of information to the government on the food situation in the *guberniia*, and assistance in the organisation of agricultural production. In order to carry out these tasks, a wide sphere of competence was accorded to the *guberniia* food committee. The committee had to ascertain the exact position with regard to the availability of food, forage, and articles of prime necessity in the *guberniia* compared with the need and demand for those products. It had to establish a timetable for the delivery of the grain to the state storehouses. The storage of grain and the supervision of enterprises processing the grain were also within its competence. The power to requisition grain, to establish the conditions for the conclusion of agreements on state procurement, to fix the sale price on goods of prime necessity, to control the cartage of food and the distribution of implements of production, and to supervise the actions of food committees within the *guberniia*, all lay within the realm of the *guberniia* food committee. Legislation thus accorded the committee an impressive array of tools for the implementation of the grain monopoly. However it was given no guidance as to what action to take if the producers were to refuse to surrender their grain. The government assumed that the producers would act in accordance with the state monopoly and made no provision for opposition to the monopoly. The *guberniia* committees were thus given everything except the power to enforce their decisions and to carry out their functions in the face of local opposition.

The real ground work for the grain monopoly was to be done by the lower level committees, those in the *uezdy* and *volosti*. It was these committees that were to perform the functions over which the *guberniia* committee had broad supervisory control. The tasks of the *uezd* committees, as outlined in the 25 March legislation, were as follows: to determine the amount of food products and articles of prime necessity on hand in the *uezd*; to determine the procedure for the state purchase of food and forage products within the *uezd* and the distribution of them by *volost*; to establish the procedure for the distribution of food and forage products and articles of prime necessity among the local population; and to advise the *guberniia* committee on the local situation to facilitate the implementation of appropriate measures. In fulfilling these functions, the *uezd* food committees were to be guided by the directives of the *guberniia* food committee. The basic role of the *uezd* food committee was to act as an intermediate organisational level between the general overall control of the *guberniia* committee and the practical implementation of measures by the *volost* committees. The *uezd* committee was to coordinate the actions of the *volost* committees in the collection of grain and to supervise the distribution of that produce among the *volosti*. The *uezd* committee was in reality to be little more than an organisational transmission belt, translating the broad *guberniia*-wide plans worked out by the *guberniia* committee into meaningful directives for the *volost* committees. Its decision-making power was circumscribed by the power accorded to committees at the *guberniia* level and it had little independent part to play in the operation of the grain monopoly.

In practical terms the most important cog in the structure was to be the *volost* food committee. The tasks allotted to *volost* committees were as follows: determination of the amount of food and forage products and articles of prime necessity on hand in the *volost*; state purchase of food and forage products and articles of prime necessity; organisation of the collection, reception and transfer of food products; determination of the amount of produce necessary for the population of the *volost* and the amount of surplus that should go to the state; distribution of produce among the local population according to norms established by the *guberniia* committee; and informing *guberniia* and *uezd* committees about local conditions to enable the higher committees to take appropriate measures. Thus the *volost* committee was designed to be the actual means through which the grain monopoly was to be implemented. This body was to acquire, transport and store the grain, and distribute it among the populace. However, like the two committees above it, the *volost* food committee was given no power to enforce its decisions. Although the right to requisition grain included in the 'Law on the Transfer of Grain into the Direction of the State' covered the *volost* committee, the committee was not given any express grant of power to force recalcitrant producers to hand over their grain. Furthermore, the failure of the government to establish any satisfactory institutional mechanism to ensure that these committees were provided with adequate supplies of articles of prime necessity ensured that they also lacked the means to offer incentives for the surrender of grain. In addition, no indication was given until 20 May[70] as to the way in which producers would be paid for their crop, thereby creating an area of uncertainty in the minds of producers about the food committees right from the start. The problem of payment for grain surrendered, or the inability of local organs to pay promptly, remained significant throughout the year. The *volost* food committees lacked both the carrot and the stick.

In the unsettled conditions of 1917 the legislation establishing the food committees was deficient in one other vital respect also. It failed to build into the food committee structure any mechanism of meaningful accountability for actions taken by the committees. Formally the lower level committees were instructed that they were to work under the supervision of the committees at higher levels, the *guberniia* committee was given the right to issue compulsory instructions on matters within its jurisdiction, committee chairmen were empowered to alter decisions taken by lower level committees, and complaints against decisions or actions by lower level bodies were to be directed toward committees at the higher levels. These provisions of the legislation established the principle of accountability of the lower level to the higher level committees. However the committees at the higher levels, the national, *guberniia* and *uezd* committees, were given no power to enforce their decisions or to bring a wayward subordinate into line. They were unable to translate the principle of accountability into practice. Furthermore this lack of effective accountability within the food committee structure was replicated by the absence of any effective external check on the actions of the food committees. It was not until September that the actions of the food committees were made subject to the judicial process. Until that time there was no mechanism for individuals to protest to an independent authority against the food organs. The legislation of 25 March thus provided no meaningful accountability, thereby building into the structure an ambiguity in relations which was fatal in the chaotic months of 1917.

The 25 March legislation provided for the establishment of food boards to act as executive arms of the food committees at all levels. The chairman and assistant chairman of the food committee were to fill the same positions on the food board. The remaining membership was to consist of two to six members elected annually by the food committee both from among its own members and from individuals outside its membership. The boards were to meet at least once a week and the sphere of their actions was to be both defined and supervised by the corresponding food committees. The food boards were conceived as operational extensions of the food committees, fulfilling the latter's functions when they were not meeting.

The final major concern of the legislation of 25 March was that of membership of the food committees at the various levels. Membership of the *guberniia* food committee was to consist of the following: three elected from the *guberniia zemstvo* assembly,[71] three elected from the municipal *duma* of the *guberniia* capital, one from the local branch of the All-Russian Zemstvo Union, one from the local branch of the All-Russian Union of Towns, one from the local branch of the War-Industry Committee, five from the local soviet of workers' deputies (or, in its absence, from the sickness funds or trade unions), five from the local Peasants' Union, six from the local cooperatives (as far as possible two each from the producers', consumers' and credit cooperatives), two from the *guberniia* agricultural societies, three from the exchange committees or commercial organisations acting in their stead, one each from the *zemstvo* and municipal statistical organisations, and one each from the agronomic, economic and public health *zemstvo* organisations where these existed. In addition, representatives from the *uezd* food committees could attend in a consultative capacity during their stay in the capital, as could representatives of the government departments of War, Finance, Trade and Industry, State Control, Communications, Agriculture and Interior. Emissaries sent by the State Food Committee could also participate.

The committees' capacity to devise realistic proposals for agriculture in the *guberniia* was inhibited by their membership. The committees were too large and unwieldy to work efficiently; without any representatives of the *uezd* committees or the State Food Committee present, attendance at *guberniia* committee meetings could be as high as 42. The composition of that membership also was significant in this regard; very few members were likely to have close and direct links with the peasants. No provision was made for peasant representation on the committee; such bodies as the Peasants' Union and the cooperatives which were active in the villages were not represented on the committee by local village delegates, but by members of those organisations stationed in the *guberniia* capital or by delegates chosen for this purpose. The resulting psychological isolation from the peasantry invariably was exacerbated by the location of the committee in the *guberniia* capital. The *guberniia* committee was a town committee, oriented more toward the problem of consumption in the towns than production in the villages, its members often motivated more by party ideology than by intimate knowledge of village life; it had little empathy with the rural producers. There was no way that the *guberniia* committee could carry out its functions successfully while it remained isolated from the mass of the grain producers and out of step with their mood.

Membership of the *uezd* committee was to consist of the following: three elected from the *uezd zemstvo* assembly, two from the municipal *duma* of the *uezd* capital, three from local soviets of workers' deputies (or, in their absence, representatives from sickness funds or trade unions), three from the local branch of the Peasants' Union, three from the *uezd* cooperatives (as far as possible one from each of the producers', consumers' and credit cooperatives), one from the local agricultural society, two from the local commercial-industrial class, and one from each cooperative, agronomic and public health organisation of the *uezd zemstvo* where such organisations existed. In addition, representatives of *volost* and regional committees and of the government departments of War, Finance, Trade and Industry, State Control, Communications, Agriculture and Interior could participate with a consultative vote. Like the *guberniia* food committee, the *uezd* committee was urban in orientation. It was situated in the *uezd* main town and very few of the large and unwieldy membership of 27 (excluding representatives of *volost* and regional committees and of the government departments) were likely to be grain producers. Even the transmission belt nature of the *uezd* committee could not offset the effect of this type of membership: lack of close familiarity with and sympathy for life in the villages hamstrung many committee members' attempts to guide and regulate agricultural life in the *uezd*.

Government reliance on the urban population for the bulk of the staff of the committees it established should cause little surprise. The government itself was primarily an urban-based and urban-oriented body. Although some of its members possessed extensive land-holdings, usually they spent a large part of their time in the cities, leaving their estates to be run by managers. This was particularly the case during the war. But the basic urban-centredness of these people alone is insufficient to explain their reliance on the urban areas and urban inhabitants for the administration of the rural areas. The central government was concerned to establish its control over Russia, and in order to achieve this it had to depend upon people who were literate and, ideally, experienced in administration. These people were found in the towns, not the villages. Furthermore it was the larger towns that were best served by the communications network, by the telegraph and occasionally the railway. Use of this network was vital to achieve the measure of control at which the government aimed. These administrative factors dictated the government's reliance on the towns, but they could not ameliorate peasant distrust of the towns and their inhabitants.

The success or failure of the government effort depended on the *volost* food committee. The membership of this body was to consist of three private land-owners elected by the *uezd zemstvo* assembly, six peasants elected by the *volost skhod*, three from local cooperatives (as far as possible one from each of the producers', consumers' and credit cooperatives), two from workers' trade unions or sickness funds where such existed, one from the local commercial-industrial class, and three from among the local *zemstvo* employees. Representatives from the Ministry of Agriculture could participate with a consultative vote. The composition of this committee appears to be far more realistic, at least on paper, than those at the *guberniia* and *uezd* levels; half of the membership would have had close links with the producers of grain, if they were not producers themselves. However in practice the legal composition of this committee was meaningless because the committee as envisaged by the government was overtaken by events. By the time attempts were made to establish these committees on a wide scale, peasant ire already had been turned toward private land-owners. Added to this, traditionally the *zemstvo* was widely unpopular among the peasants. Consequently the practical application of the legislation on membership of the *volost* food committees was undermined by peasant reluctance to work with some of the groups which should have been represented on those committees. Moreover the position the *volost* committees were to occupy already was filled by those organisations formed from below, from within the villages, discussed previously. As a result, *volost* food committees usually tended to become either appendages of already-existing peasant organisations or merged totally with those village-based bodies. In either event, *volost* food committees became more responsive to impulses from below than directives from above.[72]

By the end of March the government had formally established the framework for handling food matters that was to remain substantially unchanged until the government's fall in October. However in the early days of April, the unforeseen emergence of rural unrest stimulated the government to take further action to overcome the food crisis. This involved an expansion in the competence of the food committees as they were originally envisaged in the legislation of 25 March. In the law establishing the grain monopoly responsibility for the protection and safety of the grain lay with the owner of the crop, although food committees could relieve him of this if they deemed it necessary. By a decision of 11 April[73] the defence of all sown land was entrusted specifically to the *guberniia*, *uezd* and *volost* food committees. By mutual agreement with the farmer, the committees were to carry out the inspection and supervision of individual farms, ensuring that all measures were taken to ensure the safety of the crop. If any farms placed under the mantle of the food committees in this way sustained damage as a result of popular disturbances, the government was to reimburse the owners for the real losses thereby sustained. However, the legislation continued, compensation was to be paid only in those instances when the owner of the crop had taken all measures possible for the defence of his property. Thus while the government accepted the responsibility for the defence of all crops, the owner was expected to take defensive measures also.

The legislation of 11 April involved a subtle extension of the power of the food committees. Their control over the crop previously had existed only after that crop had been delivered to the state collection points or after the owners had called on the committees for assistance. However the decision of 11 April made the food committees responsible for the protection of the crops while they were standing in the fields; food committees no longer had to wait for the owner to request assistance but could initiate the move to establish their control themselves. The government hoped that this would increase the flow of grain into the collection points in two ways: by offering protection against popular unrest, the government hoped that land-owners would be encouraged to sow more land and thereby increase output; furthermore it hoped that its local bodies would be more effective in protecting the crops from peasant depredations than were individual land-owners. This extension of the sphere of competence of the food committees thus brought them right into the forefront of rural unrest. However by allowing food committees to establish their control over privately-owned crops themselves and by failing to specify to what extent protection of the crop constituted control over all matters related in any way to that crop, the government legislation provided cover for the 'surreptitious' seizure of land by the peasants acting through the local food committees.

As well as trying to increase the sown area by providing greater security for land-owners' crops, the decision of 11 April also made provision for the bringing into production of land that currently was not being used. If the owner refused to sow his land, the legislation accorded to the food committees the right to take over that land and either organise sowing it themselves, or lease it to local land-holders for the current harvest at a price determined by the food committees. Any rental received for such land was to be paid to the owner of the land. This decision had a number of practical ramifications, none of which was foreseen by the government. For land-owners, if they did not wish to go to the trouble or expense of sowing part of their land, they could leave it unworked in the expectation that they would still receive an income from it guaranteed by local government organs. In return, the state would gain food production from an area that otherwise would remain unproductive. However this apparently simple exchange in practical terms was frustrated by the government's inability to control the local food committees. Many peasants utilised this legislation in their 'surreptitious' seizure of land-owners' land; by preventing land-owners from sowing part of their land, the peasants could take over that land through the local food committee with an appearance of legality.

The functions of the food committees continued to expand later in the month. On 17 April the government moved to mobilise the broad ranks of the population into the struggle for grain by giving *guberniia* food committees the right to draft the entire population, beginning with those in the strongest economic position, for work in the cartage and loading of goods for state and public needs.[74] By making the entire population subject to mobilisation by *guberniia* food committees, the government extended the authority of these bodies to cover manpower distribution. Although the legislation of 25 March contained the basis for this power by according to the food committees responsibility for the cartage of grain, the establishment of the principle of food committee control over the population of the *guberniia* was a new development.

On the same date the government's concern over possible weakness in its grain procurement network was shown by the reaffirmation of its determination to use nongovernmental organisations in the state purchase of grain.[75] Food committees were told that they could use cooperatives, public organisations, private commercial and industrial enterprises and individual merchants to purchase grain and fodder on a commission basis on behalf of the food committees. The use of these institutions appeared to be a sensible move. By permitting the use of such bodies, the government gave the local food committees access to what had been a well-developed network of organisations and procurement agencies manned by people with experience in these matters. However the government did not foresee the hostility with which the peasants regarded these organisations, a hostility marked by the widespread peasant reluctance to deal with these bodies. Furthermore, the government's preference for cooperative institutions rather than individual merchants in grain procurement created widespread dissatisfaction among the latter, a development which made the necessary cooperation between these arms of government policy difficult to achieve. In practice, the use of these different bodies led to competition between them to obtain the grain in the peasants' hands, encouraging them to ignore the fixed price for grain in an attempt to outbid their competitors. Clashes between these different bodies occurred in many areas. Thus the benefits that seemed to be promised by the use of these non-governmental organs were accompanied by some considerable practical drawbacks.

These government moves to improve distribution and supply were accompanied in late April by a tentative beginning at encouraging the peasants to come forward with more of their grain. Leading circles in Petrograd had acknowledged that a major problem would be to persuade the peasants to surrender the grain that they were holding, and thereby to maximise the state procurement of grain remaining in the peasants' hands.[76] With this in mind the government took some small steps to increase the trickle of articles of prime necessity into the countryside. The first move in this respect was taken on 21 April with the establishment of a government monopoly on leather, to be operated through regional committees established throughout the country.[77] This was to be the first of many proposed steps to increase the distribution of articles of prime necessity, as indicated by the formation three days later of the Commission to Investigate the Supply of Consumer Goods to the Population.[78] The Commission's brief was to cover all consumer goods, although it was to be particularly concerned with 'industrial products, such as metals and metallic goods, leather and leather goods, sugar, tea, kerosene, soap, textiles and paper'. Working on the basis of information provided by government institutions, public organisations and private enterprises, the Commission was to determine the level of popular requirements, industry's capacity to meet these requirements, the level of existing stocks, the best mode of distribution to the consumer, and a feasible scale of fixed prices and means for regulating them. The government was now committed formally to the regulation of both aspects of exchange between city and countryside. However, in practical terms, very little was done to increase the supply of these goods to the rural population.

As well as trying to increase the flow of grain into the collection points and the cities by the above means, an attempt was made to regulate consumption throughout the country as a whole. The government tried to do this through the introduction on 29 April of grain rationing throughout the entire Russian state with the exception of Transcaucasia and the *oblasti* of the Turkestan governor-generalship.[79] This decision provided for the establishment of ration standards for the distribution and consumption of rye, wheat, spelt, millet, buckwheat, lentils, beans, peas, corn and all flour and groats. The ration system was to be implemented by the food committees. They were to ensure the equal distribution of products among the whole population, with the exception of those engaged in heavy physical labour who were to receive a higher ration. Ration cards were to be issued in the urban areas, while in rural localities 'some documentary means' of ensuring the equality of distribution had to be established. The ration amounts specified in the decision were declared to be maxima not minima, and involved no guarantee on the part of the food organs to supply the full amount. The introduction of rationing was a logical corollary to the establishment of the grain monopoly and the government's attempts to increase production and improve supply. If the government could regulate these three aspects of the food question, production, distribution and consumption, the food problem would disappear. These new regulations were also significant in relation to the powers of the food committees: they specified formally the way in which food committees were to handle the grain distribution functions accorded to them by the legislation under which they were established. Thus it had taken the government more than a month formally to outline the powers of the food committees in an area over which they were supposed to be exercising control from the time of their establishment.

By the end of April it was clear that government attempts to solve the food question were foundering on the rocks of local intransigence and institutional incapacity. In the words of War Minister Guchkov:

The situation with regard to food for the people and forage in particular, is not favourable. Here is why this is so. Under the old structure, however violent the chaos, the authorities were those who were heard, there were elements of coercion without which our struggle is impossible . . . In the region of food, local organs do not always act on the demands made to them by the central authorities. If you wish, this is fully understandable psychologically. In the localities the danger exists that the local population will remain without food if it acts on all the demands of the central authorities. The local people over-sensitively feel the interests of their region and prefer to retain their reserves for themselves . . . without a strong authority, which has subordinated the local organisations we will not manage.[80]

Guchkov put his finger on a basic weakness of the government's position: its inability to have its desires carried out at the lowest levels of rural society, manifested most clearly by its inability both to persuade the producers to give up their grain on a wide scale and to enforce its will on the lower level organs theoretically responsive to its directives. There was little hope for the government's grain monopoly and its rationing of consumption if it could neither persuade the peasants to give up their grain nor force them to surrender it.

By the time of the demise of the first Provisional Government in early May, the broad outlines of the government's approach to the food question had been established by the Ministry of Agriculture headed by the Kadet Shingarev. Despite changes in government and changes in minister, the broad structure remained substantially unchanged in principle until the bolsheviks came to power in October. A government grain monopoly with fixed prices had been established, a nation-wide rationing system had been introduced, and a three-tiered structure of food committees had been created beneath the State Food Committee to administer food matters. However by the beginning of May the problems with the government's approach were already emerging. By its failure to ensure an adequate supply of articles of prime necessity to the countryside, the government ensured that the peasants would refuse to surrender their grain. However the government did not give the food committees the power to overcome the peasant opposition to the operation of the monopoly that was thus generated. Furthermore the absence of clearly specified relations between committees at the various levels and the inability of the higher level committees to keep the lower level bodies in line undermined the structure's efficiency. However the basic weakness of the committee structure was the inability of the *volost* food committees to take root among the peasants in the form desired by the government. With the basic level committees more responsive to the peasants than to the government, the cutting edge of the government's policy was blunted: without responsive instruments at the local level, the government was unable to implement effectively the policies it announced from the capital. This was already becoming a fact of life by late April.

THE LAND PROBLEM

At the outset of its rule the Provisional Government was not greatly pressed by the land question. Unlike the food question, the land problem had not appeared directly to influence events leading to the fall of the tsar. Nor did the gradual development of rural unrest focused on the land push the food question out of the forefront of the government's attention. The land question was in many ways seen as simply an adjunct to the food question; the basic problem was not to change the formal land ownership pattern, except in so far as the lands of the former ruling family were concerned, but to increase output on the lands as they now stood. This was the major thrust of government land policy throughout 1917, a thrust which wholly ignored the wishes of the people over whom the government ruled.

The first action of the Provisional Government on land matters was the nationalisation on 16 and 17 March of the land belonging to the tsar's immediate family (the imperial appanages) and the tsar himself (Kabinet lands).[81] These were symbolic acts, signifying to the population the finality of the overthrow of the tsar, but they had little practical significance for the country's needs or the people's demands. The first detailed indication of the government's views on the land question appeared in a statement of 19 March and published two days later.[82] After acknowledging the land question as the most important task left by the old regime, the government sharply condemned arbitary and violent attempts to solve this question before it could be resolved through law adopted by the people's representatives. However before such a law could be adopted, extensive preparatory work had to be undertaken in the form of a wide-ranging investigation into the current state of land ownership, use and needs. The government recognised its major task to be implementation of these preparatory measures so that full information could be given to the people's representatives, and with this in view it pledged to establish a land committee within the Ministry of Agriculture to carry out these functions. Thus the government's basic policy on land relations was clear by mid-March: land relations were to remain frozen while investigation of all aspects of the land question was undertaken in order to present to the Constituent Assembly all the materials it would need finally to resolve the land question.

However within this static view of land relations the government pursued a policy of encouraging all efforts toward increasing the productivity of the land. Within the Ministry of Agriculture there had been concern for some time about the ability of the rural population to sow sufficient land to satisfy the demands that would be made on the crop. Consequently during March the Ministry outlined a wide-ranging scheme to improve the productive capacity of the rural sector. The local population was to be encouraged to participate in field-work as much as possible while, by agreement with the War Ministry, large numbers of reservist forces and prisoners-of-war were to be placed under the direction of the Ministry of Agriculture for field-work. Provision also was made for the use of refugees in field-work. In addition, steps were taken to ensure that agricultural workers were not called away to the war during busy periods in the fields. Supervision of the work of these extra workers was entrusted to the food committees.[83]

Formal responsibility for all aspects of agricultural production was assumed by the Ministry of Agriculture headed by the Kadet, A. I. Shingarev. The Ministry was to be responsible for

All questions of the organisation of sowing and the supply to agricultural production of metals, implements and other means of production, fertiliser, work forces, credit and buildings . . .[84]

The ministry's local organs were to be the food committees:

The implementation of measures in the localities, pending the formation of local organisations on correct democratic bases is entrusted to *guberniia*, *uezd* and *volost* food committees . . .

Administratively in the short term this was a wise move. The centralisation of total responsibility at the upper and lower levels should have promoted greater efficiency in the implementation of government programmes. However in practice this created the basis for later ambiguity. At the national level, the subsequent creation of the Ministry of Food complicated the clear administrative arrangement established above. At the local level, the situation was to become even more confused: if food committees were to exercise total responsibility until the formation of the *volost zemstvo* (the 'local organisations on correct democratic bases' to which reference was made), what was to be the function of other local bodies, such as land committees, formed before the *volost zemstvo*? The resulting ambiguity and confusion was to characterise government policy in the rural areas until the government's fall in October.

The organisations which the government perceived to be the most important instruments of government land policy, the land committees, were brought into existence on 21 April.[85] In a preliminary statement to the main body of the legislation, the government outlined the broad functions which it expected the committees to perform:

> These committees will be responsible for the collection of information on local land arrangements and land needs of the population, and the resolution of disputes and misunderstandings on land matters during the transitional period up until the implementation of land reform by the Constituent Assembly.

Reflecting the rise in land violations in April compared with March, the government statement then attacked all attempts at the arbitrary resolution of the land question, called on the population not to attempt to solve it themselves, and assured the soldiers at the front that no attempt would be made to resolve the land question in their absence. The tone of this statement clearly summarises the government's attitude to land matters. The newly-formed land committees were not meant to solve the land question at that time, but merely to create the conditions for the future solution of that question by collecting all the data necessary for that task. Their role in settling disputes and misunderstandings arising over land matters was specifically designated to be temporary; any settlements the committees brought about were to remain operative only until the final resolution of the land question by the Constituent Assembly. The immediate aim of the committees was the prevention of disruption to agricultural production arising from continuing disputes. The government's lack of a sense of urgency was highlighted by this preliminary statement. The need for careful preparation and for waiting until the troops came home were, as recognised by the government, prerequisites for a fair and just resolution of the land question in the long term. However in the immediate context of 1917, with land hunger rampant in many rural areas and the level of rural unrest steadily rising, such considerations were politically unwise.

The functions of the land committees were outlined in greater detail in the body of the legislation itself. At the summit of the hierarchy of land committees was the Chief Land Committee. Based in Petrograd, this body was to be responsible for the overall supervision of the collection and processing of the information necessary for the future land reform and for measures preparatory to it. On the basis of the information thus collected and the views of the lower level land committees, the Chief Land Committee was to draw up a general plan of land reform for consideration by the Constituent Assembly.[86] In addition to this planning role, the Committee was also to investigate and advise the Minister of Agriculture on the relevance to current agricultural conditions of earlier established laws and institutions, on coordination between land organs and the government, and on the need for other methods of regulating land and associated economic relations. The Chief Land Committee was thus meant to advise the Minister on matters of a legislative nature concerning the operation of the government's land policy, as well as processing the data for the future land reform.

In practice the Chief Land Committee was to be less important than the lower level committees. According to the legislation of 21 April, *guberniia* and *uezd* land committees were to be established everywhere throughout the country. The functions accorded to these bodies are worth quoting in full because they clearly demonstrate one of the government's major failings: its willingness to fiddle at the edges of the land problem without facing up to the core of the issue—the peasant demand for land redistribution. The most important duties of the *guberniia* and *uezd* committees were outlined as follows:

(1) The collection of information necessary for the land reform; the compilation of views and conclusions on questions related to it as well as the carrying out of necessary preparatory activities.
(2) The execution of the decisions of the central authorities on land matters.
(3) Agreement with local government organisations on questions concerning the management of lands and agricultural

properties belonging to the state, and submission to the Chief Land Committee in relevant cases of proposals concerning changes in the procedure for using and administering these properties.

(4) Publication of compulsory regulations on questions of agricultural and land relations within the limits of existing statutes and laws of the Provisional Government.

(5) Settlement of questions, disputes and misunderstandings arising in the field of land and agricultural relations, within the limits of existing statutes and laws of the Provisional Government (and) the establishment, if necessary, of chambers of mediation and conciliation for the adoption of measures to regulate relations which may arise as a result of the arbitrary violation of anyone's rights and interests.

NOTE: Cases will be submitted to such chambers, organised on the model of courts of arbitration, by agreement of the parties, on whom decisions of the chamber will be binding.

(6) Prevention of the acts of private persons leading to the depreciation of land and agricultural properties, if these acts are not justified by public needs and the needs of the state.

(7) The raising before the Chief Land Committee of questions of removing such properties from the possession of private persons;

(8) Implementation of relevant decisions of the state authority, and agreements with local food committees and other government institutions on the most expedient utilisation of these properties.

Unlike *guberniia* and *uezd* committees, *volost* land committees did not have to be established everywhere. They were to be

   . . . formed on the initiative of the local population or *uezd* committee.

and their duties were to be defined by the *uezd* committee within the limits applying to *guberniia* and *uezd* committees.

Apart from the major weakness of the land committees in the eyes of the peasants—their failure to have a mandate to carry out land redistribution—the land committee structure as established by this legislation had a number of practical problems. Within the hierarchy of land committees there was no clear demarcation of competence except that implied by the territorial divisions of *guberniia, uezd* and *volost*. The legislation did accord to the Chief Land Committee the power to define further the jurisdiction of the individual committees and to act as arbiter in their disputes, and it also gave the *guberniia* committee a temporary veto over the decisions of the lower level committees pending appeal by the lower body to the Chief Land Committee, but it gave no effective guidance regarding the limits of each committee's jurisdiction. The powers of the *volost* committee were not even defined. Furthermore this ambiguity was exacerbated by the government's failure to build any meaningful accountability into the structure: if lower level committees decided to ignore instructions coming from above, there was little the higher level bodies could do to enforce compliance. This ambiguous situation, in which both individual committee's spheres of competence and general notions of accountability were vague, created the possibility of friction which the stresses of the chaotic times translated into reality.

The ambiguity present within the land committee hierarchy was exacerbated by a parallel ambiguity in relations with the food committees established a month earlier. Although in theory the foci of these two structures were clearly distinct, in practice their areas of competence overlapped. The theoretical distinction could be maintained in practical terms only if the sphere of competence of each type of committee was defined far more precisely than the government had done. The food committees could carry out neither their investigatory nor their procurement and distribution functions without dealing with land relations, particularly after the widening of their powers on 11 April.[87] Due to the prior establishment of the food committees and the broad interpretation placed on their powers, the land committees could not carry out their appointed functions without moving into an area already occupied by the food committees. The government made no attempt to specify precise guidelines for these committees until July, with the result that the establishment of land committees led to the development of grey areas in the local administrative structure which only served to impede the efficient conduct of government policy.

Another way in which lack of clarity in the 21 April legislation caused problems involved the granting to the land committees of the power to dispossess an individual of his land if he was undertaking action leading to its depreciation. By not defining the types of action involved, the way was left clear for the seizure of property by these organs for reasons that may have been far removed from those in the minds of the framers of the legislation. This provided a ready means for the 'surreptitious' seizure of land by peasants.

The efficient implementation of government policy also was hampered by the type of relationship between committees and population that was envisaged by the framers of the 21 April legislation. True to the ideals and the perceptions of the government, they believed that the population would wait patiently for the Constituent Assembly to resolve the land question and that they would obey the organs established to regulate affairs until the Constituent Assembly was convened. Consequently they made no provision for the emergence of popular opposition to the committees or the refusal to implement their directives. The legislation did not accord to the committees' power to overcome popular opposition or to enforce their will on a recalcitrant local population. If they could not persuade the local population to comply, the committees were not in a position to force them to do so. The ambiguity in relations between population and committee which this created was compounded by another: the initial legislation provided for no independent check on the activities of land committees. Until they were made accountable to the judicial apparatus in September, land committees and their actions could not legally be challenged in an independent forum by those who felt aggrieved by them.

The operation of the committees in the context of the public mood of 1917 also was hindered by the legal composition of those committees. According to the 21 April legislation, the Chief Land Committee was to consist of the Minister of Agriculture and his Assistant Ministers, a chairman, business manager and 25 members appointed by the government;[88] one representative from each of the *guberniia* land committees, six representatives from the All-Russian Peasants' Union, six from the All-Russian Soviet of Peasants' Deputies, three from each of the Temporary Committee of the State Duma and the All-Russian Cooperative Union, one representative from each of eleven political parties,[89] five representatives from the most important scholarly societies, and experts invited by the chairman with an advisory vote. Representatives of government departments were able to sit in with an advisory vote. However membership of the committee was far too large and unwieldy for effective operation; altogether it consisted of 161 members, and with 'competent persons' over 200 attended meetings. Furthermore this situation was exacerbated by the wide variety of views represented in the committee, from the conservative right of some of the government appointees to the radical left of some of those coming as representatives from the rural areas. Moreover, given the composition of the membership, many of the members did not have the intimate knowledge of village life or the sympathetic approach necessary to appreciate fully the problems of the peasant producers. This was particularly the case in the executive committee which was dominated by SRs, many of whom were blinded by their ideological beliefs from seeing the actual situation in the countryside.[90] The executive committee remained isolated from the real world of the villages; it was only at the occasional full meetings of the Chief Land Committee that representatives from the *guberniia* land committees attended, with the result that much of the work of the committee was dominated by members who were primarily Petrograd-oriented.

Of more practical significance for the course of Russian agriculture during 1917 were the *guberniia* and *uezd* committees, and yet much of the membership of these bodies was not distinguished by intimate knowledge of peasant life either. *Guberniia* committees were to consist of four members elected by the *guberniia zemstvo* assembly, one by the municipal *duma* of the *guberniia* capital, one representative from each *uezd* land committee, representatives from the economic sections of the *guberniia zemstvo* board (to a maximum of three), a justice of the circuit court, a justice of the peace, a representative of the Ministry of Agriculture, and experts invited by the chairman with the right of a consultative vote. *Uezd* land committees were to include four members elected by the *uezd zemstvo* assembly, one by the municipal *duma* of the *uezd* capital, one from each *volost* land committee, a *zemstvo* agronomist and statistician, a justice of the peace (where there were no *zemstvo* agronomists, statisticians or justice available, appropriate people could be invited by the land committee), and experts invited by the chairman with an advisory vote. The composition of the committees at these levels was an unfortunate compromise. The inclusion of members elected from the lower level land committees who were usually both more radical and less educated than the other members, hindered the ability of these bodies effectively to conduct the investigation into the land situation which the government required. However the inclusion of these people rarely created a strong sense of empathy between the committee and the villages. The representatives of the *volost* and *uezd* committees in those at the next highest levels usually were chosen not from among those living in the villages and tilling their plots, but from the ranks of those who had left the villages and were living in the towns. Local party activists often filled these positions. The links that many of these had with the villages sometimes remained strong, but the presence of such links usually could not ameliorate the developing perception in the villages of the land committees as foreign institutions. The committees were widely seen as composed of people from the towns who had little knowledge of, or sympathy with, conditions in the villages. Furthermore in the peasants' eyes they were manned by the traditional exploiters of the men who worked the land, the land-owners and government officials whose role in the rural economy was solely to live off the sweated labour of the peasants.

This impression of foreignness was reinforced by the physical location of these committees in the major towns of the *gubernii* and *uezdy*, thereby being to some extent isolated physically from the villages and their concerns. Thus as far as many peasants were concerned, the *guberniia* and *uezd* land committees were both out of touch with, and alien to, the peasants and their interests, while on the government side their membership made the committees unable to fulfil the task envisaged for them.

The only land committees on which the peasants in the villages could play a major part were the *volost* committees, and yet under the government legislation these did not have to be established in all *volosti*. It is difficult to see how the *guberniia* and *uezd* committees could be expected to carry out their functions effectively without being rooted in the villages through *volost* committees; these were the obvious links between village and town. According to the 21 April legislation, in those instances where *volost* committees were established, their membership was to consist of five full and three alternate members and they were to be elected by the *volost zemstva*. Pending the introduction of that body, the *uezd* land committee was to determine the procedure for electing members in accordance with local conditions. However these provisions of the legislation were inoperative from the start. The *volost zemstva* were not instituted widely throughout Russia, elections for them not being held until August–September by which time all the *volost* committees that were going to be established had been established. Furthermore by the time *volost* land committees were formed in many areas, they were confronted with the prior existence of village-based peasant organisations and food committees. As a result, when land committees were formed at the *volost* level, the actual configurations of those committees were determined more by existing local power relationships than by the dictates of the *uezd* committee.

Thus during the life of the first Provisional Government, a formal administrative structure had been decreed for the rural areas and two specific institutional structures to deal with problems of food and land had been created. However the conditions had already been laid for the complete and utter collapse of the government's rural policy. The government's refusal to countenance land reform and its inability to persuade grain producers to surrender their grain in larger quantities, set the tone of a policy that was bound to evoke widespread opposition within the countryside. This could only be exacerbated by the government's reliance on people seen by the peasants as traditional exploiters to man the newly-established administrative structures. Peasant opposition was manifested in the increasing level of unrest as the government's life drew to a close. Yet in this situation the institutions developed by the government were incapable of taking any positive action to rectify the problems. Not only were the institutional structures shrouded in ambiguity, but those at the *uezd* and *guberniia* levels which tended to remain responsive to the government generally wielded little influence in the villages, while the organisations at village and *volost* levels were more responsive to the peasants than to government directives. The first government thus bequeathed to the second not only a problem that was to become of ever-increasing magnitude as the months passed, but also an institutional framework that was incapable of coping with that problem.

3 The Summer Upheaval

The uneasy balance of political forces in Petrograd was upset in April by the war issue. The war aims espoused by Foreign Minister Miliukov in his note of 18 April to the allied governments in which he reaffirmed Russia's treaty obligations, thereby pledging to remain in the war until final victory was achieved, evoked wide opposition within the ranks of both the government and the Soviet. This opposition also spilled over into the streets, with demonstrations occurring on 20 and 21 April. The dispute over war aims led directly to the question of power in the revolution. In contrast to the situation in March, the approach to this question in late April and early May was characterised by wide agreement in both government and Soviet on the need for the inclusion of members of the Soviet in the ministry.[1] As a result, the ministry that emerged on 5 May from the discussions conducted by Prince Lvov was very different from that which had ruled in the early spring; while the first government was dominated by the right with only one representative of a left-wing party, the first coalition government had five from the left—two SRs (Chernov and Kerensky), two Mensheviks (Tsereteli and Skobelev) and one Popular Socialist (Peshekhonov). Of course the Socialists were still outnumbered by representatives from the right: there were four Kadets (Nekrasov, Shingarev, Manuilov and Shakhovskoi), two Octobrists (V. N. Lvov and Godnev), one Progressive (Konovalov, who joined the Kadets in June), and three non-party (G. E. Lvov, Tereshchenko and Pereverzev) members. However of the three ministerial portfolios that were most significant for government rural policy, two were in Socialist hands: Chernov was Minister of Agriculture and Peshekhonov was Minister of Food. The third portfolio, the Ministry of the Interior, was held by the former Kadet and current non-party liberal, Prime Minister Prince G. E. Lvov. Socialists thus formed a large and important segment of the first coalition government. In the second coalition which was formed by Kerensky to succeed the first when it collapsed early in July, Socialists held a majority of the posts although the Kadets remained the largest single party. The ministry consisted of three SRs (Kerensky, Chernov and Avksentiev), three Mensheviks (Nikitin, Skobelev and Prokopovich), two Popular Socialists (Peshekhonov and Zarudnii), five Kadets (Nekrasov, Iurenev, Kokoshkin, Ol'denburg and Kartashov), one Progressive (Efremov) and one non-party (Tereshchenko) member. Furthermore all three ministries of most significance for rural policy were in Socialist hands: Chernov retained Agriculture, Peshekhonov retained Food, and Avksentiev took over Interior. Thus during the summer, when unrest reached its height, responsibility for rural affairs lay with Socialist ministers. It was at this time too that the most significant disagreements over rural policy occurred within the government.

Although the physiognomy of the first and second coalition governments differed markedly from that which immediately succeeded the fall of the tsar, the approach to rural problems adopted during late spring and summer did not differ from that adopted by the first Provisional Government. There was no fundamental change in approach in any of the spheres with which the government was concerned; a succession of *ad hoc*, unconnected, partial, half-measures and a tinkering with the established structure remained the order of the day, with the result that the basic problems were left untouched.

THE FOOD QUESTION

The food question remained the focus of government attention in the rural areas during late spring and summer. In its initial declaration on 5 May the government declared its determination to fight economic disruption by extending governmental control over the production, transportation, exchange and distribution of products and, if necessary, to resort to the organisation of production.[2] However, in the following months no sweeping changes were introduced; the government continued to tinker with the established machinery without attacking the root of the problem.

During the first week of May a number of steps had been taken to stimulate the flow of grain into the reception points and the cities. On 3 May, two days before the formation of the first coalition, the Ministry of Agriculture sent two circulars to *guberniia* food committees.[3] These were, in effect, addenda to the legislation of 25

March establishing the grain monopoly and the food committee structure. The first circular gave food committees the power to acquire by force at half the price any grain subject to alienation which the possessors refused to surrender. This decision made explicit what had previously only been implicit in the logic of the thinking behind the grain monopoly: if the provisions of the monopoly were not adhered to voluntarily, they were to be enforced, by force of arms if necessary, by the local food organisations. On paper the government food committees were being given teeth, but in practice nothing was done to overcome their impotence.

As a corollary to this, the other circular urged food committees to take steps to increase public awareness of the law on the grain monopoly. In addition, *guberniia* food committees were urged to proceed more quickly with the establishment of *uezd* and *volost* committees and to carry out the census of grain reserves and requirements in order to establish the quotas to be retained by the owners. This census was to be completed by 31 May. All committees were reminded that they were to supervise not only the acquisition of grain but its distribution also. This circular constituted a government instruction to the food committees to begin preparations for the implementation of the grain monopoly. It had thus taken the government almost six weeks from the announcement of the grain monopoly and the formal establishment of the machinery to implement that monopoly, to issue instructions to set that machinery in motion. During this six week period a vacuum had existed during which the grain monopoly was little more than a declaration of intent. Furthermore by demanding that the preparatory work for the monopoly had to be completed within four weeks, the government was imposing an impossible task upon its food organisations. If the food committees had been well-established and popularly accepted they may have been able to complete the agricultural census within the four weeks demanded, but given the actual state of affairs in the countryside, this was impossible.

Steps were taken to centralise the administration of the food question by the formation on 5 May of a special Ministry of Food. Gradually the new ministry was to take over all aspects of the food question, although initially its control was extended only to that sphere previously under the control of that section of the Ministry of Agriculture dealing with the organisation of the sown area: working out general questions for the organisation and implementation of measures for enlarging the sown area, collection and processing of statistical material, supply of workers to the agrarian economy, investigation of the seed needs of the different regions, and working out plans and conditions for financing agricultural production.[4] From this basic core of functions, the new ministry's authority was to spread gradually. On 19 May the Minister of Food was granted control over some credits for use by the lower food organisations to finance their operations. On 7 June the Minister was authorised to begin to organise the planned distribution to the population of those articles of prime necessity which were the main focus of concern of the Commission to Investigate the Supply of Consumer Goods to the Population, established a month earlier. It was not until 1 July that responsibility for food matters was passed over to the new ministry.[5] The government's decision of that date accorded the following functions to the Food Ministry: the procurement and supply of food to the army and population; in concert with the Ministry of Agriculture to assist in the production of food products and the supply to the producers of workers and such production needs as seeds, metals and implements; the procurement and supply to the population of other articles of prime necessity; the regulation of production and consumption and of the purchase and sale prices of food and articles of prime necessity; direction of food committees; and participation in the resolution of questions dealing with internal and external trade, transport and local government, and administration. The State Food Committee was to continue to exist under a separate statute, although it was to be chaired by the Minister of Food, while the food committees were to be the local organisations of the new ministry until they were replaced by the *zemstva* at the corresponding levels.

Thus the law of 1 July vested almost sole authority in food matters in the new Ministry of Food, although in some areas it was to act in agreement with the Ministry of Agriculture. In addition, the Food Ministry was to control the distribution of articles of prime necessity and the supply to the farms of the means of production which they needed. But as well as these more specific functions, the Ministry also was given a vague mandate to concern itself with all questions of transport and local government in the rural areas. In this way it was brought into direct contact with all forms of rural unrest, not just that concerned with the food question.

The delay between the formal establishment of the new ministry on 5 May and the adoption by it of full powers on 1 July was unfortunate. Certainly the government was in a difficult position. If it had established the Food Ministry and immediately accorded to it full powers over the food question, it would have created the possibility both of further disrupting the supply system because of the problems involved in establishing the new ministry, and of impeding the development of the new ministry by the imposition on it of a burden of responsibility which it was, at that stage, unable to bear. However in avoiding these pitfalls the government compounded a problem that was to afflict it throughout its life. By establishing a ministry which was not only to exercise functions that were not clearly distinguished from functions to be exercised by other ministries but which also was gradually to increase the sphere of its bureaucratic competence, the government exacerbated what was already a very ambiguous situation within the governmental bureaucratic structure. The ambiguity existing at the local level as a result of the parallel existence of government food, land and *volost* committees was both reflected and reinforced at the national level by the concurrent existence of Ministries of Food, Agriculture, Interior, Finance and War, all of which exercised functions bearing more or less directly on the food question. With the severity of the continuing food crisis, a dissipation of energies through institutional diversification was something the Provisional Government could not afford.

On 21 May the All-Russian Food Congress opened in Moscow, attended by delegates from soviets, food committees, trade unions, public and cooperative organisations, consumers' unions, economic societies, the stock exchange, government departments and commercial and industrial circles. At the congress the former Minister of Agriculture and current Minister of Finance, A. I. Shingarev, outlined his view of the food situation. While arguing that the country faced a crisis because of an apparent shortage of both food and material goods, Shingarev directed the blame for this as follows:

> The absence of a united organisation, an organised power is the source of all evils at the present moment. . . . There is grain in all the *gubernii* . . . But not enough grain has been delivered and not enough is being delivered because the local organisations are not efficient . . . the danger that faces the country is all the more grave because the country does not have the most elementary organisational control, and regardless of how deep the confidence

expressed by the masses, regardless of the endless number of welcoming telegrams they sent to the Provisional Government, these are nothing but words . . .[6]

The basic thrust of Shingarev's position was reaffirmed, albeit in a more moderate fashion, by Peshekhonov. At the Food Congress he called for state control of all branches of the economy, industry, transport, exchange and distribution, as the only way to solve the crisis. He continued to stress the organisational factor at the First All-Russian Congress of Soviets of Workers' and Soldiers' Deputies which opened in Petrograd on 3 June. He declared that ample grain existed in the country, but the major problem was obtaining and conveying it. This could be done only by the state, through the state grain monopoly. However the monopoly could be implemented only after the food committees had carried out a thorough investigation of local reserves and needs. Such an investigation had been hampered by the slow emergence of these food committees, especially in those areas from which grain had to be obtained. This situation was exacerbated by the peasant refusal to surrender their grain for money because of the current inflationary conditions. However, according to Peshekhonov, there was also a shortage in the towns of the goods which the peasants wanted in exchange for their grain, and therefore the fixing of the prices of these goods alone would not solve the problem; greater quantities of these goods had to be produced also.[7]

Thus both Finance Minister Shingarev and Food Minister Peshekhonov believed that greater organisational efficiency in the rural economy was necessary to increase the flow of grain into the state's hands. However Peshekhonov supplemented his faith in organisation by recognition of the need for increased supplies of articles of prime necessity. As we will see below, Agriculture Minister Chernov had a totally different view of the most effective means of increasing the flow of grain to the state, a means which was to cause violent dispute within the ranks of the government. But even though both Shingarev and Peshekhonov, who held two of the most important posts in the government, shared broad agreement on the need for greater organisational efficiency in the rural economy, their opinions had little practical impact on government policy.

On 30 May the government introduced legislation supplementing that of 11 April dealing with the protection of crops and the sowing of unused land.[8] The new legislation, which emanated from the Ministry of Food, once again accorded to the food committees broad responsibilities in these areas. Food committees, preferably those at the *guberniia* level, were to formulate measures for the defence of the crops based on local conditions, although committees were not to attempt to replace an owner's defence of his property. However if owners wished, they could place their crop wholly under the protection of these committees. In cases where owners retained a right to protect their crops, claims for compensation as a result of damage caused by popular unrest were to be investigated thoroughly by a commission elected from the *uezd* food committee. That part of the legislation referring to the sowing of unused land was more detailed than its counterpart of 11 April had been. The legislation began with a warning that it was not designed to bring about a change in the basic system of land organisation, but to bring into production areas of land which the legal owner currently was unable to work with his own resources. Being a measure designed to increase productivity from normally productive areas, this law was not to be taken as a direction to sow those areas which normally remained unsown — meadows, common pastures and fallow land. Land currently unproductive could be taken over by the food committees which could either supervise the working of the land themselves or lease the land to those wishing and able to work it. However food committee control over such land was to remain in force only until there was a return to normal times.

The legislation of 30 May broadly repeated that of 11 April with no substantive changes in content. However there was a subtle difference in tone between the earlier and the later pieces of legislation, with that of 30 May reflecting a more sympathetic attitude toward the private land-owners and a greater recognition of the role some food committees were playing in rural unrest than was evident seven weeks earlier. Whereas the 11 April legislation had implied that crops would come under government protection on the initiative of the food committees, the 30 May legislation emphasised that the food committees would become involved only with the agreement of the owner. This difference in emphasis was evident also when the legislation dealt with the sowing of unsown land in its stress on the temporary nature of food committee control over unsown land and the change in terminology from land which the land-owner refused to work to that which he was unable to work. This change in tone is a reflection not simply of the fact that the two pieces of legislation emanated from different bureaucratic structures in Petrograd, but from governmental recognition that it was the private land-owners who were its allies in the countryside, both in the struggle for stability and for increased food supplies, not the peasantry. But the change in emphasis in the later piece of legislation did not alter the scope which it gave as a cover for the 'surreptitious' seizure of land by the peasants.

Grain rationing had been introduced formally throughout the country on 29 April but it was not until 6 June that the methods of applying the card system in 'cities and areas of an urban character' were prescribed.[9] Distribution by means of a ration card system was to apply to the whole population with the exception of the military which was to be supplied direct by the War Ministry. Ration cards were to be issued in a number of categories: individual cards, collective cards issued for a family or other group of people, extra cards for those engaged in heavy physical labour, cards with a limited number of coupons for residents who were only temporary in the area, and cards entitling the holder to portions in restaurants. Although the cards were to be issued without charge, the cost of their production was to be added to the price of the article. Transfer of cards was prohibited. Bread and flour were to be issued only on presentation of a card at stores, cooperative societies and other institutions officially registered for this purpose. Consumers were to be attached to particular distribution points from which they had to obtain their ration. The whole operation was to be supervised by the food committees.

The situation outlined in these instructions was to be the model for the whole country, variations being permitted only in response to local conditions. The major problem with the legislation did not concern any of its specific provisions, but related to its timing: officially grain rationing had been in existence for five weeks before the basic guidelines outlining how it was to operate were laid down by the government. In this five-week period rational implementation of the decision of 29 April had been impossible. Uncertainty and ambiguity had been created and widespread hoarding encouraged as people tried to build up reserves before rationing began. Furthermore by adding the cost of the production of the ration cards to the prices of the goods involved, the government stimulated further price rises.

On 26 June formal responsibility for grain rationing throughout the country was passed from the Ministry of Agriculture to the

Ministry of Food.[10] Reflecting the deteriorating food situation, this transfer of responsibility was accompanied by a lowering of the norm of the *per capita* monthly flour ration. However, more serious for the government's long-term prospects in this field was the implication behind the set of instructions to food committees issued at this time. The food committees were called upon immediately to conduct a comprehensive survey of population size, food needs and resources. The fact that this instruction still had to be issued at the end of June shows how little the preparations for the government's grain monopoly had been implemented. The conduct of such a census was a necessary prerequisite for the implementation of the monopoly. Unless the government could ensure supply, which in effect meant the efficient operation of the grain monopoly, the rationing of grain products could not be implemented. The government's failure adequately to control supply meant that its rationing plans were undermined. Not only could the government not provide the population with food, but the existence of the rationing system highlighted this failure and directed popular antagonism toward the government, which was held directly responsible for food shortages in the towns.

During June it appeared that the government may have been going to take some decisive action to implement the type of control over all branches of the economy that had been mooted in the government's initial declaration and that Peshekhonov had called for at the Food Congress in May. On 21 June an Economic Council and a Chief Economic Committee were formed.[11] The former body was to work out a general plan for the organisation of the national economy and was to plan general measures for the regulation of economic life. The latter body was to coordinate the implementation of all measures by government departments and institutions which aimed at the regulation of economic life in the country; it was to institute the programme worked out by the Economic Council. Membership of both bodies was to come from government departments and public organisations. However in practice neither body was rooted firmly in the bureaucratic structure of the capital and neither had very much influence; both consistently were ignored and by-passed in decision-making matters. Consequently neither body had any significant effect on government policy, their presence simply adding to the bureaucratic complexity and confusion in Petrograd.

A third body also was established at this time, designed to deal specifically with the problem of supply to the army. By the middle of the year the army, like many other areas of Russia, was experiencing difficulties in obtaining sufficient supplies. In an attempt to overcome this, on 30 June special advisory bureaux were established to coordinate and supervise the supply of food-stuffs to the troops at the different fronts.[12] However such bureaux were limited in their effectiveness; they existed only in an advisory capacity and they relied on the food committees for the procurement of the grain. This attempt by the government to overcome the food problem, like all its efforts in this field, was undermined by the two essential weaknesses of its general policy: popular rejection of the grain monopoly and the government's inability to gain control of the low level organisations in the countryside.

By mid-July the food situation was critical and rural unrest was at a peak. On 18 July, in response to a circular of 16 July by Agriculture Minister Chernov discussed below, Food Minister Peshekhonov sent a circular to all food committees in Russia.[13] It began by reminding the committees of the earlier decisions relating to the establishment of the grain monopoly, the food committee's duty to protect the crops, and the state's obligation to reimburse owners for losses. The circular then went on to berate actions by the populations of many localities which prevented land-owners from harvesting and sowing their fields, and the reluctance on the part of some land-owners and tenants to harvest the grain and prepare their land for the following season's crops. After stressing the critical nature of the situation, Peshekhonov went on to instruct *guberniia*, *uezd* and *volost* food committees:

(1) Immediately to take the most energetic and decisive measures for the prevention and termination of . . . wilful and illegal acts on the part of the population . . .

(2) Under no circumstances can decisions be taken giving cause to the population to commit violent and criminal actions against land-owners . . .

(3) To inform land-owners and tenants that they must exert all their efforts to harvest their fields and crops and sow winter plough lands. If they cannot manage this through their own efforts and resources . . . the food boards . . . must take appropriate measures for the harvesting of fields and meadows and the sowing of winter crops . . .

(4) To inform the population that for wilful and illegal acts

preventing land-owners from managing their farms properly, the guilty, as well as reimbursing the losses caused, will be strictly accountable to the law . . .

Members of food committees who refused to abide by the instructions in paragraphs (1) and (2) were threatened with dismissal and criminal prosecution. Peshekhonov's circular continued:

All measures for the settlement of questions concerning the sowing and harvesting of fields must be taken exclusively by food committees and boards . . . No other committees have the right to take on themselves settlement of the above questions, and their decisions are not binding on the population.

In this circular Peshekhonov tried to eliminate some of the ambiguity in relations between government food, land and *volost* committees by defining exclusively a sphere of food committee competence, that concerning the sowing and harvesting of fields. However he left many other areas of dispute between the different types of committee unclarified. But the most significant aspect of the circular was the attitude adopted by the Food Minister to the question of rural unrest. Peshekhonov placed the food committees in the forefront of the struggle with rural unrest. The ambiguity in the relationship between food committees and land-owners present in the legislation dealing with the protection of sown lands was gone. It was the food committees' duty, clearly expressed by the Food Minister, to bring about 'the prevention and termination' of all acts hindering the production of food. But although Peshekhonov envisaged the food committees exercising a 'law and order' function in the countryside, in the circular he gave thinly-veiled acknowledgement that food committees were often instrumental in bringing about the unrest they were now being urged to prevent.

With the summer eruption of rural unrest having a significant effect on the flow of grain into the government's hands, the government continued to tinker with the established structure. Rationing was expanded to limit the consumption of a wider range of food goods, an attempt was made to make some articles of prime necessity easier to obtain, and directions were given to food organs on the choice of mills for the processing of the grain.[14] In an attempt to increase the flow of grain into the collection points the government set in motion a course to train agitators to go into the countryside to encourage the peasants to surrender their grain, and it established regional committees to coordinate the transport of supplies.[15] However, major technical problems remained unresolved and in the forefront of official concern at this time: by early August the comprehensive census of population, needs and resources had still not been completed, there was widespread refusal among the population to cooperate with private firms acting for the government in grain procurement,[16] and government food committees had developed on a far smaller scale in the southern producing area than in the northern consuming region. Thus not only was the necessary data for the operation of the grain monopoly not available, but the mechanism for implementing it was clearly deficient.

On 4 August the government made the following announcement:

In view of the rumours circulating on the possibility of raising the fixed prices of grain of the 1917 harvest, the Provisional Government states that all fixed prices on grain established by the law of the Provisional Government of 25 March 1917, on the current and previous years' harvest, will under no circumstances be raised. If an attempt is discovered by the people in some places to hold back delivery of grain for the army and the needy localities, the Minister for Food will set certain dates for delivery, at the expiration of which fixed prices on grain will be lowered and payment for grain, both voluntarily released and confiscated, in accordance with article 8 of the law of 25 March 1917, will be made at the new lowered fixed prices. Moreover the Provisional Government announces that, in accordance with government instructions, the Minister of Food is urgently at work on measures to supply the population in so far as possible with objects of mass consumption (textiles, iron, kerosene, etc) at fixed prices.[17]

This announcement has a plaintive ring about it. The government was adopting a hard-line approach in the face of increasing pressure for a rise in the fixed prices of grain, blustering that those who did not surrender their grain at the fixed price prevailing in their area would lose it for a lowered price at a later date. This was the same basic position adopted by the government when it introduced the grain monopoly. It had not worked then and there was no reason to see why it should work now, especially since popular confidence in both the government and the currency was at a much lower level than it had been in March, and the government's inability to carry

its threats into practice in the rural areas was clear. The last
sentence appears to have been thrown in as a form of encouragement to the peasants to deliver the grain: the peasants should
surrender the grain to the government because all steps were being
taken to provide the peasants with the goods they required. If the
government had been able to improve the supply of these goods to
the peasants, the latter may have surrendered their grain in greater
quantities. However the government had been saying the same
thing since the announcement of the grain monopoly more than
four months earlier, and there had been little real improvement in
the situation. The government's credibility was negligible in the
villages.

But the government's problem was not only one of credibility.
The unreliability of the lower-level government organs was acknowledged in Petrograd, and yet the government realised that it
was primarily upon these organs that its food policy depended. This
dilemma was clearly demonstrated by government actions during
middle and late August. On 18 August the responsibility of local
food organs for the preservation intact of goods in transit was
reaffirmed; any losses incurred as a result of plunder or of
carelessness were to be retrieved by the food boards. Two days later
Peshekhonov told the *guberniia* food committees that they were to
use all measures, including the use of force, to obtain grain.
However on 21 August, under pressure from the Stavka, a
government directive was issued vesting control over the movement
of food-stuffs and articles of prime necessity in the region of the
theatre of war in a person specially appointed to control the flow of
supplies to the front. Special powers, including the right of armed
requisition, were vested in this office to carry out its functions. In
addition, local food organisations explicitly were denied the power
to delay or vary the destination of food or articles of prime necessity
in transit, this power being vested in the Food Minister alone. On 24
August a government decision vested in the Food Minister the
power to suspend completely or temporarily any food committee or
group of food committees acting contrary to the interests of the
state.[18] On one hand the government recognised its dependence
upon the food committees, but on the other it realised that food
committees were an important factor in the disruption of supply
which it was trying to overcome. The government was caught on
the horns of an insoluble dilemma.

With little faith left in many of its food organs at the local level, and with no end in sight to the grain crisis, the government felt it had little alternative but to make the following announcement on 27 August:

(1) Fixed prices on all grain of the harvest of 1917 and of past years will be calculated in an amount twice that shown in (the law of 25 March) . . .

(2) The Minister of Food is authorised to change the prices for the milling and processing of grain and to establish new fixed prices for flour and groats corresponding to the new prices for grain and grain processing. . .

. . .

(6) Payment for grain received in deliveries beginning on 1 August is to be made at the prices laid down by the present law.

(7) The Minister of Food is authorised to establish time limits for the compulsory delivery of grain, at the expiry of which grain due for delivery which has not been delivered may be requisitioned with a reduction of 30 per cent below established prices.[19]

Two days later the government made a long announcement explaining the reasons for the doubling of the grain price. The government declared that the flow of grain was insufficient to satisfy the demands of the country: large areas of Russia were experiencing catastrophic grain shortages and yet there was sufficient grain in the country to satisfy minimum demands. Not only was the current harvest not coming in sufficient quantities, but the government was still trying to acquire grain from the harvest before, which in normal times would have been in the granaries long ago. Moreover weather conditions would soon halt water transport, the means of supply upon which many areas were heavily dependent. While declaring that it would not hesitate to use 'extreme measures of coercion' against those disobeying the law or negligent in the execution of it, the government acknowledged that its main chance of success lay in persuasion, not coercion. Consequently it declared that it was doubling the grain price in order to decrease the differential between the price of grain and that of articles of prime necessity, thereby placing those articles more within the reach of peasant producers. It was hoped that this would encourage them to give up their grain.[20] However even the doubling of the grain price often was not sufficient to enable the peasant producer to produce his grain at a profit, or at least without a loss, in many areas; rising prices throughout the year had increased the cost of production so much that even with the doubling of the grain price many peasants could still produce only at a loss. Moreover the doubling of the grain price did not make articles of prime necessity substantially easier to obtain; production was not increased simply by raising the grain price and, despite a government injunction to the contrary, the rise in the price of grain was certain to drive up the production cost of those articles even more, thereby putting them further out of reach of many peasants.[21] Furthermore for those not engaged in the production of grain, the doubling of the price caused greatly increased food bills and therefore greater hardship. The government's decision provided a great stimulus to the already rampant inflation.

In view of the government's firm declaration of 4 August that the price of grain would not be raised under any circumstances the panic move in doubling the grain price further undermined its credibility in the eyes of the population; the government's dithering was clear for all to see. The decline in the government's credibility would not have been so bad had it been accompanied by clearly positive results. However this was not the case. To the extent that the government grain monopoly was designed to make more grain available to consumers, the government decision was at least in part contrary to this by pricing large parts of the consumer population out of the market. To the extent that it was designed to dampen down inflation, the decision to double the price totally undermined this aim. The success of the major aim, that of increasing the flow of grain into state coffers, is difficult to gauge. In many instances committees set their own price levels and ignored the new figures.[22] Certainly increases in delivery were reported in the southern *gubernii* and parts of the Middle Volga region, although lack of funds prevented many food committees from taking advantage of this.[23] However increased deliveries had begun to occur during the second half of August, prior to the doubling of the price, solely as a result of the agricultural cycle; the period just after harvesting was always characterised by increased deliveries to collection points. Nevertheless the doubling of the price was responsible for part of the increase in volume of grain flowing to the state during the remainder of the life of the Provisional Government. According to Food Minister Prokopovich speaking on 16 October, during September 1916 only 19 million *pudi* of grain were received from vendors, while in September 1917 incomplete reports showed that 43 million *pudi* had been received.[24] Although part of this increase reflects the March 1917 rise in the grain price compared with that prevailing during 1916, it must in part also have resulted from the recent doubling of the grain price. However the increase in the volume of grain going into government hands was not nearly sufficient to fill the need that existed in the country. Food shortages continued. Consequently in retrospect, the gains stemming from the decision to double the price of grain were more than compensated for by the losses the government sustained as a result of that decision: a little extra grain in exchange for a further loss of credibility and a lot of extra hostility from consumers who had to pay the increased prices.

By the end of the life of the second coalition government in late August the government was facing a food crisis of major dimensions. Widespread food shortages were contributing to the developing sense of popular alienation from the government, and yet the government was able to do nothing to overcome the problem. Despite the doubling of the grain price the government monopoly remained unpopular among producers; low-level organisations remained more responsive to the peasants than to the government, thereby undermining all government actions in this area; and the resultant failure of the grain monopoly undercut the government's plans for the rationing of grain. The government was in an impasse from which it was unable to escape.

THE LAND QUESTION

Despite the increased level of socialist participation in the two coalition governments, the land policy followed by both was nothing more than a continuation of that of the first government. That little was going to change was evident from the declaration of the first coalition government issued on the day of its formation, 5 May:

> Leaving it to the Constituent Assembly to decide the question of the transfer of land into the hands of the workers, and carrying out the preparatory work for this, the Provisional Government will take all necessary measures to ensure the greatest production of grain to satisfy the needs of the country, and to regulate the utilisation of land in the interests of the national economy and the working population.[25]

The second coalition government also reaffirmed the principle that final resolution of the land question could only be implemented by the Constituent Assembly, although, in a statement which was the subject of bitter dispute within government ranks, it acknowledged that the future reform should be based on the principle of land being in the hands of those who work it and promised to draft a law for the Constituent Assembly on this basis.[26] However in the immediate sense, the policy of both coalition governments remained unchanged from that which they had inherited from the first government: there was to be no change in land relations, but efforts were to be made to increase grain production within the existing pattern of those relations.

The government position as outlined in these declarations must be seen in the light of the official positions on land adopted by the two major government parties at their congresses in May. When the VII Kadet congress had met in March, a bitter debate on the land question had been left unfinished. Pressure by many provincial delegates for a radicalisation of party policy was opposed by the more conservative central committee headed by Foreign Minister Pavel Miliukov. No resolution was adopted on the land question, further debate being postponed until the next party congress in a few weeks time. When the VIII congress opened in mid-May, the question of agrarian reform was again the subject of bitter and vitriolic debate. While all speakers in the debate acknowledged the need for some changes in the structure of land relations, there were violent disagreements over both the scope and timetable of such changes. However when it came to the adoption of a formal resolution, the conservative element in the party triumphed; on virtually all parts of the resolution, the more conservative position was carried by more than a two to one majority.[27] Official Kadet policy favoured the state acquisition of privately-owned productive land which exceeded the labour norm, with the payment of financial compensation to those whose lands were acquired. The acquired land was to be placed in the usage of the peasants. The Kadets reaffirmed their support for the principle of private land-ownership, but they decided officially to leave determination of this question up to the individual communities to decide. The official Kadet position thus favoured land confiscation, but at a price. The position went part of the way towards meeting the demands of the peasants, but it still fell far short of their maximum demand: the passing of all land into peasant hands without payment of any compensation.

In late May the Socialist Revolutionaries gathered to hold the III congress of their party. During the congress, debate on the land question was overshadowed almost completely by other issues. The debate on agrarian matters was characterised more by somnolence than by the fires of passion as the congress passed the responsibility for updating the party's original agrarian programme drafted by Chernov to an agrarian commission of the Central Committee. However this body never addressed itself to the agrarian question with any positive, programmatic result, which meant that the party as a whole was bound officially for the remainder of the year by what was essentially a stop-gap resolution from the III Congress. It was a resolution that covered over wide differences within the party. The resolution on land called for the abolition of private ownership in land throughout Russia with all land being placed in the hands of the people for equal productive use. A law to this effect should be introduced in the Constituent Assembly. Eventually the land should be socialised, or placed in the state of being owned by no-one, used equally by all, and broadly regulated by the local administration.[28] In the meantime, before the convocation of the Constituent Assembly, the peasants should refrain from land seizure, all land should be placed in the management of democratised land committees, all productive implements and livestock in the agrarian economy should be distributed to best productive advantage, and tree-felling should be regulated with a fixed price established on timber. This programme did not have universal support within the party, but it was supported by Agriculture Minister Chernov.

There were thus major differences between the formal programmes espoused by the Kadets and the SRs. Broad agreement existed on the need for the distribution of state-acquired privately-owned land to the peasantry. However the two programmes differed greatly from this point on. While the Kadets favoured compensation for lands acquired, the SRs vehemently opposed it; the SRs favoured the abolition of private land-ownership while the Kadets supported the principle of land being held in private hands; the Kadets believed that only agriculturally-important land exceeding the labour norm should be subject to redistribution, while the SRs expounded the view that all land, including that in the cities, forests, and agriculturally useless land should be so subject.

However despite these formal differences, the main divisions within the government during the lives of the two coalition governments which ruled between May and August were not based on a clear split along party lines between Kadets and SRs. The most significant division which rent the government during the summer was that between Chernov and a few supporters on the one hand, and on the other the Kadets, large sections of the leadership of the PSR (including Kerensky), and most of the government. Reflecting official SR policy, Chernov favoured the immediate transfer of all land into the hands of the land committees for distribution among the peasants, not only because he believed in the intrinsic justice of the principle of land being in the hands of those who worked it, but also because he felt that this would increase grain production and encourage grateful producers to surrender their grain to the state, thereby helping to alleviate the food crisis. As Chernov doubtless understood, this was a formula for the passing of all land into the hands of the peasants since it was they who controlled most of the lower level land committees. But Chernov did not support the arbitrary seizure of privately-owned land by the peasants, as he was frequently accused of doing; consistently throughout 1917 he condemned arbitrary seizures undertaken by the peasants. He acknowledged that the transfer of land to the peasants could formally be done only by the Constituent Assembly, but he argued that since that body would work on the basis of land being placed in the hands of those who worked it, the passing of that land to land committees at this time would not usurp the functions of the Assembly but would implement the decision it was yet to reach.[29] This position raised a storm of disapproval within the government; when Chernov tried to implement this policy by extending land committee control over all agriculturally significant land, the move was rejected by the government, and on at least one occasion Prime Minister Lvov attempted unsuccessfully to persuade Chernov to disavow the 'illegal actions' taken by land committees in the sphere of land relations.[30] Chernov was roundly condemned for 'broadening and deepening' the revolution, destroying respect for law, encouraging anarchy in the countryside, pursuing a partisan rather than a national policy, and presenting the Constituent Assembly with a *fait accompli*. Both Prince Lvov and the Kadets resigned from the government early in July largely as a result of Chernov's policies.[31] Indeed the Kadets, many of whom had been alienated from Chernov almost from the first by the internationalist position he had adopted on the war issue in April, were so opposed to the policies he pursued that in the negotiations taking place in July for the formation of the second coalition government they made his exclusion a condition of their participation in the new ministry.[32] However Kerensky could not withstand the pressure from the PSR CC for the retention of Chernov in the government, while the Kadets realised that any government in which they participated was likely to be more moderate than one from which they were absent. Consequently both Chernov and five Kadets took up ministerial positions in the second coalition. Throughout Chernov's tenure of the Ministry of Agriculture, Kerensky and most of his SR colleagues actively opposed Chernov[33] even though the Agriculture Minister was doing little more than attempting to implement the formal PSR programme. Chernov was virtually isolated in the government. One effect of this high level of overt conflict within the government was that after the formation of the land committees on 21 April, there was little government activity in the sphere of land relations.

However despite the low level of government activity on the land question, some measures were introduced in this field. The most important of these, and one which precipitated a major argument in the government, was the decision to restrict land transactions. Since the fall of the tsar the peasants had been demanding that the government take action to preserve the country's land fund intact through the imposition of a total prohibition on privately-owned land changing hands, either wholly through sale or partly through mortgage. The peasants' assumption was that such land could find its way into the hands of foreigners through purchase or into the hands of major financial institutions, either domestic or foreign, through mortgage and that such land could be excluded from the general redistribution fostered by the Constituent Assembly. Chernov agreed with the peasant analysis, favouring the imposition of a total prohibition on land transactions as a means of overcoming this possibility. This was a logical position in the light of the government's expressed desire to freeze all land relationships so as not to complicate the final resolution of the land question by the Constituent Assembly. However the Kadets and most non-party members of the government did not adopt this position. Instead they argued that such a move would infringe the owner's inherent right to dispose of his property, it would depreciate land values and thereby impair the credit structure of the banks and the savings of many small investors, and it would threaten the whole basis of production in the rural economy. In his desire to have such a measure adopted by the government Chernov was faced with a solid phalanx of the right in the government including Prime Minister Prince Lvov who, up until that time (early May), had refused to adopt the more generally hard-line position of the Kadets.[34]

Confronted with this solid wall of opposition within the government, Chernov turned to a more indirect means of achieving his aim. At his urging, on 17 May Minister of Justice P. N. Pereverzev despatched an administrative order through his department to notaries throughout the country instructing them not to acknowledge land transactions until further notice. This was, in effect, a ban on land changing hands. However when Pereverzev's action was brought to the attention of the government as a whole, it came under intense criticism, and was rescinded officially on 23 June. The matter remained under debate within government circles, culminating in an official government decision restricting land transactions on 22 July.[35] According to this decision, all instances of land changing hands had to be approved by the *guberniia* land committee and confirmed by the Minister of Agriculture. The Ministry of Agriculture, upon consultation with the *guberniia* land committee, also had the right to withdraw land submitted for public auction and turn it over for temporary economic management to the Peasants' Land Bank, the Nobles' Land Bank, and the Administration of the National Domains. The provisions of this decision were greatly different from the total prohibition both popularly demanded and favoured by Chernov. They were also inconsistent with the government's stated desire to freeze all land relationships because they provided a means for private landowners to dispose of their land. In the struggle within the government the popular aspirations, in this case personified by Chernov, were crushed by the Kadet-led conservative elements. The government's unwillingness to move very far toward the peasants' aspirations was thus again clear in this, the only substantial piece of legislation dealing with land relations passed after the formation of the land committees.

Despite an undertaking by the second coalition government to widen and strengthen the land committees, nothing substantial in this line was achieved by either government. Although a number of changes were made to the land committee structure, they made little difference to the operation of these bodies. By a government decree of 28 June, the Land Organisation Commissions established to administer the Stolypin reforms were abolished and their powers passed to the *guberniia* and *uezd* land committees. This decision marks the formal end of Stolypin's land reform programme and it reflects an end to government issuance of titles to individuals confirming them in the possession of plots carved out of communal land. The formal government programme encouraging the individualisation of communal land was ended. On 13 July Agriculture Minister Chernov instructed land committees to take all measures possible to defend in their entirety the agricultural experimental stations and their lands, since it was through the research of these bodies that it was hoped the future development of Russian agriculture would proceed. In addition to these decisions relating to the powers of the committees, the government also enlarged the size of the committees. In early June representatives of soviets of peasants' deputies and soviets of workers' and soldiers' deputies were added to committees at the *guberniia* and *uezd* levels, while on 25 August representatives of the Nobles' and the Peasants' Land Banks formally were added to committees at all levels.[36] In these three decisions the government was doing little more than tinker with the established framework. No attempt was made to get at the root of the government's problem, the lack of responsiveness on the part of local committees to the government and the unpopularity of the government's policy.

If the government was unable to achieve anything substantial through the lower level land committees, the record of the Chief Land Committee was equally bare. The major purpose of the Committee was the collation of material and the drafting of projected laws on land relations for consideration by the Constituent Assembly. In addition, it was to peruse existing laws in the light of their relevance to the current situation. The Committee met in full session on only three occasions, all during the tenure of the first two coalition governments: 19–20 May, 1–6 July and 25–29 August.[37] Nothing of any substance emerged from these meetings. This is not surprising considering the large number of delegates present at such a meeting and, according to one delegate,[38] the poor quality of many members of the committee; he declared that many were incapable either of understanding or contributing in a worthwhile way to the Committee's work. Although such criticism may be excessively harsh, it does highlight one characteristic of the Committee: the broad spectrum of the membership represented at a full meeting involved such a wide diversity of views that agreement on specific questions and issues was impossible. The size and nature of the membership and the infrequency and short duration of meetings ensured that the full meetings of the Chief Land Committee produced little in the way of concrete policy proposals.

Far more work was done by the Committee's executive committee. Consisting of right wing populists and Kadet agrarian experts, this body held lengthy, and sometimes acrimonious, discussions through the year. During those discussions a number of broad schemes for the future of land were worked out and a number of proposals for more specific changes were formulated. However on many occasions the Committee ran into stern opposition to its proposals from other sections of the government,[39] particularly while Chernov was Minister of Agriculture. The rightist orientation of the Committee jarred on Chernov's more radical disposition, while many positions adopted by Chernov aroused the ire of members of the Committee; Chernov's circular of 16 July (discussed below) almost precipitated the resignation of the chairman of the Committee, Professor Posnikov.[40] However despite its difficulty in obtaining acceptance of its proposals, the executive committee of the Chief Land Committee was an important element in determining the government's approach to the land question. Its acknowledged pool of expertise enabled it to act as a conservative counter to the Ministry of Agriculture under Chernov, while its conservative outlook gained it a receptive hearing among many leading politicians. Consequently through its role in the agrarian debate within the government it played a significant part in formulating the government's broad approach to rural problems; Chernov himself implicitly acknowledged the part played by the Committee.[41] Thus the executive committee of the Chief Land Committee was a significant factor in government land policy and in frustrating V.M. Chernov in his attempts to implement segments of the official SR land programme.

The government was more active in trying to increase the productivity of the land than it was in dealing with land relationships. However its activity in this field was very haphazard, action being taken with little thought of a rational overall approach, and designed purely to meet a current exigency. The government's attempts to increase productivity focused on the supply of labour power, both mechanical and human, to the rural areas. In an attempt to boost the production of agricultural equipment, the government tried to relieve the fuel shortages being experienced by industry by granting to local fuel committees the right to seize privately-owned forest land to augment local sources and to by-pass peasant opposition to timber-felling, and by prohibiting the export of timber. The government also took upon itself the responsibility for constructing factories specifically to produce agricultural equipment, and proposed a new scheme of distribution of such goods to overcome the inefficiency of the current one. Along with these attempts to improve the situation in the capital, the government also tried to ensure the maximum utilisation of agricultural equipment already in the countryside by granting explicitly to food committees the power to take over equipment not being used to its full capacity for use in field-work. Turning to human labour power, the government tried to encourage its citizens, and particularly the unemployed and the young, to go to the countryside to assist with the field-work; in some instances soldiers were given leave to assist with the harvest. Special organisations were formed to coordinate the activities of the vast influx of recruits which the government expected,[42] a development which achieved little apart from exacerbating the institutional proliferation which characterised the government's rural policy. There was little overall planning or system in the government's efforts. However even if the government had expended much time and effort in planning its moves in this field, its efforts were bound to be frustrated by its inability to establish control at the lowest levels of rural society.

The history of the handling of the land question by the first two coalition governments is thus a dismal one. The two governments simply followed the lead given by their predecessor, trying to retain land relations unchanged while increasing production and improving distribution and supply within the existing land ownership pattern. Only Chernov and some supporters wanted to make a major change by passing all land into the hands of the land committees but this aim was firmly rejected by the conservative majority in the government. It is striking that the major move in the sphere of land relations taken during this period, the restriction on land transactions, was taken ten days after the Kadets officially left the government on 2 July. However the government could make no progress in its broad aim of retaining the *status quo* intact for the Constituent Assembly. Its policy was unpopular in the rural areas and its low level organisations could not strike roots in the villages. The majority in the government had no solution to offer to this *impasse*. Only Chernov had an alternative but the government as a whole would not countenance his proposal.

LOCAL GOVERNMENT

Little progress was made in the construction of a country-wide administrative structure responsive to Petrograd during the period of rule of the first two coalition governments. At the national level the convening of the Constituent Assembly seemed as far removed from reality by the time of the second coalition government's fall as it had when the first came to power. The question of the convening of the Constituent Assembly was not considered to be one of major urgency, despite the oft-expressed platitudes regarding its convocation at the earliest possible moment. It was not until 25 May that the Kadet-dominated Special Commission of the Constituent Assembly convened for the first time. Following its deliberations during late May and early June, it was announced on 14 June that elections for the Assembly would be held on 17 September and the Assembly would convene on 30 September. However on 9 August this decision was revoked and the government announced that elections for the Assembly would begin on 12 November, followed by the convening of the Assembly on 28 November.[43] The government's continued procrastination on this issue ensured the ultimate irrelevance of the Constituent Assembly.

At the local level the government legislated for the establishment of the apparatus of local government foreshadowed in the initial declaration of the first Provisional Government on 6 March. Since the fall of the tsar discussions had been taking place within the government on the question of local government and administration. This culminated on 21 May in a government decision on the establishment of *volost zemstva* throughout European Russia. This legislation was followed on 13 June and 26 July by more precise directions for the conduct of elections to these bodies.[44] Elections took place for the *zemstva* in the second half of August and the first half of September throughout most of the country. However by the time the elections were held, peasant disenchantment with the government, allied to traditional distrust of the *zemstvo* for its landowner connections, produced a very small turn-out of voters; only three people voted in Bel'sko-Sebezh *volost*, Petrograd *guberniia*, while in some areas of Vitebsk no-one voted at all.[45] Those *volost zemstva* that did manage to struggle into existence exercised only negligible influence in the rural areas and were of little use as instruments of government policy. Thus the government was unable to introduce the system of local administration throughout the country which it desired.

The main question facing the government in the sphere of local administration in the May–August period was that of rural unrest, which rose to a crescendo during the summer. The government's ability to handle this problem was hampered by the absence of a firm institutional base upon which a policy could rest. Formally responsibility for dealing with unrest prior to the establishment of the *volost zemstvo* was fragmented, shared between five bodies: food committees, land committees, commissars, *volost* committees, and the militia. The spheres of competence of these bodies overlapped; there was no clear demarcation of their powers in relation to one another. The result at the local level was hesitancy, ambiguity and conflict as this institutional diversification sowed the seeds of confusion.

The overlap in functions reflects two themes characteristic of the Provisional Government. Firstly, it highlights the distrust widely felt in many government circles of the loyalty to the government of these lower level organisations in the countryside. This distrust is clear from some of the government's actions and statements during the summer. In early June Interior Minister Avksentiev called for the abolition of committees encouraging illegal actions, a call that was reflected in mid-July by a decision to take all possible measures against wayward committees. Later that month the Ministers of Interior and War were given the power to act against meetings which could pose a threat to state security or military matters, a move directed in part against independently-minded committees. In August the Food Minister was given the power to suspend entirely or partially insubordinate food committees.[46] There was ample cause for official distrust of many of these lower level organisations.

The second theme which this overlap illustrates is the basic lack of agreement within the government on the desired relationship between these bodies and the functions they should exercise. This lack of agreement resulted primarily from the fact that there was no unanimity among the views of the different government departments and their ministers, nor was there any single authority which could impose consistency on these diverse views. This is highlighted by the different tones evident in the circulars sent to local organisations by the Ministers of Agriculture (16 July), Interior (17 July) and Food (18 July). Although the circulars of the Ministers of

Interior and Food were reactions to that of the Minister of Agriculture, we will look at them first.

In the circular of Interior Minister Tsereteli,[47] the types of agrarian unrest occurring in the countryside were outlined and the danger these posed to the country was emphasised. The government could not allow this to continue, and Tsereteli stressed that all attempts at arbitrary land reform were inadmissable and must cease. Tsereteli called on food committees to carry out the decision of 11 April and reaffirmed on 30 May on the protection of crops and the sowing of idle land, while land committees were instructed that in the question of land rental they were not to exceed their powers as defined by the decision of 21 April and by the 16 July circular from the Minister of Agriculture discussed below. Tsereteli also called on the commissars to take 'quick and decisive measures' to end arbitrary actions over land, to struggle with anarchy in the localities, and to implement the decisions of the government to the fullest extent. The Minister of the Interior thus emphasised the danger posed by rural unrest and called on government commissars, food committees and land committees to do all within their power (as defined by government decisions) to suppress that unrest.

Food Minister Peshekhonov[48] repeated the broad summary of unrest given by Tsereteli, and then, as indicated above, called on food committees at all levels to take 'the most energetic and decisive measures' to end rural disturbances. He also urged them not to encourage illegal acts against private land-owners, to encourage land-owners to sow and harvest their fields, and to inform the populace that those guilty of wilful acts against land-owners would be 'strictly accountable to the law'.

The basic thrust of the circulars by Tsereteli and Peshekhonov was the same: rural unrest was an immensely dangerous problem for Russia and local organisations were expected to do all in their power to bring that unrest under control. Both circulars emphasised the rights of private land-owners and berated those who infringed those rights, thereby giving expression to the broad governmental policy of retaining land relations intact until the convocation of the Constituent Assembly.

However the unpublished circular sent by Agriculture Minister Chernov to the land committees,[49] which constituted the only set of comprehensive instructions given to land committees apart from the legislation which established them, did not have the same emphasis as the circulars of his two ministerial colleagues. Chernov's circular attempted to demarcate areas of responsibility for land relations between land and food committees. Prisoners-of-war were to be under the control of food committees, although land committees were to ensure that no 'arbitrary removal of prisoners-of-war' took place. Food committees were responsible for ensuring the correct exploitation of plough and pasture lands and for harvesting the grain that land-owners could not harvest; land that could not be used by the owner was to be placed under the control of the *volost* land committee for distribution to the peasants or for utilisation under public ownership. Local land committees were to control access to and exploitation of forests, and, in agreement with food committees, work animals and farm implements unused by the owners. Land committees also were responsible for protecting model farms from destruction both on the part of illegal actions by the peasants and 'selfish actions' by the owners.

Chernov then continued:

Land committees (*volost, uezd* and *guberniia*) must look upon themselves as organisations of state power, and in all of their measures must first of all have state interests in view. Committees can go a long way in satisfying the just demands of the working peasantry, but under the absolute condition that this does not lead to the disintegration of the national economy, to the dissipation of productive forces, to the destruction of highly intensive farms, to the lowering and loss of the harvest so necessary to Russia. In this framework land committees will find energetic support in the Ministry of Agriculture . . .

In the context of the heightened levels of rural unrest in summer, Chernov's emphasis provided a stark contrast to that of Tsereteli and Peshekhonov. While the Interior and Food Ministers railed against rural unrest and called on all local organisations to do their utmost to end such disturbances, Chernov called on land committees to go some way toward satisfying the 'just demands' of the peasants, the demands motivating the actions about which the other ministers expressed concern. While Tsereteli and Peshekhonov emphasised the inviolability of privately-owned land under cultivation, Chernov stressed the inviolability only of those model farms which in the future would help to improve the standard of Russian agriculture. He made no mention of the rights of private land-owners. Chernov's view of the role and function of the lower level organisations differed fundamentally from that shared by the majority of his government colleagues who saw this circular as clear evidence of the 'socialist minister's' desire to 'broaden and deepen' the revolution. With such wide disagreement within the ministry over the proper role and functions of government organs operating at the lower levels of society, no precise guidelines could be formulated for local government and the functions it should perform. In any case with most low-level organs in the countryside more responsive to the peasants than to the government, even if agreement could have been reached within the government on their proper roles, it is unlikely that it would have had much practical effect in the rural areas.

Government attempts to deal with rural unrest also were hampered by the absence of a clear and consistent policy on how to handle that unrest. The government's reluctance both to accede to the peasants' demands and to use force of arms on a wide scale severely constricted its alternatives in dealing with the popular disturbances sweeping across the countryside. Government action mainly took the form of appealing to the populace to have patience in waiting for the final resolution of the land question by the Constituent Assembly, and of urging its own representatives to bring about a restoration of order in the unsettled rural areas. In the words of the first Minister of Agriculture, A.I. Shingarev, because the government lacked both the capacity and desire to use physical force on a wide scale, it had to

> . . . resort only to a moral influence on the population. Therefore to all the complaints sent to the Ministry, the department has turned both to subordinate *guberniia* and *uezd* commissars and directly to the *volost* committees with requests to explain to the population the inadmissability of arbitrary actions in relation to private land-owners and equally the criminal and civil responsibility for such actions, and with a directive on the necessity, in connection with the preservation and support of civil peace, to wait quietly for a just solution to the land question in the forthcoming Constituent Assembly.[50]

Although spoken in the early part of the year, Shingarev's words remained an accurate summation of the major approach of government policy in the countryside throughout the year.

However the government could offer no firm guidance to its

harassed representatives in the face of popular rejection of its appeals for patience. Illustrative of the type of guidance given by the government is the instruction from the Temporary Militia Administration of the Ministry of the Interior to *guberniia* commissars on 12 May:

> I ask you to take, with the assistance of the public committees organised in the localities, the most resolute measures for the liquidation of the phenomena indicated, which are disorganising the country, and for securing normal conditions of life.[51]

The government repeatedly failed to give any specific guidance or leadership to its local organisations, virtually leaving them to find the best means of dealing with the problems they faced. In this way the government failed to give any overall direction or stimulus to the struggle with unrest. Local authorities were left to cope with little more than the government's urgings for greater effort ringing in their ears.

This situation is highlighted by the government's continued hesitant attitude toward the widespread use of force. The reluctance to sanction the use of armed force on a wide scale meant that the government had to rely on the cooperation of the population. As soon as this cooperation disappeared, the government was faced with two equally unpalatable alternatives: it would have to use force to attempt to maintain its position, or it would have to relinquish its governing role. This dilemma, which confronted the government throughout the year, was summarised by the Menshevik Food Minister in the third coalition government, S. N. Prokopovich, when he declared, in relation to the doubling of the grain price in August:

> We were confronted by a dilemma: either we could attempt to obtain grain by voluntary means, by means of this doubling, or we could turn directly to repressive measures, to the use of armed force, and confiscate the grain from the people with the help of this force, because the people would not deliver the grain at the old prices. We could not bring ourselves to use armed force. But if now, after doubling the prices, we still do not obtain the grain we need, then of course we will be compelled to resort to the use of force. This is an absolutely definite statement. . .[52]

However the government's principled opposition to the use of armed force had been undermined by its actions earlier in the year; the use of armed force had already been sanctioned where other methods of maintaining order were insufficient. During the lives of the first two coalition governments this was reaffirmed, particularly in the wake of the July Days in Petrograd. However the use of armed force was rarely referred to directly. On 13 July Kornilov is reputed to have threatened 'without hesitation to use military force' to restore order, but this was exceptional. Government spokesmen, and also Kornilov in his more famous circulars of 8 and 31 July,[53] were usually more circumspect, preferring to talk in terms of the bringing of criminal proceedings to bear against disruptive elements, and the need for a 'resolute struggle', the 'taking of all measures', and 'the necessary steps' when referring to rural unrest. Of course the threat of force was thinly disguised by such statements, but the government was unwilling to commit itself openly and unambiguously to the widespread use of force as a means of stemming the tide of unrest surging across the country. Nevertheless such means were resorted to increasingly as the year went on; according to one estimate, armed force was used 17 times between March and June, and 39 times during July and August.[54] Although the scale of the use of troops in July and August does not constitute the wave of repression which some historians claim the government unleashed at this time,[55] it does represent a hardening of the government's position: as unrest increased, force was resorted to on a wider scale in an attempt to re-establish government control.

Thus by the end of August, when over the preceding four months Russia had experienced two broad coalition governments separated by an interregnum of three weeks, the government's position in the rural areas was no more healthy than it had been at the beginning of May. Food shortages were acute, peasants increasingly were seizing the land, rural unrest reached its peak for the year, and the local organisations of administration remained ineffective. The government continued to pursue the original policies which had alienated the peasants initially, preferring to fiddle with the framework as it existed rather than to seek solutions outside the limitations which they set for themselves. When one member of the government tried to implement measures that would have changed the framework, he was overwhelmingly rebuffed. Caught in an *impasse*, the government struggled on, with the weight of ruling becoming more onerous as the days passed.

UNREST IN THE VILLAGES

Peasant unrest reached its peak in the summer, coinciding with the collapse of the first coalition government and the negotiations preceding the establishment of the second coalition; the level of unrest rose steadily during May, June and the first half of July, followed by a temporary decline in late July and August. In this period the contours of that unrest changed considerably, compared with the first two months after the fall of the tsar.

During the late spring and summer the main form of peasant action against landed property was seizure through occupation. Rejecting all semblance of legality, in increasing numbers the peasants moved onto privately-owned land and began to cultivate it or to graze their livestock on it. They repudiated rental agreements and moved to seize land not previously covered by agreements with the owner, simply asserting their right of control by virtue of occupancy and of traditional considerations. Although such forms of 'surreptitious' seizure as the taking of stock and implements and the removal of labour power remained significant, the incidence of the establishment of rental rates declined precipitously. With the growth of the open seizure of land, 'surreptitious' methods became less important as a form of land seizure.

During the early summer the level of destruction declined, but in late July and August this began to rise once again. The level of personal violence, although fluctuating month by month, remained significant through the period. This is not surprising since each instance of the open seizure of land created an overt conflict situation between the peasants and the land-owner and his supporters. However in this type of situation there was, by the middle of the year, little the land-owner could do to defend his land. The following report from Novgorod *guberniia* in July is indicative of the state of public security:

> In Belebelkov *volost*, Starorus *uezd*, robbery, murder and arson have occurred. The peasants, gaining no satisfaction from the authorities, resort to arbitrariness. The other day a thief was killed who, according to the population, had terrorised the peasants. The local militia was not armed.[56]

Such reports of the powerlessness of the local authorities in the face of peasant depredations abound in the messages from the localities to the militia headquarters during late spring and summer. With the local authorities virtually helpless, not only did the land-owners have little defence against the open seizures of the peasants, but the way was left clear for the venting of deeply-rooted prejudices and personal antagonisms. Murder, assault, arrest and robbery were common occurrences in many villages. When the authorities tried to use armed force to quell these disturbances, armed clashes between peasants and militia frequently resulted.

While the bulk of peasant actions during spring and summer concerned the seizure of arable or pasture land, in May, June and early July the effective seizure of forest and woodland remained an important strand of rural unrest. As earlier in the year, peasant control was established by the imposition of both blanket and partial prohibitions on access to the timber on the part of everyone who was not a member of the local peasant community. In imposing such bans the peasants rejected established defence requirements, commercial contracts and city and railway needs for fuel as well as, in many cases, the requirements of private land-owners. As an alternative, or sometimes a supplement, to the placing of a prohibition on access to the timber, the peasants in many areas went into the forests and felled the trees themselves. Such felling was aimed at providing fuel for use at home as well as, in some cases, for speculative sale to the fuel-hungry towns.

As the significance of the seizure of timber declined in late July and August, the peasant seizure of private land-owners' crops reached major proportions; in both July and August this form of action registered more than one-fifth of all instances of peasant actions against land and was second only to the open seizure of land as a constituent part of unrest as a whole. The peasants seized control of the crops either by preventing the land-owner from harvesting his crop or by carrying the crop off themselves. In cases of the latter type of seizure, the peasants sometimes left the land-owner with sufficient grain for his family's needs, sometimes even paying a nominal sum for the grain.[57] However on most occasions the peasants appear to have seized control of the whole of a land-owner's crop leaving him nothing to provide for his needs. By thus seizing the produce of the estates, the peasants completed the noose around the necks of the land-owners whose land they had not seized. Seizure of the produce meant that the peasants were, in effect, taking control of the land out of the hands of its legal owners; formal ownership meant nothing if the owners gained no benefit from such ownership. Land-owners everywhere were in a position from which they could not escape: if the land-owner did not work his land, the peasants would seize it; if he did work his land there was no guarantee that the peasants would not seize it anyway, and even if they did not take over the land physically, they would seize the produce from that land; and finally, caught in this vice, the land-owner was not able to dispose of his land because of a shortage of buyers, peasant prohibitions on the sale of land, and, after 12 July, the government restriction. There was no way the land-owner could make his estate pay.

Increased peasant crop seizure in July and August was linked to the steady increase over the whole period of peasant actions in relation to the food situation. Although the establishment of the grain monopoly originally coincided with a surge of grain into the reception points, in the long term its effect was the exact opposite of that desired by its framers: the peasants widely refused to cooperate with the monopoly. The peasant producers refused to deliver the grain at the new price: from Orel *guberniia* in mid-May came the report:

> The peasants do not want to supply grain at the established fixed price.[58]

Blaming the towns for the situation they found themselves in, the peasant producers frequently placed a total embargo on the provision of grain to the towns. Many urban dwellers migrated from the cities into the countryside in search of food, often being forced to barter consumer goods for the grain they needed. As the year went on, this embargo was more and more frequently extended to the front as well. Attempts on the part of the government to break this embargo by requisitioning the grain from the owner often met with armed resistance on the part of the peasants.

The refusal on the part of the peasant producers to supply grain to the towns not only deprived the urban inhabitants of food, but it was also instrumental in preventing the northern non-grain-producing *gubernii* from receiving the necessary supplies of grain; there was no way of collecting grain for shipment to the north unless it was first collected in the major transport centres in the towns or larger villages. The impact of this was heightened by the widespread introduction by local peasant authorities of prohibitions on the export of grain from the region of origin. Militia reports record the following message from Simbirsk in May:

> In Sengil *uezd* the local Popov and Dvorian *volost* committees forbid the removal of grain from the surrounding villages.[59]

Peasants were not only refusing to send grain to the towns and to the army, but also to peasants in neighbouring areas. The unity of the country was disintegrating; Russia was breaking up into separate economic units. However, many of these economic units had insufficient food for their populations; they were not economically self-sustaining. Consequently peasants from these areas frequently intercepted grain being shipped from production to consumption areas and seized it for their own use, or mounted expeditions into neighbouring grain-producing regions, either to buy food on the thriving black market, thereby increasing its price and undermining their own future position as purchasers,[60] or to take it by force.

During July änd August peasant actions against the grain monopoly were stepped up. The vast increase in peasant crop seizure during these months noted above was significant because, allied to the widespread refusal on the part of the peasants to supply the grain at the fixed price, this removed from government access a large amount of grain which otherwise it could have used. Peasants individually hoarded grain on a massive scale and collectively they continued to prohibit the removal of grain from the immediate area. They sabotaged the grain census that was necessary for the monopoly to work, refused to cooperate with food committees which were attempting to carry out the functions the government accorded to them, and frequently acted violently toward those trying to implement the monopoly:

> 'On 25 July at 9 a. m., in the village of Alikovo, Iadrin *uezd*, Kazan *guberniia*, under the influence of agitators disturbances occurred against the introduction of the grain monopoly. A crowd of soldiers and peasants armed with sticks and bottles, evidently incited by deserters who also took part, cruelly beat up the chairman of the food board Mr Zubkov (and) the captain in command of the soldiers charged with assisting the introduction of the monopoly in the *uezd* . . .'[61]

In many of those areas where peasant organisations permitted the export of grain from their immediate region, they ignored the price set by the state and established their own price.

Just as many peasants in the grain-producing areas reacted violently to attempts to collect the grain, those in grain-deficient regions frequently reacted in a similar way to the food shortages that inevitably were occurring. The immediate effect of such shortages often was violence and destruction. Food riots were becoming more common during the late summer, the focus of this discontent almost inevitably being the government officials and instrumentalities established in the local areas to deal with food matters: grain storehouses and the property of the food authorities was plundered and their employees were beaten up. From Vladimir came the report:

> On 8 August in Shuia serious disorders, including the destruction of the *uezd* food board, occurred due to an acute shortage of foodstuffs.[62]

Thus during July and August peasant activities increasingly were directed toward some aspect of the food situation, either acting in a way which decreased the general supply of food to Russia as a whole or reacting to that decreased supply.

The upsurge of rural unrest during the summer was linked to deepening peasant disillusionment with the Provisional Government and its actions. This is reflected in the changing basis of peasant actions during this period. During early spring, when the peasants' faith in the government was at its height and they were confident that they would soon achieve their demands through the government, their actions were motivated in large part by a desire for the amelioration of their immediate economic position and the avoidance of an open confrontation with the government. The importance of 'surreptitious' methods of land seizure and of the seizure of only parts of landed estates during this earlier period indicates this twin desire. However by mid-summer the fragile peasant faith in the government had evaporated in many areas. Economic motives had been replaced as a basis for peasant actions by a desire to settle old debts against former oppressors and to achieve their demands now, through their own actions. The significance of 'surreptitious' methods of seizure declined, particularly during July and August, as the peasants no longer tried to avoid conflict with a government they no longer believed in. No longer were the peasants willing to seize only that amount of land they needed in the short term: during the summer the seizure of entire estates was widespread, even if this meant in many cases leaving much of the seized land unworked. The rise in destructive activity in late July and August is further evidence of the decline in economic motives. Having given up all hope for the satisfaction of their demands through government action, the peasants were now willing to embark on a course of open confrontation with the government, to seek their own solutions to their problems. As a report from Poltava in late June asserted:

> The agrarian movement in the *guberniia* has become stronger. Consciousness that the land question can be resolved only by the Constituent Assembly has been strongly shaken.[63]

From the peasants' point of view their continued disillusionment with the government was well-founded. On the land question, the government went no way toward satisfying the basic peasant demand. Government policy remained one of postponement of the final solution of the land question until the convocation of the Constituent Assembly. However the continued postponement of that body could do nothing but alienate even further a peasantry whose distrust of the government was growing daily. The government's land policy was interpreted in the villages as amounting to little more than a disguised attempt to defend the private land-owners and to prevent the peasants from gaining what rightfully belonged to them. The government's commitment to the freezing of land relationships was perceived to be double-faced: land relationships were to be frozen completely in the sense that the peasants could not obtain the legal title to land they currently did not own, but despite the government restriction on land trans-actions of 12 July, land-owners still possessed the formal right to buy and sell land. To the peasants it appeared that there was one law for the peasants and another for the private land-owners. Continued government strictures against arbitrary action in land affairs reinforced such a view. The government appeared unsympathetic to peasant needs and demands.

On food matters too, government actions and their effect during the summer were unlikely to regain the peasant faith lost during the spring. It was in the middle of the year that the government's food policy really began to bite home. Late July and August were months

when the peasants were busy harvesting the grain and preparing it
for the market. Consequently it was a time when the peasant
producers were acutely aware of grain prices and the way they
related to the other sectors of their economic life. It was also a time
of year when local government organisations were intent on
collecting the harvested grain. Consequently it was at this time that
grain producers began to feel the full effects of the fixed price and the
grain monopoly. With the price offered for the grain at such a level
that the peasants could not realise sufficient from their produce to
enable them to purchase articles of prime necessity on the open
market, with explicit government rejection in early August of any
possibility of an increase in the fixed price, and with government
inability to supply articles of prime necessity in the required number
at any price, the peasants refused to surrender their grain. The
increased government attempts to collect the grain in the villages,
normal for this time of the year, highlighted this situation and, in
July and August, acted as a catalyst to the emergence of a more
active form of opposition to the grain policy than had been evident
earlier.

In the grain-consuming areas too, the summer period was vital; if
the government could not secure sufficient grain during this period,
the peasant consumers would starve in the coming winter. However
it was clear from early in the year that the government's procurement programme was running into difficulties. Already in May the
food situation in Kaluga was described as 'close to catastrophe',
while in Nizhegorod it was 'difficult'; by July – August reports of
food shortages were coming from many parts of the country.[64] The
bankruptcy of the government's policy was clear in the effect it was
having of antagonising producers and failing to supply consumers.
In response, both groups indulged in heightened levels of disruptive
activity and rejected even further the authority of the government,
one because it saw Petrograd as a predatory ogre willing to take all
and give nothing, and the other because the government was unable
to guarantee that most basic necessity of life—food.

Another element relevant to the course of unrest during the
summer was the apparent increase in the flow of agitators, and
therefore of propaganda, into the villages. While agitators had been
a significant influence throughout the earlier part of the year,
accurate measurement of the number of agitators at work and the
effect they had is impossible. Nevertheless it does seem that the flow
of agitators increased during the late summer, primarily in the form

of deserters from the front, although the extent of this should not be exaggerated. Reacting to the turbulent conditions in the country-side and the opportunites these created, seasonal demands of field-work on the family plots, and a general war-weariness heightened by the beginning of the summer offensive in mid-June, many soldiers poured out of the trenches and into the countryside; according to an official in Podolsk during July, the number of deserters in the rural areas was increasing daily.[65] Many peasants were still violently opposed to desertion and to deserters: on 5 July peasants in Kazan decided to send all deserters back to the front, while three days later peasants in Tula detained a deserter and beat him to death.[66] However by this time the general feeling in the villages was far more receptive to deserters than these instances indicate, and in many areas soldiers returning from the front constituted a significant radicalising influence. This often was linked to an increase in destructive activities. In a despatch from Nizhegorod on 26 July it was declared that:

> All the unrest and lawlessness is linked with the appearance in the boundaries of the *guberniia* of deserters, soldiers on leave or delegates from regimental committees, and also sometimes even delegates of the Soviet of Peasants' Deputies. Under the influence of the agitation of the above-mentioned delegates and soldiers, the consciousness of the local peasants that all civil laws had lost their force and that all legal relations must be regulated by peasant organisations, has been strengthened.[67]

Although this report exaggerates the role of the soldiers, in essentials it is accurate; they radicalised the peasants when they appeared in the villages. The increased rates of desertion in the summer and the consequent influx of large numbers of deserters into the seething countryside provided a stimulus for rural unrest. The enormous increase in the level of destruction in the peasants' actions from July to August may in part be a reflection of this fact.

The sharp decline in the level of unrest in August compared with June and July has been attributed by some Soviet historians to the government's policy of adopting a hard line toward rural unrest at this time.[68] Certainly in the wake of the July Days the government was loud in its condemnation of disruptive actions of all sorts. In some areas of the country, primarily the urban areas, 'bolsheviks' and 'Leninists' were harassed, arrested and driven underground.

However the effect of this in the countryside was patchy. Punitive action was taken against disruptive elements in some areas, including in some instances functionaries of land committees,[69] while in others no action was taken at all. In some instances troops sent to put down rural unrest deserted the government side and joined the peasants. Thus although government action played a role in the temporary setback suffered by rural unrest in some individual areas, on the national scale it was only of minor importance.

The major factor in the decline in the level of unrest during late summer was the seasonal effect of the normal course of agricultural life. During May and early June hay-mowing and the gathering-in of fodder occupied most of the daylight hours in the villages. This was followed in most of June and early July by a period during which the intensity of field-work declined very greatly and the peasants no longer had to be almost wholly concerned with the demands of production. Late July and August witnessed a sharp increase in the amount of time the peasants had to spend in the fields: crops planted in the previous autumn had to be harvested, the soil prepared, and crops for harvesting in the following summer had to be planted. This pattern of the intensity of field-work was reflected in the level of unrest: rural disturbances reached a peak in late June and early July during the slack period in the villages, and then declined as field-work became more demanding in late July and August.[70]

The seasonal pattern of agricultural life also conditioned the contours which rural unrest took during this period. These four months were all characterised by a very high incidence of open land seizure. Meadow and pasture land was seized in large quantities; with the peasants unable to satisfy their requirements for fodder from the common pastures alone, their attention naturally turned to the meadows held by private land-owners.[71] Much arable land was seized during this period too, of course; the disappointing size of the harvest in many areas and the need to sow land for the future crop being significant as motivating factors. The high incidence of crop seizure also reflects the fact that it was harvest time, when peasant attention was turned to the crop. Furthermore this was the time when the maximum economic advantage could be gained from the seizure of crops, given the normal market situation. Moreover with crop failures occurring in many areas, peasants hoped to recoup the deficit in domestic production by seizing crops belonging to private land-owners. Crop failure also stimulated destructive activity and *pogroms* as peasant producers vented their frustration and disappointment in a wave of violence.[72] The seizure of livestock and agricultural implements and the withdrawal of labour power, although declining in significance over the period, also had seasonal ramifications: by carrying out such actions in June and early July, the peasants could use the resources thus gained in their own field work. Finally, the decline in peasant timber seizure is explained by seasonal considerations: with the warm weather there was little need for firewood, while the completion of repair work around the villages had reduced greatly the need for timber for constructional and maintenance purposes. Thus both the level and configuration of rural unrest during the summer were determined, within the context of increasing disillusionment with the government, to a significant degree by the seasonal pattern of rural life.

THE PATTERN OF ORGANISATION

One of the most striking characteristics of the Russian revolution was the immense proliferation of voluntary or non-governmental organisations which developed at all levels of society. The patterns of organisation that emerged during the late spring and summer accurately reflect the disintegration of national economic unity and the increasing alienation of the urban-based government from the villages occurring at that time.

The *volost* committees discussed in the preceding chapter theoretically were the base of a three-tiered pyramid of committees in the countryside, with committees at the *uezd* and *guberniia* levels comprising the upper two tiers. However this pyramid was internally fractured from the start; the two upper levels rarely were firmly rooted in the base, in most cases being almost completely isolated and alienated from the *volost* committees. The major reason for this was the primarily urban nature of these bodies.

The weakness in links between committees at the village and *volost* levels and those at the *uezd* and *guberniia* levels is clearly evident in the membership of the latter; rarely were peasants working in the fields prominent among the membership of these bodies. The *uezd* committees consisted of representatives of the *volosti* (normally appointed by the *volost* committees), including the towns, and members of public organisations and institutions. Membership was not elected directly and popularly, but represented other organisations. In practice, committees at the *uezd* level were the lowest level bodies in which the interests of both rural and urban dwellers were involved. The balance between these different groups varied from instance to instance, but the general situation in Tula and Riazan as described by a representative of the Moscow Soviet of Workers' Deputies was not unusual:

> *Uezd* committees have been elected primarily in this way: from each *volost*—1 deputy; from the town—five times as many as necessary; in addition there were representatives of the priesthood, *zemstva*, cooperatives and others. It turns out approximately thus: 17 from the peasants, 12 from the town (merchants), 3 from the *zemstvo*, 2 from the priesthood, and another person and, in this way the peasantry are not in the majority.[73]

In most instances the *uezd* committees were not broadly representative of the population of the *uezd* because peasants were rarely in the majority of the membership. A similar situation existed in the *guberniia* committees. The composition of the Voronezh *guberniia* committee is typical of the type of membership these committees usually had. Established in June, this consisted of the following: two representatives from each *uezd* committee, six from the Soviet of Workers' and Soldiers' Deputies, three from the *guberniia* committee of peasants' deputies or the Peasants' Union, three from the cooperatives, two from the *guberniia* food committee, and one from each of the *guberniia* zemstvo, stock exchange committee, regional railway committee, city administration, institute of higher education, and committee of the united organisations of Voronezh.[74] In practical terms this membership included no one who was necessarily closely linked with the villages: those organisations which were active in the rural areas, the cooperatives and the Peasants' Union, normally were represented in these committees by urban-based functionaries rather than by workers in the villages. Even when the villages were well-represented numerically in these committees, this was rarely by peasants working in the fields; at the *uezd* and *guberniia* levels it was common practice for the peasants to be represented by urban-based intellectuals, divorced from the villages. In many of these bodies, as in the government food and land committees, the representatives of the villages were local party activists who were more concerned with events in the towns and with trying to follow and reflect the party politics of the capital than they were with events in the countryside. In the rhetoric of party politics which frequently dominated the meetings of these committees, the reality of the land question and of rural unrest was transformed into a question of theoretical principles and dogmatic assertions. The ideological tenets of the major political groups tended to obscure rather than enlighten events in the villages for those who held those beliefs.[75] Despite the air of unreality that this generated, these committees did sometimes act as a stimulant to unrest. News of their proceedings and decisions often was spread throughout the villages through newspapers and agitators. When radical resolutions on matters concerning the peasants were adopted, they often stimulated unrest in the villages by encouraging the peasants to take unilateral action to achieve their demands. The prominent position occupied by SRs in many of these committees and their role in fostering the passing of resolutions which mirrored that adopted on the land question by the congress of the All-Russian Soviet of Peasants' Deputies discussed below was significant in this regard.

Located in the *guberniia* or *uezd* seat and formed and manned by urban-based and urban-oriented activists, these committees were widely seen by the peasants in the villages as alien and hostile. According to one report

> The peasants say that apart from the *volost* committees they do not acknowledge anyone, and once the *volost* committee has decided, then that is correct, and it is necessary to implement the given decision; all the *uezd* and city committees work in the hands of the land-owners.[76]

These committees exercised little continuing influence in the villages, often remaining out of touch with developments in the rural areas and being far less in tune with the changing moods of the peasantry than the village and *volost* bodies.[77]

Uezd and *guberniia* committees usually were formed by *uezd* and *guberniia* congresses of peasants' deputies. These bodies were large meetings convened irregularly throughout the administrative regions of Russia. Delegates to the congresses, most of whom were not peasants, were drawn from all areas of the *uezd* or *guberniia* and from as many of the organisations deemed relevant to the peasants' lives as possible. The only major exception appears to have been the village committees which were deemed to be represented through the *volost* committees. Taking place in the *uezd* or *guberniia* seat, these assemblies also tended to become arenas for political combat between local representatives of the political parties struggling for power in Petrograd. For most of the year SRs tended to dominate the proceedings of these bodies. Those present who were not members of any of the political parties, who usually were the representatives from outside the urban areas, generally tended to follow where the party activists led. This factor gave many of the congresses an air of unreality, making them more aware of, and responsive to, events in Petrograd than to developments in the surrounding villages. However, in the course of the wide-ranging discussions characteristic of these congresses, radical positions were often adopted and similar resolutions were passed. Such decisions, when published in local newspapers and carried into the villages by agitators, on many occasions stimulated the peasants to re-volutionary action in the countryside.[78] Nevertheless these bodies were not of great significance for the course of rural unrest in 1917.

The history of the Russian revolution has become linked indissolubly with the concept of the soviet. Perceived as the spontaneous organisation of the oppressed in their struggle for freedom, the soviet has been depicted by many historians as the most important organisational form of 1917. However most historians have focused on Petrograd where the soviet has most closely approximated to the role commonly attributed to it. In the rural areas the soviet did not closely approach the popularly accepted view. As low-level organisations, the soviets were by no means unique in the Russian countryside, except perhaps in that they had a nominal summit in the All-Russian Soviet of Peasants' Deputies. In terms of organisational structure, membership and role, there was little to differentiate between soviets of peasants' deputies and other peasant organisations.

Unlike the formation of village and *volost* committees, which were a direct and immediate response to the needs of the people, independent soviets rarely sprang unaided from the womb of village society. They were far more likely to emerge as a result of the efforts of an outside agitator going into the rural areas with the specific aim of organising soviets among the peasants. The concept of the soviet as the best form of independent organisation for the peasants was shared by the cooperatives, the Peasants' Union, the SRs and the bolsheviks, although they differed on the form the soviet should take.[79] It was these bodies, plus the soviets in the cities whose commitment to the concept of the soviet goes without saying, which were most active in sending agitators into the countryside to proselytise the virtues of this particular type of organisation. The most important of these was the SRs. This mode of development of the soviets, by external stimulus rather than internal generation, meant that the distribution of soviets at village and *volost* levels depended upon such chance elements as the appearance in the region of a skilled agitator, the strength of the existing local peasant organisation, and the state of the finances of the local Peasants' Union, cooperative, or SR party branch.

Soviets were not widely developed at the village and *volost* levels before the bolsheviks came to power. Although accurate figures are not available, it is the general consensus among historians that village soviets were not established on any large scale until after the bolshevik *coup* in October. At the *volost* level the development of soviets was both uneven and limited. In Vladimir the unevenness was very pronounced: in one *uezd* there were soviets in all *volosti* except one, in another there was a soviet in only one *volost*, in a third there were 13 soviets in 28 *volosti*, and in the fourth nine *volosti* our of 13 had soviets; in Voronezh there were soviets in one-third of the *volosti* of the *guberniia*, while in Birsk *uezd* Ufa *guberniia* nine *volosti* out of 14 had soviets. On the national scale, it has been calculated that no more than 11 per cent of all *volosti* had soviets by October 1917.[80]

It was at this local level that the distinction between soviets and other peasant organisations was most blurred. In most cases attempts to form soviets at village and *volost* levels occurred after village and *volost* committees had developed, with the result that the reservoir of people toward which the soviet appealed was the same one toward which the existing committees looked. The local population usually was not large enough to support two completely independent bodies, especially when the aims of both were broadly the same. Furthermore there was a drastic shortage of able people to serve in local committees, with the result that those who had any ability were forced to serve in virtually all low-level organisations.[81] With the ground thus cut from under their feet by the prior existence of village and *volost* committees, there was generally little scope at the village and *volost* levels for the existence of independent soviets. Only when the population was disillusioned with the prior-established institutions was the ground fertile for the growth of soviets. When there was no widespread dissatisfaction with these organisations, in most cases either no soviet was formed or, if it was, it soon merged with the already existing committee. The organisation resulting from this merger was sometimes called a 'soviet', but it differed little from organisations at the same level which did not undergo a merger and which were known by a different name. However mergers, although common, did not always occur. There were instances of soviets and peasant committees existing side by side, sometimes in a state of approximate equality and sometimes with one subordinate to the other.[82] However this was not the usual state of affairs. Soviets were not widely significant as independent entities at the lower levels of rural life.

At the *uezd* and *guberniia* levels soviets of peasants' deputies were formed in the main regional towns under the inspiration of representatives of the same institutions that were instrumental in the organisation of soviets at the lower levels: cooperatives, Peasants' Union, SRs, bolsheviks, existing soviets, and, near the front, soldiers. Soviets at these levels were far more widespread than those in the *volosti* and villages, reflecting the larger human resource base provided by the *guberniia* and the *uezd* and the greater concentration of organised political forces in the city than the countryside. By mid-July 317 *uezdy* out of a total of 813 possessed soviets; by October this had risen to about 422. By October *guberniia* peasant soviets existed in all *gubernii* of European Russia with the exception of Volynsk and Estland.[83]

Uezd and *guberniia* soviets often were formed at the *uezd* and *guberniia* congresses referred to earlier, although in some instances soviets were elected directly by the memberships of soviets already existing at the *volost* and, in the case of the *guberniia* soviets, at the *uezd* levels. The membership and size of the soviets varied enormously because there were no precedents or established standards to follow. However the soviets were almost invariably large bodies; the Bogorod *uezd* Soviet of Peasants' Deputies in Moscow *guberniia* consisted of 105 members while that of Kostroma *uezd* consisted of 115. The size of the soviets usually necessitated the development of a smaller executive committee to guide the work of the soviet as a whole. The soviets of Moscow *guberniia* seem to have been particularly well structured in regard to the internal organisation of their work, largely owing to the interest in the lower level soviets taken by the Moscow *Guberniia* Soviet of Peasants' Deputies. As a result of the efforts of the Moscow Soviet of Workers' Deputies, the Moscow Soviet of Soldiers' Deputies and the Moscow Union of Cooperatives, the *guberniia* peasant soviet formally was brought into existence on 18 March. Once established, it was very active in sending agitators into the countryside to foster the development of lower-level soviets. The *guberniia* soviet itself had not only an executive committee but also a three-man presidium and various sections designed to deal with specific areas of life: organisational, representation, finance and economy, literature-publishing, and consultation. The soviets in Moscow, Bronitskii, and Bogorod *uezdy* had executive committees numbering respectively twelve (with a presidium of three), five and seven. The Petrograd Guberniia Soviet of Peasants' Deputies, formerly the Soviet of Peasants' Deputies of the Petrograd Garrison, had an executive committee of 14, while that of Kostroma *uezd* had one of four.[84] Executive power generally tended to be stronger in the *guberniia* soviets where the scope of work was wider and the numbers present larger than in those at the *uezd* level.

Like the *guberniia* and *uezd* committees discussed above, the soviets at these levels tended to have little direct relevance for events in the countryside. The soviets were situated in the urban areas and were therefore as physically isolated from the villages as the *guberniia* and *uezd* committees. Links with the lower levels of rural life were usually very weakly developed. This was exacerbated by the fact that very few delegates from the villages exercised substantial influence in these soviets, particularly those at the *guberniia* level. The peasants normally were represented by non-peasant intellectuals whose attachment to the peasants frequently was based on ideological misconceptions rather than knowledge or understanding of the situation in the villages. Peasant consciousness was diluted even further in these soviets by the organisational links which many of them possessed with soviets of workers' and soldiers' deputies, particularly at the *guberniia* level. Although the majority of peasant soviets did not merge with the other types of soviets to form a single soviet of workers', soldiers' and peasants' deputies,[85] many did merge either their executive committees or presidia. In other instances the different types of soviets held united congresses or joint discussions on matters of common interest; alternatively a permanent commission with observer status could be attached to the other soviets. All of these forms of contact turned the attention of the soviet away from being exclusively bound up with peasant affairs and made it more conscious of the problems of the urban workers and of politics on the national scale. To the extent that these considerations occupied their attention, they became less sensitive to the peasants they were claiming to represent.[86]

Another major factor causing the increasing irrelevance of the *guberniia* and *uezd* soviets as a whole was that many of these bodies were dominated by the SRs. As the influence of the cooperatives and the Peasants' Union declined in the countryside, the SRs were left with no serious opposition in their attempt to extend their influence into the peasantry through the soviets. As a result, many soviets became virtually PSR organs because of the strength of SR influence in them: all five members of the executive committee of the Bronitskii Uezd Soviet of Peasants' Deputies and all seven members of the executive committee of the Bogorod Uezd Soviet of Peasants' Deputies were SRs, to cite but two examples.[87] Many observers testify to the strength of SR influence in the soviets, even into September and October. Some of these SRs adopted radical positions and, as in the *guberniia* and *uezd* committees, stimulated unrest by doing so. However most of those exercising major influence within the soviets tended to take their lead from the SR-dominated All-Russian Congress of Soviets of Peasants' Deputies, which met in May. The result was that these *guberniia* and *uezd* soviets espoused a policy opposed to arbitrary actions in the countryside allied to continued support for Kerensky, policies which reflected the stated views of the All-Russian Soviet. However in so doing, these soviets tied themselves to a static view which, by mid-summer, had no relevance at all to the views of the majority of the peasantry. In this way many *uezd* and *guberniia* soviets were by-passed by the course of revolution in the rural areas.

At the summit of the hierarchy of soviets was the All-Russian Soviet of Peasants' Deputies, a body which met in full session on only one occasion prior to the bolshevik seizure of power. The relevance of this body for the course of rural revolution virtually was decided by the time the delegates met in Petrograd on 4 May for the first session of the First Congress of the All-Russian Soviet of Peasants' Deputies. Elections throughout the country had returned to Petrograd a total of 1115 delegates of whom 537 were SRs, 136 were non-party, 329 of unknown affiliation, 103 SDs, 6 Trudoviks and 4 Popular Socialists. With this large base and the support of many of the formally uncommitted, the SRs were able to impose their imprint on the formal congress resolutions. Moreover through their dominance of the congress sessions, the SRs were able to gain a commanding position on the executive committee of the soviet elected at the congress; of the 30 members of the committee 25 were

SRs, of whom four would hold ministerial positions before October (Kerensky, Chernov, Avksentiev and S. L. Maslov). Of those 25 SRs, the majority were to the right of centre of the party, and therefore did not share the views of V. M. Chernov. In addition, 12 members of the executive committee were members of the Chief Land Committee. Thus while the effective SR majority in the congress as a whole ensured the passing of SR flavoured resolutions, the SR-government flavour of the executive committee ensured that in the absence of another congress, the expressed will of the All-Russian Soviet as formulated by the executive committee would not stray too far from the official government line. Consequently as the peasants became increasingly disillusioned with the government and what it was doing, they moved further away from the All-Russian Soviet of Peasants' Deputies and those who took their lead from it.

Like the situation in the urban-based bodies at the *guberniia* and *uezd* levels, peasants working in the fields were not the most significant part of the membership of the All-Russian Soviet. The peasants tended to be represented by non-peasant intellectuals, a fact reflecting both the traditional peasant search for leadership from above and the regulations relating to representation at the soviet which specified that peasants' deputies did not have to be peasants, but only elected by peasants. Despite the non-peasant nature of the membership, the decisions of the soviet broadly reflected the sentiments expressed on behalf of the peasants as a whole by peasant organisations at lower levels. The congress resolutions broadly corresponded to many resolutions passed by peasant bodies at that time. The resolutions also were very similar to a model instruction compiled on the basis of 242 sets of instructions given by local communities to their deputies at the congress.[88]

Both the congress resolution and the composite instruction on the attitude to the war refer to the need for a quick but fair peace without annexations, and for the need to continue to support the front until such peace was achieved. Both also commend attempts by the Soviet of Workers' and Soldiers' Deputies in Petrograd to bring an end to the war by uniting the workers of the world.

On food matters, both agreed on the need for the grain monopoly and the fixed price on grain, on the need for fixed prices on articles of mass need and improved distribution of them in the countryside, on the need for a ration system, and for the requisition of grain at the old price from those with more than 50 *dessiatiny* of land, banks, commercial entrepreneurs, and merchants. Both also agreed that food organisations should be based on democratic principles, on the need to struggle with speculation, and on improving the labour situation.

On the land question too there was broad agreement although, as indicated below, the congress took a more radical position on one aspect of this than that contained in the model instruction. Agreement existed on the following principles: private ownership in land should be abolished with all land being alienated without compensation for division on an equal basis among those who wish to work it; final resolution of the land question must be carried out by the Constituent Assembly; pending the convocation of that body, a number of interim moves should be taken to preserve the economic wealth of the country and to alleviate the lot of the producers: prohibition on land transactions, widening the scope of the power of the land committees to include the exercise of control over the economic resources of Russia (for example seed, fish, timber), better distribution of farm implements, and the fixing of rent and wage levels. Both also contained a condemnation of the arbitrary seizure of land.

A survey of these, the most important congress resolutions as far as the peasants were concerned, shows that the congress resolutions broadly reflected the instructions given by local communities to their delegates. However the resolutions did not mirror the instructions exactly. The resolution on the *volost zemstvo* emphasised the need for a democratic base for that organisation while the composite instruction, without forgetting about the need for democracy, emphasised the functions that body should play in the agrarian sphere. On the role of land committees, the congress resolution was more radical than the composite instruction: while the latter called for the transfer of unused land into the control of land committees prior to the final resolution of the land question by the Constituent Assembly, the congress resolution demanded that all land should be placed 'in the management' of land committees, which were to control all aspects of land usage.[89] Apart from these exceptions, the congress resolutions broadly reflected the instructions coming from below.

The congress resolutions were quite radical in the context of May 1917. They went further than government policy in a number of respects, particularly on the question of the power of land committees over all land in which the soviet's position mirrored that of Agriculture Minister Chernov. However this resolution was not interpreted by all at the congress and in government as a radical step. Many preferred to interpret it as meaning that land committees would work out a *modus vivendi* between peasants and landowners while preserving the juridical rights of the latter. However it was widely interpreted by the peasants to mean that all the land should be placed in their hands. The resolution was spread throughout the countryside by agitators and by delegates returning home, and it gave a significant stimulus to land seizures in many areas. However with this exception, the congress resolutions were neither radical nor in tune with peasant sentiment later in the year, by which time the peasants had rejected the premise of the continued authority of the Provisional Government upon which the congress resolutions were based. No further congresses were held at which the mood of the peasants could make itself felt, and the executive committee was tied too closely to the government to gauge and express peasant opinions accurately. As a result, the soviet became increasingly out of step with the peasants as the year wore on; it remained rooted in the psychology of the spring. This is graphically illustrated by the fact that it was not until 5 October that the executive committee prepared a draft law bringing all land 'in the management' of land committees, to implement the decision adopted in May.[90] The position of the soviet was largely rejected by the peasants by the middle of summer, with the result that it was, in practice, largely irrelevant to the course of developments in the rural areas.

Another type of organisation in the countryside has been emphasised by many Soviet historians of the period, organisations of poor elements within the peasantry, the poor and landless peasants and the hired labourers. The formation of special organisations of farm workers and of the poor peasantry was a major plank in Lenin's agrarian policy, stemming from his view of the developing class differentiation within the peasantry. Although such bodies did develop, they were not very widespread. The only areas in which they appeared on anything but a negligible scale as independent entities were in the Baltic region and in parts of the Ukraine, and even here they were an insignificant factor in rural unrest. Soviets of landless deputies were formed in Lifland, Estland and Kurland while organisations of agricultural workers appeared in Minsk, Poltava, Kiev, Kursk, Kharkov, Taurida, Kherson, Ekaterinoslav and Moscow. All of these were organised on a very small scale, frequently being limited to a union of workers on one estate. The main form of action initiated by such organisations was the strike over working conditions or pay.[91] Their significance in 1917 was very limited.

Peasant committees and soviets were not the only organs of a non-governmental nature in the rural areas during 1917. An organisation which appeared to have the potential for immense power among the peasants was the All-Russian Peasants' Union. Originally formed in 1905, this organisation virtually disappeared in 1906, only to be revived during March 1917. The aims of the Union were expressly stated at the Union's congress in early August:

> The All-Russian Peasants' Union is a wide professional – political organisation and has as its main aim the general organisation of the citizen peasantry, as the labouring agricultural population, for the organised expression of its will, the organised defence of its interests and rights and for enlightenment and education.[92]

There was nothing unique about these aims; they were shared, in essentials, by the peasant committees and the soviets. This was a major source of weakness for the Peasants' Union, and it tried to overcome this by gaining control over what it perceived to be its main competitor, the soviets.

The Union had played an active role in the convocation of the All-Russian Congress of Soviets of Peasants' Deputies. On 15 March it announced that it had obtained the permission of the Prime Minister and of the Petrograd Soviet to organise an All-Russian Congress, and it donated 500,000 roubles to the SRs for this purpose. It then set about preparatory work, entering the organisational bureau established in early April to prepare for the congress.[93] However in both the organisational bureau and the congress, the Union was in a weak position; it had only about one-third of the members of the organisational bureau, and although many of the delegates to the congress were members of the Union, they did not act jointly in that capacity. The president of the Union, S. L. Mazurenko, did not even gain election to the executive committee. Nevertheless despite this failure at the national level, the Peasants' Union persevered in its aim of taking over the soviet structure and making the lower-level soviets executive organs of the Union. This view was expressed clearly in a resolution of the Union's congress in August:

The organisations of the working peasantry—the All-Russian Peasants' Union and the Soviet of Peasants' Deputies—are extremely necessary for the achievement by all the working people of 'land and freedom', but under the condition that the Soviet of Peasants' Deputies acts in accordance with those positions which the Peasants' Union adopts at the congress, and also that members of the Soviet of Peasants' Deputies not elected from the Peasants' Union, must stand for election again.[94]

The leaders of the soviets struggled against such institutional imperialism; they called on the peasants to boycott the Peasants' Union Congress and they worked hard in the localities to undermine local organisations of the Union and to swallow them up in the soviet structure.[95]

It is difficult to gauge the strength of the Peasants' Union in the villages. There were many instances of the formation of Peasants' Union organisations in the local areas; meetings were convened, and 32 *gubernii* were represented at the congress in the middle of the year. It was claimed at the congress that branches had been formed in 265 *volosti* of Ekaterinoslav.[96] However these figures are misleading. The basis upon which the Union stood in the countryside was fragile. It had nothing to offer the peasants which they could not gain through their own institutions rooted in the villages, the peasant committees or the soviets. Moreover the Union had adopted a moderate, pro-government 'law and order' stance in March and it had not substantially modified this by October. As the mood of the peasants moved to the left, the moderate stance of the Peasants' Union lost its relevance to the situation in the villages. By October, the influence of the Peasants' Union in the villages was negligible.

An important organisation in the villages early in 1917 was the cooperative. The cooperative movement had flourished after 1905, and particularly during the war years, but its position was not established legally until 20 March 1917.[97] There were three main types of cooperatives operating in the countryside during 1917, the producers', consumers' and credit cooperatives. Producers' cooperatives were based on a similar idea to the traditional peasant *artel'* and were the medium through which production could be organised collectively. Consumers' cooperatives provided goods the peasants needed, usually through a local store run on a shareholding basis, while credit cooperatives were a source of finance for improvements to the farms or for the gaining of more land. Like the Peasants' Union, cooperative associations in the villages also became centres of education and enlightenment, providing reading rooms, lectures, and other similar facilities.

However in the highly-charged political atmosphere of 1917 the cooperatives ceased being purely economic and educational institutions and entered the political sphere. Accepting the importance of soviets as organisations of the peasantry, the cooperatives undertook to assist in the organisation of soviets at all levels. At the national level they were instrumental in the convocation of the All-Russian Congress of Soviets of Peasants' Deputies. As well as appealing to the peasants to prepare for and support the congress, individual cooperatives played an organisational role in the genesis of the congress: the Moscow Credit and Loan Association joined the organisational bureau to help to prepare for the congress, and it donated 5000 roubles toward covering the expenses of the congress[98] Financial support for the soviets was a continuing feature of the activities of the cooperative movement; the executive committee of the All-Russian Soviet of Peasants' Deputies received a large part of the finance for its continuing needs from the cooperatives. This work at the national level was repeated at the lower levels; organisational stimulus and financial contributions from the cooperatives were important factors in the genesis of soviets in many areas of the country. However this was the extent of the cooperatives' political activity. Members of the cooperatives in local committees and soviets did not act jointly in their capacity as cooperative members. As organisations, the cooperatives could offer the peasants nothing politically that could not be obtained through other organisations. Thus although the disturbed economic conditions favoured the growth of cooperatives, in terms of on-going political influence, they were relatively insignificant in the countryside.

In analysing the part played by different organisations in the countryside in 1917, a word must be said about the political parties. It was only after the fall of the tsar that political parties of all shades of opinion became legal in Russia. Prior to this time many of them, including the SRs and the bolsheviks, had been characterised by a truncated, clandestine existence. Their formal leaderships and chief theoreticians were either in Siberian exile or abroad, while underground party cells remained in existence in Russia, harassed by the police and in only intermittent contact with the formal party leadership and with similarly situated clandestine groups elsewhere in the country. As a result of this situation, when party leaders returned to Russia after the fall of the tsar and tried to build up their parties in the new conditions of legality, lower organs and party functionaries frequently were reluctant to accept party discipline. Intra-party links between all levels remained weak: for all practical purposes the party name constituted an umbrella based on a few prominent personalities under which a wide range of groups and individuals sheltered. None of the parties was clearly defined, frequently merging with other parties at virtually all levels except the summit; the close interconnections between bolsheviks and mensheviks is but the most well-known example of this phenomenon. With each party consisting of a comparatively clearly-defined leadership group surrounded by an indeterminate grey mass of party organisations and followers, the accurate measurement of a party's political influence among the peasants is virtually impossible.

The weakness in links between levels is clearly evident in the Socialist Revolutionary Party. Traditionally acknowledged as the peasant party, the PSR played a prominent role in the Provisional Government, with a member of that party leading the government during the last four months of its life. It was thus a government with substantial SR participation that continued to frustrate the peasant's demands. Nevertheless people calling themselves SRs continued to exercise influence at the village and *volost* levels, and in the election to the Constituent Assembly the peasants expressed their faith in these low-level functionaries by returning an SR majority. Despite disillusionment with the party at the national level, the peasants continued to place their faith in those nominal SRs at the village and *volost* levels.

SR influence was spread into the countryside primarily by way of the developing network of soviets. The SRs placed great emphasis on a network of soviets under party control, seeing these as the instruments for representing the peasants' interests, controlling the acts of temporary organs, preparing the peasants for the Constituent Assembly, explaining the agrarian question and taking whatever interim measures were necessary before the final resolution of the land question by the Constituent Assembly.[99] Through their dominant position on the All-Russian Soviet and through an extensive array of functionaries in the rural areas, the SRs frequently were in the forefront of the formation of soviets at all levels of rural society. Once these soviets were formed, SRs often continued to exercise some form of guiding role in these bodies, particularly at the *guberniia* and *uezd* levels. Therefore at these levels the degree of influence exercised by the soviet among the peasants often depended upon the political outlook of the local SR group dominating the soviet. If the local group continued to support the government and Kerensky, the influence of the soviet waned over the year; if the group was of a more radical incline, the soviet could continue to exercise some influence in the villages right up until October.

From this power base in the soviets, the SRs sought to extend their influence throughout the countryside, primarily through agitators and the printed word. According to one report, only SR literature was printed and was known in Iamburg *uezd* Petrograd *guberniia*. Around Saratov the SR newspaper circulated in 25,000 copies compared with 9000 of the bolsheviks. From Kursk it was reported that the PSR was the only party of which anything was heard. From Saratov it was reported that the SRs had organised 50 village committees in Kamyshin *volost* alone.[100] To the extent that any party exercised influence in the villages, that party was the SRs. But despite the impressive figures of SR strength in the rural areas, the influence of the PSR at the village level was of marginal significance in 1917. Low level activists claiming to be SRs frequently neither understood official party policy nor tried to implement it on a wide scale.[101] Such individuals could retain political influence in the villages only by moving with the radicalisation of the peasant mood. When they ceased to move in this way, or when they tried to enforce government policy, they were discarded and lost what influence they had wielded. However when they did move to the left with the peasants, they ceased to exercise any influence that was markedly SR-government in tone. It was for these nominal SRs who were responsive to their demands that the peasants voted in the Constituent Assembly election, not the party at the national level. Thus, for all practical purposes, influence in the villages that can be characterised as PSR was minimal in the months immediately preceding the bolshevik coup.

Bolshevik influence in the villages was even less significant than that of the SRs. A shortage of party workers with experience of working among the peasantry, lack of funds, an initially un-attractive land policy, and the skill of the SRs in gaining control of the soviets were all factors hindering the extension of bolshevik influence into the countryside. Important too was the basic bolshevik orientation toward the cities, a factor highlighted by the recommended distribution figures of some bolshevik publications: 360 of the 3200 copies of *Privolzhskaia Pravda*, 5000 of the 47,000 copies of *Sotsial Demokrat*, and 100 of the 3,000 copies of the Saratov *Sotsial Demokrat* were to go to the countryside. Nevertheless, despite the basic concentration on the urban workers and the cities, the bolsheviks did try to extend their influence into the rural areas, primarily through the despatch of agitators and literature into the countryside. However there was little planning or systematic organisation in these attempts.[102] Prior to the October *coup*, bolshevik organisations were seldom found below the level of the *uezd* town. Cells were established in some villages; according to one source 343 bolshevik organisations were established at the regional and sub-regional levels between the two revolutions, but such a figure is minuscule compared with the almost 10,000 *volosti* in European Russia. Furthermore, many of the party organisations that were established lacked both initiative and effectiveness, refusing to act on their own without guidance from the Central Committee. The isolation of the bolsheviks from the peasants is highlighted by the small peasant membership of the party prior to the October *coup*; there were no peasant delegates listed at the VI Congress of the party in July–August 1917.[103]

The bolsheviks also tried to spread their influence into the countryside by means of the *zemliachestva*, or association of countrymen. These were originally non-party organisations which developed among the workers and the garrison troops of Petrograd, Moscow and Kronstadt, uniting people from the same *volost, uezd* or *guberniia* resident in the town. By the end of July there were 25 *volost*, 23 *uezd* and 10 *guberniia* organisations in Petrograd uniting 10–15,000 workers and soldiers, while in Kronstadt there were 44 *guberniia* and *oblast'* associations by July.[104] These organisations did not become entirely bolshevik-dominated, but the bolsheviks were able to exercise considerable influence in many of them; their struggle to increase their influence in these organisations was a major factor in the weakness of the *zemliachestva* in Moscow. In August a central bureau of *zemliachestva* was elected in Petrograd consisting of representatives from 12 *gubernii*.[105] This was dominated by bolsheviks and headed by Sverdlov. The bolsheviks tried to use the *zemliachestva* as channels through which to direct their agitators and their message into the countryside, thereby making use of the contacts that such organisations naturally had. However there is no evidence to show that the use of the *zemliachestva* increased bolshevik influence in the countryside. They remained a small urban group isolated from the mass of the population.

Most of these non-governmental organisations operating outside the capital, the *guberniia* and *uezd* committees, *guberniia* and *uezd* soviets, the Peasants' Union, cooperatives, and the political parties, suffered the same fate as the organs established by the government in the countryside. As peasant disillusionment with the government grew, peasant communities turned inward, seeking to solve the problems confronting them through their own institutions. In doing so they turned their backs on the towns and the rest of Russia. On a large scale they refused to provide grain for the urban dwellers. They destroyed the official rural power structure and rejected the authority of virtually all institutions that were not rooted in the villages; those organisations at the *uezd* and *guberniia* levels could hope to exercise influence only if they moved with the changing mood of the villages. The peasant committees situated in the villages were the real powers in the rural areas, taking over the functions, and frequently the titles, of the committees established by government decree. The government could do nothing about this massive loss of peasant support because it was unwilling to change the basic policies to which the peasants objected. It was during the summer period from May to August that the die was cast for the Provisional Government; in the face of active peasant opposition, the government could not last.

4 The Dénouement

The last period of Provisional Government rule, September and October, began in a crisis atmosphere. Bitter opposition to Chernov and the policies he favoured in the rural areas and profound distrust of Kerensky, engendered by the fear that he would support the socialisation of the revolution, encouraged the Kadets in the cabinet to proffer their resignations on the night of 26–27 August in the hope of promoting the establishment of a new, 'stronger' cabinet more in tune with their own point of view. However their resignations were overrun by the Kornilov affair. It is not necessary to probe the murky depths of this still contentious question here. Suffice it to say that at this time of internal instability within the government, an external threat loomed up which was to have important longer-term consequences for the fate of the revolution. However the Kornilov episode was also important in the short term, in determining the contours of the new government to replace the second coalition. The Kornilov episode reinforced in the minds of many on the left the distrust of the Kadets which had always been a prominent strand in their political outlook. This was reflected in the adoption of resolutions by the Petrograd Soviet and by the SR Central Committee and the Mensheviks on the night of 31 August calling for the exclusion of the Kadets from the government Kerensky was currently trying to form. Kerensky could not afford to ignore the wishes of these bodies.

Consequently after attempts to draw some prominent indus-trialists into the cabinet failed (they refused to participate in a cabinet which excluded the Kadets), Kerensky was forced to announce the formation of a rump 'Directory' government consist-ing of five people. The SR Kerensky remained Prime Minister, the Menshevik Nikitin became Minister of the Interior, while the other three posts, Foreign Affairs, Army, and Navy, were filled by non-party figures.[1] Thus in this crucial period, when rural unrest was again on the rise and when the government had gambled every-thing on the doubling of the grain price, neither the Ministry of

Agriculture nor that of Food was represented at the highest government levels. These positions in the government were not filled until 25 September when a new cabinet, the third coalition, was formed. The left remained the single biggest group, although they were no longer in the outright majority as they had been in the second coalition. The ministry consisted of four Mensheviks (Nikitin, Prokopovich, Maliantovich and Gvozdev), three SRs (Kerensky, S. L. Maslov and Liverovskii), four Kadets (Konovalov, Smirnov, Kishkin and Kartashov), one Radical Democrat (Bernatskii), and five non-party (Tereshchenko, Verkhovskii, Verderevskii, Salazkin and Tretiakov) members. Kerensky remained Prime Minister and Nikitin remained Minister of the Interior, while the right SR S. L. Maslov became Minister of Agriculture and the Menshevik S. M. Prokopovich took over the Food Ministry.

PARALYSIS OF THE GOVERNMENT

In these last two months, while the Provisional Government slowly slid to its doom, it did virtually nothing in the rural areas to try to arrest that process. Having effectively gambled everything on the success of the doubling of the grain price, the government was left with little alternative but to wait and hope that the price increase would bear fruit. Only a few minor moves were made in an attempt to make the food supply system more efficient; fixed prices were established on a whole range of items, and a state monopoly on eggs and sugar was imposed.[2] However such moves were a case of too little too late, as the government continued to tinker with the established structure without doing anything about the basic cause of the structure's inefficiency.

The unresponsiveness of the lower organs to the government's directives remained clear during the autumn. A decision of 7 September made the low-level government organs formally responsible to administrative courts:

Decisions, orders, actions and derelictions of duty on the part of food and land committees and their boards . . . may be the subject of protests by commissars and complaints by appropriate organs of municipal, *zemstvo* and *volost* administrations, as well as by private persons, companies, and establishments whose interests or rights have been infringed by illegal decisions, orders, actions or derelictions of duty of a food or land committee or board . . .[3].

This decision gave those who felt aggrieved by the actions of food or land committees an opportunity to protest against those actions and to bring their protests before the courts. The land and food committees were thus being made formally accountable to the judicial process. However, apart from the enormous problem of translating this formal accountability into practical application, there was often also the very real problem of deciding what constituted an illegal action: the failure to complete the agricultural census prevented the formulation of clear guidelines for grain procurement, thereby forcing food committees to use their own standards in carrying out the functions accorded them by the government. In this situation it was not clear when actions were illegal and when they were not. The lack of clarity in government directions to its lower-level organs in general compounded this problem.

Despite the distrust of many of the lower-level organs in the countryside evident in this decision, the government had little alternative but to rely on those organs for the implementation of its policy. On 24 September a decision was announced expanding the power of the *guberniia* food committees: they were granted the right to permit the export of food from their *guberniia* without official sanction from the centre in each case.[4] This was a weakening of the previous policy, which had vested sole control over the movement of grain in the Food Minister, and a recognition of the unwieldiness of such attempts to control everything from the centre. However the decision did nothing to increase the flow of food from the villages into the collection points; if the peasants could not be encouraged to surrender their grain in greater quantities, such adjustments to the transport system alone had little prospect of success in overcoming the prevailing food shortages.

The government's final major decision on the food question was contained in a circular published in the official press five days before the government was pushed from power.[5] It reaffirmed the government's conviction, expressed at length a few days earlier before the Council of the Republic by Food Minister Prokopovich, that the basic problem was no longer procurement of the grain from the peasants, but transportation of it to areas of need. The circular urged commissars to use armed guards to protect the grain, both while it was in the storehouse and in transit. In this way it was hoped that popular interdiction and plunder of the grain would be prevented. However this decision remained a dead letter; the government had been pushed into obscurity before it could have any effect.

This decision is interesting for the continued hardening in government attitude which it signifies. As its time was drawing to a close, with the food crisis in the cities increasing and the level of rural unrest once again rising to a crescendo, the government was more willing to resort to military means in an attempt to re-assert its dominance. Armed force was resorted to more often during September and October than during the spring and summer combined; according to one study it was used on 56 occasions between March and August and on 105 in September and October.[6] Although the number of instances in which armed force was used during the autumn was small compared with the size of the village population and the number of individual instances of unrest, the increase in its use over the year shows that under the pressure of events, the government's principled opposition to the use of armed force, undermined as early as March, was now collapsing about its ears. However the government was reluctant to acknowledge this by giving a blanket sanction to the use of force to stem the tide of unrest. The government's position remained what it had been throughout the year: force could be used to suppress unrest if other methods were found to be insufficient. On 8 September Kerensky instructed commissars to call in military assistance in time of necessity. Later in the month the government urged the formation of local committees consisting of representatives from central and local government and from local public organisations connected with the land question. These committees were to suppress all manifestations of rural unrest, seeking the assistance of the military in those cases where martial law had been declared. During October special powers, limited in both time and place, were granted to *guberniia* and *oblast'* commissars to deal with rural unrest, and they were encouraged to call in the army if they deemed this necessary; army commanders were instructed to place units from cavalry reserve regiments at the disposal of *guberniia* commissars for this purpose.[7] However the more frequent resort to the use of armed force was coming too late to be of any benefit to the government; its reluctance to sanction the widespread use of armed force and its unwillingness to accede to popular demands in other areas had produced effects which could not be reversed at this late stage. Government control in the countryside had disappeared and there was no way that it could be restored.

In land matters the government's position did not change during the final two months of its tenure of office; it remained unwilling to make any major concessions to popular opinion over the structure of land relations. Indicative of the government's position is the bill, introduced by the SR Agriculture Minister S. L. Maslov, under consideration at the time of the government's fall. This bill did not propose to bring all the land under the control of the land committees as the All-Russian Soviet of Peasants' Deputies and Maslov's own SR Party had demanded. Instead, reflecting the Kadet programme and the broad views of the executive committee of the Chief Land Committee, the bill proposed to establish a land fund for future redistribution which excluded land being cultivated personally by the owner, except in those areas where there was an acute shortage of land generally. The principle of private ownership was to remain intact.[8] Thus the bill not only did not closely approximate the contemporary views of the peasants, but did not even accord with the views expressed by peasant organisations in May, four months earlier. In October the government was still rooted firmly in the positions it had adopted in March.

The rural policy of the Provisional Government lay in ruins at its feet at the time of the bolshevik *coup*; the government had achieved none of the aims it set itself in the rural sphere. The chronic food shortage had been exacerbated, land relations had undergone a fundamental change at the hands of the peasants, and rural unrest had gripped the country in a whirlwind of lawlessness. The government's failure in the rural areas was the result of a complex of factors which, taken in isolation and given more time, the government may have been able to overcome, but which in the conditions prevailing in 1917 were too overpowering for the government to handle.

The government's position in the countryside was undermined by its failure adequately to deal with the problems confronting the peasants. The government could neither profess nor implement a clear and positive policy in the rural sphere, an inability which was linked to the conditions under which it came to power. The fall of the tsar had caught all political groups by surprise; none had expected it and none had formulated a comprehensive programme to be put into effect once power had been achieved. Furthermore although those who formed the nucleus of the first government had participated in the Duma during the last years of tsarist rule, they had only very limited administrative experience upon which to draw when they had to face up to the problems of governing the country. Thus with Russia in a situation where decisions of national importance had to be made quickly and competently, the government was in the hands of a group of men who lacked both a clear conception of what should be done on the national level and the administrative background to fit easily into the role of government decision-makers. In the initial period the government was feeling its way, uncertain of the reliability, the capacities and the limitations of the bureaucratic machine with which it had to administer the country and possessing no agreed blueprint to follow. Under such conditions the formulation of clear, concise and effective legislation was impossible.

The effect of the administrative inexperience of these men in a situation which required clear and commanding government was exacerbated by the conception of the government's tasks shared by many members of the government. Perceiving the government to be a temporary, stop-gap administration and viewing the continuation of the war as its prime responsibility, members of the government were unwilling to implement measures which would have fore-closed options for the Constituent Assembly when it met to decide Russia's future, or which would have disrupted the war effort.[9] The government was intent on maintaining the established structure intact and only taking measures which would further that aim. Comprehensive planning and the implementation of a consistent programme of action was something which the government did not attempt.

Government action in the rural sphere, and especially in regard to land relations, also was hindered by the chronic lack of unity which plagued successive cabinets. The perceived need to placate extremes of both left and right meant that people of widely differing political views and philosophical positions shared ministerial responsibility. The presence in governing circles of various parties, factions within parties, informal cross-party alliances, personality conflicts between members of the government, and bureaucratic rivalries between government departments (particularly Agriculture, Food and Interior) made a unified approach to issues almost impossible to achieve. Furthermore this fragile structure of unity was continually being put to the test by the development of rural unrest. The disturbances in the countryside confronted the government with a basic question of principle; should armed force be used against the sovereign Russian people in an attempt to suppress disorder and preserve the established structure which the government had pledged to protect, or should the government acknowledge the justice of some of the peasants' claims and pass the land—around which most of the disturbances centred—into their hands? With the basic *raison d'etre* of the government continually being challenged in this way by rural unrest, the fragile unity within government ranks was placed under constant stress, particularly while Chernov was Minister of Agriculture. Discord was always just below the surface, with the result that the government frequently could reach agreement only by leaving specifics unspecified.

The government's capacity for action in rural affairs also was affected by its isolation from the villages and their concerns. Without remaining abreast of the swiftly-running currents of opinion in the countryside, the government had no chance of making decisions that would accord with the ever-changing situation. The government consisted of men who, for the most part, were urban-based and urban-oriented, whose direct experience of the villages in recent times was limited. Furthermore government ministers took much of their advice from people similarly far removed from the villages and their concerns: the executive committee of the Chief Land Committee was dominated by people whose background was predominantly urban and it was isolated in the Petrograd bureaucracy; the executive committee of the All-Russian Soviet of Peasants' Deputies also was centred in Petrograd and although the views it expressed in May reflected organised opinion in the villages, by October they had ceased to do so; and the *guberniia* committees which sent reports into the centre were situated in the *guberniia* main towns and therefore outside the mainstream of rural developments. Furthermore it was these bodies that were most characterised by the distorting effect of party ideology. The isolation from the peasants that characterised this urban-based government was not insurmountable. With effort, the gulf could have been bridged. However the government lacked the drive to do this and remained isolated, both physically and psychologically, from the peasants and their concerns.

The combination of administrative inexperience, an overwhelming desire to maintain the *status quo* intact, a chronic absence of unity and isolation from the peasants undermined completely the government's ability to act with any purpose in handling the problems it faced. Consequently the government's whole legislative programme in the rural sphere lacked a sense of overall coordination and consistency; it had the mark of the hasty implementation of insufficiently-considered decisions in reaction to a current difficulty. This is highlighted by the frequent occurrence of the announcement of a government decision followed some time later by directives as to how that decision was to be implemented. Two instances will suffice. Food committees were established on 25 March. They could not fulfil their functions until a grain census was carried out, but the committees were not instructed to conduct such a census until 3 May, six weeks later, and then the census had to be completed by 31 May. In another instance, grain rationing was formally introduced on 29 April, but it was not until 6 June that details of how this was to be implemented were issued. In both of these instances important decisions were announced, and yet the means of carrying out those decisions were not outlined until some time later. Government policy as a whole lacked planning and coherence and consisted of a series of almost unconnected decisions. Decisions in relation to food and land were given some coherence by the existence of institutional frameworks of food and land committees, but even this coherence was minimal. Without a definite programme of its own, attempting to implement a holding operation while dealing with crises which could not be avoided, the Provisional Government could do little but react to situations over which it had no control.

The absence of a clear and coherent approach to rural affairs was reflected in the proliferation of institutional structures in both Petrograd and the countryside that were designed to handle some aspect of life in the rural areas. Stemming from the existence of a wide diversity of views in the government in Petrograd, including differences between government departments, political parties, and cabinet ministers, and from a lack of coordination of those views, this institutional proliferation was marked by the absence of a clear demarcation of responsibility between the different structures. Ambiguity between these structures was matched by ambiguity within the structures as committees at different levels shared areas of responsibility and function without any clear notions of accountability. Friction and rivalry were the result of this institutional ambiguity. The multiplicity of institutions and the ambiguity of relations between them hindered the effective implementation of government policies at the local level and dissipated government energies by providing too many possible channels through which measures could be introduced. The most obvious example of this was the handling of rural unrest. Responsibility for dealing with rural disturbances was not rooted firmly in any one institutional structure, but existed amorphously in the grey area between seven different bodies. With responsibility for handling rural unrest dispersed in this way, government policy was characterised by ambiguity, inconsistency and ineffectiveness. A similar situation existed in relation to land and food matters where the close connection between these areas of concern meant that, in order to promote efficiency and avoid confusion and conflict, the government should have defined the spheres of competence of the two institutional structures far more carefully than it did.

The ambiguity and lack of coherence characteristic of the governmental structure in the countryside was compounded by the inability of low level government committees to strike roots among the population. The small number of representatives from those working their farms and living in the villages in committees at the *uezd*, *guberniia* and national levels not only hindered these bodies in understanding the desires of the peasants, but also made them appear foreign to the peasants. They were 'city committees', having little knowledge or understanding of rural problems as far as the peasants were concerned. Government committees at the *volost* level were unable to gain widespread peasant support because of the prior existence of peasant bodies at that level. The government committees could not gain the confidence of the population without rejecting government authority altogether and becoming more responsive to impulses from below than directives from above, which means that in effect they would have ceased to be government bodies in everything except name. The government's inability to strike firm roots on a wide scale at the local level deprived it of those organisations upon which it depended for the implementation of its decisions.

Popular lack of faith in the government committees was balanced by the powerlessness of those bodies. Lacking any effective means of enforcing their decisions, government committees had to rely on the cooperation of the populace to achieve their ends; if the populace refused to cooperate, the local committees could do nothing to force it to do so. This was a fundamental problem in the implementation of the grain monopoly; the local committees could neither persuade nor force the peasants to give up their grain.

However the crux of the government's problem in the rural areas was the unattractiveness of its policy. It was this which alienated wide sections of the peasantry, and which was responsible for the government's inability to establish any long-term control in the villages. The details of the law on the grain monopoly made that policy unworkable by providing no incentive for the peasants to give up their grain. Government land policy was inflexible and made no concessions to the land-hunger evident throughout the peasant population. The newly-formed local administration was undermined by peasant distrust of the types of people with which the government tried to staff the new administrative structures. By not being responsive to the wishes of the bulk of the populace, the Provisional Government ensured the development of widespread popular opposition to its moves in the rural sphere. The government's refusal to budge from the positions it had adopted and its reluctance throughout most of the period to contemplate the widespread use of armed force against the population, even if it had been able to draw on such force, meant that the government could do nothing about the hostility its policies provoked. The unacceptability of the government's policy was the major factor in the government's fall.

THE VILLAGES IN THE AUTUMN

Popular opposition to the government, evident throughout the year in the changing level of rural unrest, surged up again in September and October after the temporary decline of late July and August. During these last two months the most significant development was the enormous increase in the destructive strand of rural disturbances; by October such actions comprised almost a quarter of peasant infringements against landed property. The following despatch to the Ministry of the Interior gives an indication of the destructive force of peasant activities in Tula:

In the first days of October individual communities began to make demands to estate owners to transfer the estates (into) the direction of the communities and (in cases of) non-implementation of the demands they threatened *pogrom*. Up to this night there have been thefts of harvested grain and live and dead stock from the farms, and the felling of trees has taken on a general epidemic character. The estates of Tulinov, Veresh-chagin, Levshin, Unkovskii, Kremlev and Trishatnii have been destroyed; grain, livestock and implements have been plundered, and information has been received about the destruction of other estates also in Efremov, Bogoroditsk and Venev *uezdy*. Trees have been felled within the bounds of every wooded area of the *guberniia*, with the difference that in one place it is less, in another more. Trees are destroyed in the most rapacious way, not taking account of the age and worth of the trees.[10]

Eloquent testimony to the form the movement was taking is the stark report from Saratov in September:

The local authorities are helpless. The *pogrom* movement is spreading.[11]

It has been estimated that in peasant disturbances in Tambov in September 105 estates were destroyed; in September – October 164 were sacked in Penza and at least 20 in Voronezh, while during October more than 20 were destroyed in Nizhegorod, more than 30 in Tula, and 98 in Orel.[12] Such figures cannot be accepted as entirely accurate; for example another report from Tula indicated that 10–20 estates were being destroyed daily in Efremov *uezd* alone.[13] Nevertheless the figures still indicate that during September and October, peasant unrest was characterised to a high degree by the destruction of the bases of the established land-owning system in the countryside.

The landed estates were not the only ones to suffer in this upsurge of peasant violence. Instances of the plundering of liquor stores and the breaking of shop windows, the looting of the contents, and even the destruction of the building were features in some villages.[14] Personal violence against land-owners, government officials, persons perceived to be opposed to the peasants' aims, and targets chosen indiscriminately and arbitrarily, accompanied the widespread destruction of landed property. Although significant, especially during September, this strand of rural unrest remained a subordinate element of the broader, violent, destructive theme. The increased level of destruction in the rural areas led to greater efforts being made by some local authorities and military leaders to suppress the disorders through the use of troops. On many of these occasions the troops refused to act against the peasants, preferring to join them in their illegal actions. However there were many instances of clashes between troops and peasants;[15] such events only served to enhance the violent tenor of the period.

An important aspect of the destructive strand was the heightened level of tree-felling during September and October. In both months it was the largest single strand of rural unrest. Most of the timber felled during these months was carted away to the villages to be hoarded by the peasants. Scant consideration was given to the needs of the fuel-starved towns and the transport system.

Land seizure remained significant throughout autumn, although in the face of the increasing significance of the destructive and tree-felling strands of unrest, its importance was declining as the bolshevik *coup* drew nearer. In keeping with the tenor of the summer, 'surreptitious' methods of seizure continued to decline in significance; as all notion of land-owners' rights disappeared in most areas, open seizure became even more the norm than it had been during the summer. With the local authorities powerless in most instances and troops brought in from outside the region rarely able to dampen down the unrest they were called in to face, private land-owners remained highly vulnerable to peasant depredations.

In September and October the food crisis deepened. Although the seizure of crops became less significant, other actions with regard to food assumed a prominent place in the countryside. The peasants in the grain-producing areas continued to refuse to supply grain at the fixed price central to the operation of the grain monopoly. They refused to cooperate with the conduct of the grain census or to supply grain to the army and towns. They forbade the export of grain from the immediate vicinity, plundered grain *en route* to other areas, and refused to hand grain over to government food organisations, preferring either to hoard it or to distil it into alcohol. On occasions, the peasants even preferred to destroy the grain rather than to hand it over to the government. The result was an increased sharpening of the food crisis as wider areas of the country experienced an acute grain shortage. During September and October food shortages were reported from about two-thirds of the *gubernii* of European Russia: Orel, Simbirsk, Kazan, Volynsk, Moscow, Kaluga, Mogilev, Vilensk, Olonets, Novgorod, Estland, Penza, Nizhegorod, Tambov, Orenburg, Kostroma, Minsk, Vladimir, Pskov, Viatka, Petrograd, Saratov, Tver, Astrakhan, Yaroslav, Vologda, Smolensk, Bessarabia, Arkhangel, Samara, Lifland,

Perm, Tula and Riazan.[16] This situation was reflected in increased outbreaks of violence against those who could in any way be connected with the deteriorating situation: food boards and other organisations either were closed down or were destroyed, grain stores were plundered, and employees of food organs were beaten up or killed. Peasants from grain-deficient areas frequently mounted expeditions into those areas where grain was more plentiful: one report asserted that peasants from Kaluga were taking 8–9000 *pudi* from Orel daily. Similarly expeditions from cities and troop garrisons went to the countryside in search of grain, frequently leading to open clashes between those in search of grain and those in possession of it.[17] Violence was the overwhelming response to the food crisis.

The upsurge of unrest during September and October reflects the continued deepening disillusionment of the peasants with the government and its policies. Of course, not all peasants had rejected the government; in early October a *volost skhod* in Smolensk was still willing to work through the government, calling on it to hand over all private and monastic land to the peasants prior to the convening of the Constituent Assembly.[18] However such instances were rare. Most peasants had rejected governmental authority and sought to satisfy their demands through their own means. The government still had taken no concrete steps toward the satisfaction of the peasants' basic demand, the legal control of all non-peasant land. No large-scale land confiscation had taken place under government auspices and the Constituent Assembly seemed as far away as it had ever been. Government land policy still appeared to the peasants to favour the large land-owners rather than the small rural cultivators; government policy continued to emphasise the need for 'law and order' and the absolute inadmissibility of arbitrary actions in relation to land. This thrust of government policy was accentuated for the peasants by the government's increasing resort to the use of military force to suppress unrest and by its continued refusal to make the organisations of local administration more responsive to the peasants. Local government institutions continued to be characterised by a patently land-owner flavour in the eyes of the peasants. Thus both government land policy and those the government relied on to implement that policy remained major sources of peasant discontent.

On the food question too government actions did little to win back the support it had enjoyed initially in the rural areas. The doubling of the grain price, a desperate move by the government, could not retrieve a situation which already had been lost. Without the earlier regulation of the cost and supply of articles of prime necessity to the farms, the cost of such items in the autumn was so high that even the doubling of the grain price left many of them out of the reach of peasant producers. The producers widely preferred to keep their grain rather than surrender it at a loss, leading to the increasingly severe food shortages referred to above. As the government's inability to rectify the breakdown in the market mechanism for grain became more readily apparent to peasants in all areas of the country, the government's credibility and support reached its nadir. Both peasant producers and consumers reacted violently to the effects of the government's policies, venting their frustrations on local land-owners and government functionaries. In the words of a Tambov peasant:

> I want to ask you to explain to us, the dark people, the peasants, who is responsible for the pogroms? You think that this is done by hooligans and vagrants and drunk ragamuffins, but you are a little mistaken. This is not vagrants and ragamuffins, but people drunk from hunger.[19]

The peasants' frustration at the government's policies was reflected, at least in part, by the increased levels of property destruction and of tree-felling.

The seasonal nature of rural life remained a major determinant of both the timetable and the configurations of rural unrest during the autumn. With the bulk of winter sowing completed in August and early September, the peasants' focus shifted from being one almost exclusively bound up with the immediate necessities of field-work. As a result, the peasants had more time to engage in disruptive activities, and the level of rural unrest accordingly rose.

Turning to the configurations of rural unrest, seasonal factors were once again evident. The sharp decline in the seizure of crops reflects the end of the harvest season, with the result that by this time there were comparatively few crops left standing in the fields for the peasants to seize. Moreover by September–October peasants in some areas already had sufficient grain for their needs, and therefore had little incentive to seize any crops that remained unharvested. This was reflected in the occasional destruction of the grain. In contrast, the harvest failure in part of the Central Agricultural –

Middle Volga Region stimulated producers to engage in a heightened wave of *pogrom* and destruction. The decline in land seizure also was related to seasonal factors. With sowing completed, there was little the peasants could do with the land that remained outside their control even if they did seize it. The land would be unproductive until the spring and therefore there was little immediate advantage in bringing it under their control at that point. The enormous increase in the seizure and felling of trees was due in large part to the fact that with the impending onset of winter the need for firewood was felt in the villages with an immediacy that was absent at other times of the year. The peasants felled trees almost at will in an attempt to ensure that they had sufficient to last them through the long winter ahead. Furthermore they could exploit the acute need for fuel in the urban areas by selling at highly inflated prices the timber they had cut. Seasonal factors thus played a very large part in determining the contours of rural unrest in the autumn.

Another element affecting the course of rural unrest during 1917 was peasant consumption of alcohol. This had always been a major item in the peasant's budget, but with the outbreak of the war the tsarist government had imposed a ban on the sale of vodka. Although this measure could not eliminate the consumption of alcohol, it did restrict that practice. With the fall of the tsar, the loosening of government authority in the countryside led to a resurgence of alcohol consumption in the villages. From Letichev *uezd* Podolsk *guberniia* came the report:

Secret distilling occurs almost everywhere in the *uezd*.[20]

In some instances this had become by the autumn an important factor in rural unrest, reflecting the increased hoarding of grain on the part of many peasants. With more than enough grain in their hands for their own needs and vodka still legally unavailable, many peasants distilled their excess grain into alcohol. In the words of a report from Orel in September:

The number of thefts, plunders, murders and, mainly secret distilling is growing noticeably.

While under the influence of this alcohol, the Orel peasants went on a rampage of violent, destructive action.[21] Volkonskii gives eloquent testimony to the effect liquor could have in the villages:

> The cisterns and casks were ablaze and the mob, regardless of the flames, ladled out the spirit, drank it and got drunk. Men, women and children, and even old women, all wanted to have their share of the fete . . . They climbed on the cisterns, and pressing their breasts to it—drank. Some fell into the burning alcohol: human fat floated on the surface, but they continued to drink. They carried away the burning liquid in pails . . .[22]

The effects of alcohol on the population were so severe that a report from Podolsk in September asserted that alcohol

> . . . is the greatest threat to order. It is necessary to take energetic measures to destroy alcohol throughout the *guberniia*.[23]

Increased levels of alcohol consumption often led to disturbances and riots, particularly in the southern parts of the country. This is reflected in the greater incidence of destruction and anarchic violence during the autumn.

A final factor influencing the course of unrest, and one which increased in significance as summer turned to autumn, was the government's inability to provide an adequate counter to the peasants' actions. If the government made little headway in coaxing the peasants to behave, its record in compelling obedience was equally poor. From Penza in October comes a typical report:

> *Uezd* and *guberniia* commissars are powerless to end the anarchy.[24]

With the government unable to suppress rural unrest through force of arms because of its lack of adequate means, reflected most spectacularly by the desertion to the peasants' side of many troops in punitive expeditions, rural unrest developed unchecked; it rolled on by force of its own momentum. As the peasants achieved one aim, they were encouraged to make further, more extreme demands. The level of the aims sought by the peasants in individual areas rose as the year passed. Furthermore just as success in achieving primary aims encouraged peasants to strive for secondary aims, peasant success in one geographical area stimulated actions in neighbouring districts. Rural unrest spilled across regional boundaries. Once it began to expand, rural unrest continued by virtue of its own success.

A conscious effort to halt that expansion early in the year by meeting the peasants' demands might have been able to stem the unrolling of that unrest. A firm policy of suppressing rural unrest through the use of armed force, if implemented in March, might have had some effect in limiting the growth of the disturbances. But the government was unwilling to take up either alternative. Consequently rural unrest grew, in part at least, as a result of the lack of effective opposition on the part of the government.

Thus the course of development of rural unrest was conditioned primarily by the traditional pattern of rural life and by the process of increasing popular disaffection from the government. The former factor was decisive in the configurations that rural unrest took and the levels it achieved at different times of the year. The latter was fundamental for the existence and continued development of rural unrest. However although popular disillusionment with the government was a major feature of the Russian countryside during 1917, this disillusionment did not extend to the Socialist Revolutionaries, despite the participation of members of the PSR in that government. The PSR remained the single most popular party among the peasants despite its prominent role in the unpopular government. The extent of this support is shown by the results of the election to the Constituent Assembly: the SRs gained 42.6 per cent of the votes of those outside the armed forces and the two major cities, compared with a figure of 20.6 per cent for their nearest rivals, the bolsheviks.[25]

The reason for the continued SR support despite the party's government affiliations lies in the dichotomous view of power structures possessed by the peasants. As the year advanced the peasants increasingly viewed organisation as existing at two levels. At the *volost* and village levels organisations were responsive to peasant demands and representative of their interests. Organisations above the *volost* level were more distantly removed from the immediate life situation of the peasants, and were therefore less reflective of their desires and more responsive to other elements. The greater the disaffection from the government, the more the peasants looked to their own resources to solve their problems, and therefore the greater was the reliance they put on local organisations. This was accompanied by increasing rejection of the authority of organisations above the *volost* level. However in the local situation only those organisations and individuals which kept pace with the peasants' demands could exercise any influence and retain any popularity. In such organisations SRs, or people claiming to be SRs and accepted as such, often played a major role.[26] When the peasants voted in the election to the Constituent Assembly they were voting for someone who would be responsive to their demands and in tune with their feelings. Consequently when they voted for SRs, just as when they voted for members of other parties, the peasants were voting for their local SR or bolshevik, not for those at the national level. The SR success in the election broadly reflects the extent of the network of nominal party workers at the local level rather than the extent of support for the party at the national level. Thus while government actions in Petrograd tarnished the top-level SR leadership, it did little harm to SRs in the villages.

THE ORGANISATIONAL DICHOTOMY

The peasant view of a bifurcated organisational structure which so aided the PSR in the Constituent Assembly election should cause little surprise. The lower level committees were rooted in the traditional peasant environment; they were situated in the villages and were manned predominantly by local peasants. In contrast, the higher level organisations rarely arose on the initiative of the peasants, they were situated in the urban centres and were therefore to some extent insulated from the villages and their concerns, and their membership consisted predominantly of non-peasant intellectuals (albeit low-powered in most cases) and former peasants now resident in the towns. The higher level organisations tended to be out of touch with the immediacy of the concerns of the villages while those at the lower levels were right in the midst of those concerns. This distinction is clear in the different roles played by organisations at these levels during 1917.

The assemblies and committees in the villages and *volosti* were important as forums within which the peasants gained knowledge about the outside world and took decisions to act on the basis of information thus gained. The widespread illiteracy characteristic of the villages meant that peasants for the most part had to rely on word of mouth to find out what was happening throughout the country. It was at meetings of these organisations that such information usually was passed on. Agitators from outside the village would address the peasants, telling them of the latest events in the capital, the content of resolutions adopted by peasant organisations elsewhere in the country, and revolutionary action taken by peasants in other areas. After listening to the speakers, such gatherings usually engaged in wide-ranging and free-flowing discussion of the situation, often ending with a decision to take some action against the local land-owner and his property.

Early in the year these lower-level bodies rooted in the traditional peasant milieu were important as the instruments through which the peasants carried out their actions against land-owners. Throughout European Russia it was these bodies formally that placed limitations on the land-owners' use of their land, established rent levels, decreed the confiscation of crops and land, and generally advanced the peasants' interests in their dealings with the land-owners. When property was confiscated, usually it was done under the aegis of the peasant committees; confiscated property was placed under their broad jurisdiction and its use was determined by them. Taxes and fines imposed on land-owners were levied by these bodies and the proceeds thus gained were used by them. These peasant committees remained important as instruments of action while the peasants continued to use 'surreptitious', and therefore primarily non-destructive and non-violent methods of land seizure. However their significance in this respect declined later in the year as the peasants turned to more direct and open methods of action. The physical seizure of land-owners' property does not appear to have been orchestrated by the low-level peasant organisations. Although the decision to seize property often was taken within these bodies, a comprehensive plan of action rarely was formulated. Most peasant seizures appear to have had little logistical planning and to have been victorious by virtue of lack of opposition and weight of numbers rather than by superior tactical scheming. The course of individual peasant actions was influenced far more by a special type of leader than by the considerations of a local organisation. Such a leader was thrown up by the course of events and was both local and temporary in his effect. His leadership consisted less of giving orders than of stimulating the others to act by ostentatious or courageous action on his own part. Such ephemeral leaders, many of whom appear to have been deserters from the front, may have been particularly significant in those highly-charged situations characterised by violence.

The decline in the overt role of the low-level peasant organisations as instruments of peasant action should not lead one to assume that these organisations lost all significance late in the year.[27] Although their role as instruments of peasant action declined as 'surreptitious' methods of seizure became less common, they remained important as forums for information-gathering and decision-making throughout the year. As the peasants rejected the nominal peasant organisations at the *uezd* and *guberniia* levels along with their alienation from the government, and as outside influences from the village were rejected, the significance of the traditionally-based lower-level bodies grew; they become the dominant decision-making bodies in the rural areas during 1917, exercising effective administrative control over all aspects of rural life. Their position rested on the fact that they represented and responded to the views and interests of the peasants. They were responsible directly to the peasants; if an organisation did not work in the peasants' interests and accede to their demands, a new election was held and a new membership elected. It was to these low-level peasant organisations, springing from the heart of the village, that the peasants looked for guidance and direction.

This created a major problem for the government when it tried to extend its authority into the countryside. The government hoped to extend its control into the lowest levels of rural life by the establishment of the various types of committees at the *volost* level discussed in previous chapters. However if the government-sponsored bodies were to exercise governmental control effectively, they had to win popular allegiance away from the already-existing peasant organisations. The only way the government bodies could win popular allegiance was through supporting peasant demands. During the early part of the year when the peasant position was generally more moderate than it was to become later, broad support for the peasants' demands did not necessarily involve the complete and utter rejection of government policies. At this early stage the peasants frequently acceded to the strictures of government organisations. However later in the year as the peasant position became more radical, there was no way such committees could exercise any widespread influence without abandoning completely the government line. They were faced with an insoluble dilemma: either obey the government and be rejected by the peasants, or gain popular support by rejecting the government and, with that, their own *raison d'etre*. In practice, most low-level committees followed the latter course.

This development should cause little surprise. It has been noted above that there was a shortage of able personnel to man the lower-level committees in the countryside, a shortage exacerbated by the peasant practice of rejecting non-peasants increasingly as the year passed. Consequently when attempts were made to establish the *volost*-level committees provided for under government legislation, membership of the new bodies overlapped considerably with that of the existing peasant bodies. The government-sponsored committees often appear to have developed purely as adjuncts to existing peasant organisations. In the words of an official report early in the year:

> The organisation of food matters in the countryside is handled by *volost* committees into which the food committes enter as an integral part.[28]

Most committees established at the village and *volost* levels as a result of government legislation were swallowed up by the peasant organisational structure arising out of the villages, thereby becoming instruments of peasant unrest rather than of government authority. The peasant capture of these bodies is reflected in the government's refusal to provide any finance for many of the *volost* land committees nominally established under its aegis.[29] The government was unable to break through this layer of peasant bodies or to prevent the capture of government committees by the peasants in order to establish grass-roots control. The peasants, effectively, were autonomous, governing their lives primarily through their own village-based institutions.

The final function performed by the committees at the *volost* and village levels was intangible. By proclaiming peasant opinions on the whole range of questions of the day,[30] these committees helped to create the environment within which all the actors in the drama of 1917 had to act. In this way these low-level committees influenced actors and decisions over which otherwise they would have had no direct effect. The expression of peasant demands from all corners of the country reported widely in the Russian press, and the move to the left in the tenor of those demands as they remained unsatisfied, contributed to the developing feeling of tension in the countryside which exploded in a rash of destruction and open seizure late in the year. Significant in this regard was the infection effect, as decisions of individual meetings in one area were taken up and adopted as models by meetings elsewhere. A circulation of ideas between different areas of the country thus developed. The clearest example of such a circulation of ideas and concepts was the country-wide appearance in peasant resolutions of the phraseology of the political parties in Petrograd. These were spread in the same way that the decisions of local peasant meetings were spread, through local newspapers and the actions of agitators. Local bodies thus acted as motor forces of infection, spreading radical ideas across the countryside and thereby helping to determine the climate within which people acted and decisions were made. Part of the tragedy of 1917 as far as the Provisional Government was concerned was that it was not sufficiently sensitive to the impulses coming from these peasant committees.

Nominally peasant organisations at the *uezd*, *guberniia* and national levels also contributed to the creation of an atmosphere throughout the country. However while organisations at the lower levels in general reflected the prevailing anti-government mood in the villages, the nominally peasant organisations at these higher levels tended to exude a conflicting image. A few projected a similar type of message to the village and *volost* committees, a move to the left being evident in their successive meetings; some higher-level committees passed radical resolutions and encouraged illicit seizures. However most of these organisations tended to lag behind the changing mood in the villages, in varying degrees admonishing open land seizures and calling upon the peasants to wait for the solution of the land question by the Constituent Assembly.[31] The prime example of this was the executive committee of the All-Russian Soviet of Peasants' Deputies, but other examples abounded at the *guberniia* and *uezd* levels. As the year wore on, most of these bodies were rejected by the peasants. However they may have remained significant in 1917 in another respect. By placing a moderate visage on peasant aspirations at the lowest level at which the government had any widespread control, these organisations may have hindered the government in its attempt to gain an accurate picture of the mood in the villages. The radical views characteristic of the lower level peasant bodies could be offset and balanced by the more moderate views of the higher bodies. It would not be surprising if the government was taken in by this fact, preferring to live with the decisions of those higher organisations that were closer to its own position than to pay due consideration to the radical views coming from the villages. It would have been a blind minister who could see none of the reality through this façade, but it would have needed a very perceptive one to ignore the facade altogether.

One of the major characteristics of 1917 was thus an enormous proliferation of organisations in the countryside. However only those at the village and *volost* levels retained a high degree of relevance to developments in the rural areas throughout the year. These bodies emerged from within the womb of the village in response to the peasants' needs. They were manned by peasants, they advanced the peasants' interests, and they retained the allegiance of the village population. In this way the organisations at the village and *volost* levels formed by the peasants left little room in the rural areas for the exercise of influence by other organisations: with peasant needs being met by village and *volost* committees, there was little scope for independent soviets, party organisations, government bodies, or city-based *uezd* and *guberniia* committees to wield much influence in the countryside. Organisations from outside the village generally remained irrelevant to the peasants' needs, not only because those needs were met fully by the lower-level bodies, but also because they were wholly out of touch with the villages. Certainly some of these organisations at the higher levels retained some relevance by moving with the changing mood in the villages, but the vast majority got out of step with that mood and ceased to have any real influence in the countryside. The period between the two revolutions thus saw the rejection by the peasants of all forms of authority that were not firmly rooted in the traditional peasant environment, the villages.

The traditional nature of the peasants' actions is evident in their approach to the land question. All land that was not subject to the traditional forms of peasant land tenure was subject to peasant attack: landed estates owned by private land-owners, those owned by the state, those attached to ecclesiastical institutions and, in the areas dominated by the repartitional commune, those separated from the commune under the aegis of the Stolypin reforms. One study of peasant unrest has asserted that peasant actions were directed against these different types of landed property in the following proportions: against private land-owners 85.7 per cent, against 'village bourgeoisie' (including separators) 5.6 per cent, against the government 4.6 per cent, against the priesthood 3.6 per cent, and others 0.9 per cent.[32] Although such figures cannot be accepted as precise indicators, they do show the broad sweep of unrest. The three traditional exploiters in the peasants' eyes, private land-owners, government and church, were attacked by the peasants and their land-holdings were seized, while the government-inspired attack on the traditional communal framework was vigorously repelled throughout large areas of Russia.

The strength of traditional considerations is clear in the attitude toward the form and extent of land tenure common in the countryside. The peasants' approach to this question was based on a principle that stemmed from traditional practice and which was clearly summarised in the resolution of a congress of delegates of *volost* committees in Novouzen *uezd*, Samara *guberniia* in April:

Land, as a blessing created by nature, can be used by all who wish to work it with their own personal strength, without hired labour, but not more than the labour norm.[33]

The key to the possession of the land for the peasants was use and labour:

The land must belong to those who work it with their hands, to those whose sweat flows.[34]

In practice this principle was translated into a belief that each household should only have sufficient land on which to support itself through its own efforts.[35] In the areas where hereditary land tenure was dominant, this principle did not involve a rejection of the notion of private property; rural unrest constituted an enforcement of this principle upon all who infringed it because only that land which the owner could not work himself was seized. The land which he was working himself remained his private property. However in the areas characterised by communal tenure, which included those with the highest levels of unrest, this principle involved a rejection of private property in land:

Land, not being created by the hand of man, can neither be sold nor bought.
All forms of private ownership in Russia are henceforth and forever abolished.[36]

Private land tenure, with the exception of the traditional *usad'ba*, was opposed because it interfered with the process of repartition, which in essence was a mechanism for ensuring the continued operation of the principle outlined above. In this region private land-ownership was destroyed. The peasants' assumption in 1917 was that land seized would become an extension of the land already under cultivation, with the traditional patterns of land tenure applying; they envisaged the imposition of the pre-revolutionary system of land tenure on the seized lands through the reapportionment of those lands on the basis of the traditional norms. Immediate action to implement this system of tenure was not always taken with regard to newly-seized lands, but it was the pre-revolutionary system which was imposed on the land when the peasants formalised land tenure on the seized estates.[37]

The reversion to the pre-revolutionary system is brought into sharp relief by the treatment accorded to many of those who had separated from the commune under the aegis of the Stolypin reforms. In the words of one peasant decision:

> All who took their portion and separated from the commune into an *otrub* are granted the right to return to the commune, having given up their *otrub* and received their strip in the commune. In each village with adjoining settlements, new villages, *khutori*, farmlets and other populated places, one agrarian community with one elder and with one *skhod* is to be formed.[38]

In the Central Agricultural and Middle Volga regions and in some of the *gubernii* in the south, where the repartitional commune was most strongly rooted, the effects of the Stolypin reform were swept away; those who had left the commune with their land were reintegrated into it, often with greater violence than the above resolution indicates. In the *gubernii* of the north and the west, the peasants' attitude toward enclosures was more positive; all *otruby* were destroyed, but most *khutori* appear to have been preserved, probably reflecting peasant recognition of the benefits of this type of tenure in the unfavourable conditions.[39] Nevertheless the extent of the re-emergence of the traditional structure, bringing with it a re-assertion of traditional patterns of land-holding, is remarkable; it has been calculated that after 1917 as much as 98 per cent of the agricultural land in some *gubernii* of the RSFSR was held by the commune, while as late as 1928 the *skhod* still settled most questions of vital interest to the peasant.[40]

The strengthening of the traditional framework resulted both from a conscious desire on the part of the peasants to reinforce the communal structure, and from the fact that, in the new and uncertain situation of 1917, the peasant relied even more heavily on the long-established structures with which he was familiar than he did in normal times. The peasants' reaction to 1917 was overwhelmingly traditional in nature. The seizure of land on the basis of user rights and the refusal to surrender grain to an overbearing and demanding government were sanctioned by the traditional mores of Russian peasant life. The timetable of rural unrest was determined largely by the traditional pattern of rural life. The most important organisations in the countryside were those rooted in the traditional fabric of village society. One effect of the traditional nature of rural unrest was that the question of private property as a form of peasant land tenure did not arise throughout much of Russia; it was not a viable alternative within the bounds of the dominant repartitional communal framework, and was therefore not even a matter for debate. It is in terms of the traditional nature of peasant unrest that events in the countryside are best seen.

THE GEOGRAPHICAL DISTRIBUTION OF RURAL UNREST

The traditional nature of peasant disturbances in the countryside is evident from their geographical distribution. Analysis of the militia reports shows that of all instances of rural unrest between the two revolutions, the geographical regions of European Russia provided the following proportions:[41]

	Per cent		Per cent
Central Agricultural	21.8	Lakes	6.2
Middle Volga	16.6	Lower Volga	4.9
Little Russia and the S.W.	14.3	Urals	4.1
Byelorussia and Lithuania	13.9	Baltic	3.0
Central Industrial	7.4	Northern	0.5
New Russia	7.3		

Of the 50 individual *gubernii*, almost 50 per cent of all rural unrest was provided by 12 *gubernii*:

	Per cent		Per cent
Kazan	5.4	Mogilev	3.5
Penza	5.0	Kursk	3.4
Orel	4.9	Tula	3.2
Riazan	4.4	Tambov	3.1
Minsk	4.2	Volynsk	3.1
Podolsk	3.7	Samara	3.1

Gubernii experiencing highest levels of unrest

Gubernii of European Russia, 1917

Northern
1. Arkhangel
2. Vologda

Lakes
3. Olonets
4. Novgorod
5. Petrograd
6. Pskov

Baltic
7. Estland
8. Lifland
9. Kurland

Byelorussia & Lithuania
10. Kovno
11. Vilensk
12. Vitebsk
13. Smolensk
14. Mogilev
15. Minsk
16. Grodno

Little Russia & the
Southwest
17. Volynsk
18. Podolsk
19. Kiev
20. Chernigov
21. Poltava
22. Kharkov

New Russia
23. Bessarabia
24. Kherson
25. Taurida
26. Ekaterinoslav
27. Don Oblast'

Lower Volga
28. Astrakhan
29. Samara
30. Orenburg

Middle Volga
31. Saratov
32. Simbirsk
33. Kazan

34. Nizhegorod
35. Penza

Central Agricultural
36. Tambov
37. Voronezh
38. Kursk
39. Orel
40. Tula
41. Riazan

Central Industrial
42. Kaluga
43. Moscow
44. Vladimir
45. Tver
46. Yaroslav
47. Kostroma

Urals
48. Viatka
49. Perm
50. Ufa

As one would expect, these two tables have a broad correspondence; of the *gubernii*, only Samara does not come from one of the four most restive geographical regions. Furthermore, five of the *gubernii* come from the Central Agricultural region. Significantly, ten of these most restive *gubernii* share common boundaries, forming one long serpent dominating the heartland of Russia. The other two, Kazan and Samara, form a block close by.

A comprehensive explanation of the reasons for regional differences in rural unrest cannot be attempted because there is insufficient data available for each area for the micro-level analysis necessary for such an enterprise. Nevertheless an indication of the broad factors which influenced the geographical distribution of rural disturbances can be made.

As indicated above, the main elements of rural unrest centred on the traditional peasant concerns, land and food. These also constituted the main determinants of the geographical distribution of rural unrest. Although the figures of the 1917 census must be treated with some caution, they do supply a picture of the land ownership position in most of European Russia.[42] Looking at the broad sweep of land ownership in the 34 *gubernii* for which the census gives figures, a general pattern emerges: the stronger the position of non-peasant land-owners, measured in terms of the proportion of the land they owned, the higher the level of unrest, and vice versa. All the *gubernii* in which the peasants owned more than 80 per cent of the land, with the exception of Riazan, were characterised by comparatively low levels of unrest, while those in which peasant ownership was at a lower level generally experienced higher levels of disturbances. Two factors are relevant in this. Firstly, the stronger the position of the private land-owners, the higher the level of peasant action had to be to displace those people, and vice versa. Secondly and more importantly, the less land in peasant hands, the greater peasant land-hunger was likely to be, with a resultant high level of peasant frustration and antagonism toward the private land-owners.

There was a clear link between a high level of unrest and the existence of acute population pressure on the peasants' landed resources; with the exception of the sparsely-populated Northern region, the four geographical regions providing the highest levels of unrest were those in which the pressure of the peasant population on their productive land was most severe. This is illustrated by the following table which compares the proportion of European Russia-wide unrest occuring in each region with the regional level of land-hunger expressed in terms of the average *dessiatiny* of exploitable peasant-owned land per peasant:

	Unrest	Land		Unrest	Land
Central Agricultural	21.8	0.9	Lakes	6.2	2.7
Middle Volga	16.6	1.2	Lower Volga	4.9	2.5
Little Russia and the Southwest	14.3	0.8	Urals	4.1	2.3
Byelorussia and Lithuania	13.9	1.2	Baltic	3.0	No information
			Northern	0.5	1.1
Central Industrial	7.4	1.5	All European Russia		1.3
New Russia	7.3	1.3			

Of the nine *gubernii* with the highest levels of unrest for which the census gives figures, in seven the average area of peasant-owned land per peasant was less than the average for European Russia as a whole:

	Unrest	Land		Unrest	Land
Kazan	5.4	1.1	Mogilev	3.5	1.3
Penza	5.0	1.0	Kursk	3.4	0.9
Orel	4.9	1.0	Tula	3.2	1.0
Riazan	4.4	1.0	Tambov	3.1	1.0
Minsk	4.2	No information	Samara	3.1	1.8
Podolsk	3.7	No information	Volynsk	3.1	No information

Although not all *gubernii* characterised by acute population pressure on peasant landed resources experienced high levels of unrest,[43] the vast majority did so. Where population pressure on landed resources was pressing, the level of unrest tended to be high.

The presence of strong population pressure on the peasants' landed resources traditionally had stimulated attempts by the peasants to increase the area of land at their disposal. In general terms, the less land the peasants owned, the more inclined they were to seek to rent land from the private land-owners. The peasants owned least land in the more valuable grain-producing belt of the

Central Agricultural, Middle Volga, Little Russia and the South-west, and New Russia regions. It was in these areas, and particularly the Central Agricultural and Middle Volga regions where the unrest reached its greatest intensity, that peasant rental of non-peasant land appears to have been most widespread.[44] Of the twelve *gubernii* which provided the bulk of rural unrest, only Minsk and Mogilev were in areas in which peasant rental of privately-owned land does not appear to have been widely developed. Land rental engendered feelings of bitter antagonism among the peasants because of its conflict with their basic philosophical position on the land: they were being forced to pay for land which they felt belonged to them by the legal owners of the land who refused to work it productively. These feelings were reinforced in this central black earth area by the continued strength of the traditional repartitional commune and the bitter opposition to separators that this involved.[45] It was here where communal sentiment was strongest and land rental was extensive that the highest levels of unrest, and of the destructive element within that unrest, occurred. There was thus a broad correlation between the incidence of peasant land rental and the level of rural unrest. This was one element of the phenomenon of land hunger that was central to rural unrest, with the attitude toward the private land-owner engendered through land rental giving that sense of land hunger an extra dimension of viciousness.

The food crisis from which Russia was suffering during 1917 was a major factor influencing the distribution of unrest. It is impossible to isolate the effect of this in the consuming area of the north because food shortages were experienced in all *gubernii* of the region.[46] However its impact in the south can be isolated. During the August–October period when the food shortage was most acute, deficits were reported from the following *gubernii*: Orel, Nizhegorod, Astrakhan, Mogilev, Simbirsk, Kazan, Volynsk, Penza, Tambov, Orenburg, Minsk, Saratov, Samara, Bessarabia, Tula and Riazan.[47] Of these sixteen *gubernii*, ten were among those most characterised by unrest, while another two, Saratov and Simbirsk, experienced high levels of disturbances.

The geographical distribution of these hungry *gubernii* is signifi-cant. They stretch from Russia's western border in Bessarabia and Volynsk east to the boundary of European Russia in Orenburg, and south from Ufa along the Volga to the Caspian Sea. Southern Samara and Astrakhan situated in the belt extending south from

Ufa were not very fertile, being devoted primarily to pastoral activities rather than to agriculture. They were thus marginal to the grain heartland of central Russia. The *gubernii* comprising the eastward sweep from Bessarabia and Volynsk to Orenburg also were marginal. They were situated on the boundary between the rich black earth of the southern regions and the poorer soils common further north. Consequently the fertility of the soils in this belt was lower than that of the soil of the black earth heartland further to the south, but higher than that to the north. Moreover in the Middle Volga area (Simbirsk, Penza, Nizhegorod, Saratov and Kazan) weather conditions were not always reliable. This broad area thus constituted a transitional belt in which farming, although usually dependable, sometimes was subject to sharp fluctuations. In 1917 one of those fluctuations occurred. Large areas of the black earth region experienced a drought during the spring and early summer, followed in July by torrential rains. The result was widespread crop failure.[48]

Peasant reaction to the crop failure was important in the heightened levels of rural unrest during the summer and autumn. Unlike the peasants further to the north, those in this region had high expectations in relation to their crop yields. Most of the *gubernii* were characterised by substantial pre-war grain surpluses.[49] The fertile soil made the peasants of these *gubernii* expect continued high returns. Moreover they relied on high returns for their very survival. When these expectations were frustrated by bad weather conditions and the peasants found themselves faced with acute grain shortages, their sense of land hunger and of antagonism toward the private land-owners became more acute. Their reaction was violent, expressed in a rage of destruction and *pogrom* against symbols of established authority and private land-holding interests; this region provided more than half of all instances of the destruction of property and almost a third of all cases of personal violence occurring in the countryside between the two revolutions.[50] In the newer grain-producing area of Little Russia and the Southwest where the level of population pressure on landed resources was greater than in the traditional growing area but where there was no crop failure to give a heightened sense of urgency to this situation, the level of unrest was lower and the violent, destructive element was less marked. Wherever land-hunger was pressing, peasant unrest occurred, but when that land-hunger was joined by unexpected food shortages, the level of unrest was raised and its viciousness was increased.

Although it was the traditional considerations of land-hunger and food needs which played the most important roles in determining the distribution of rural unrest, a number of other factors were significant also. One of the most important of these was the war and close proximity to the front. The presence in any area of an enormous army on a semi-permanent basis imposes great strains on the economic infrastructure of the region. Its presence disrupts normal economic life, places increased demands on local food production and, with the enormous retinue that accompanies an army, often occupies valuable agricultural land thereby decreasing regional productivity. In addition, social strains usually develop between the local populations and the soldiers, particularly if the latter are not well-disciplined. This was certainly the case in Russia in 1917 where discipline among the soliders in many areas had clearly broken down by the middle of the year. The hungry army was disintegrating. Parties roamed the countryside in search of food, sometimes leading to clashes with the peasants. Tired of the war and not wanting to miss out on the land redistribution occurring in their villages, many soldiers left the ranks, taking with them into the villages the gospel of revolution. The state of the army made the whole near-front area ripe for the outbreak of widespread disturbances. This is partly reflected in the fact that three of the most volatile *gubernii*, Podolsk, Volynsk and Minsk, were situated in this area.

The disturbed state of the near-front area as a result of the disintegration of the army was transmitted throughout rural Russia by the passage of deserters from the front to the villages of the hinterland. These deserters took with them the message of revolt, frequently accompanied by some organisational experience which could be put to good use in the villages. It is impossible to plot accurately the influence exerted by these deserters because there are no accurate records of those areas they penetrated. Nevertheless it can be assumed that those *gubernii* situated immediately behind the front and those in a north–south band immediately to the east of the near-front *gubernii* all would have been affected significantly since it was through these areas that deserters heading for the rear had to pass. With the exception of Vilensk, Kovno and Kurland (most of which was occupied by the Germans) all of the *gubernii* in these areas experienced substantial levels of unrest:

Near-front gubernii		Band to east	
Bessarabia	1.6	Kherson	1.8
Podolsk	3.7	Kiev	2.1
Volynsk	3.1	Poltava	1.9
Minsk	4.2	Chernigov	1.8
Lifland	1.7	Mogilev	3.5
		Smolensk	2.8
		Vitebsk	2.1
		Pskov	2.7

In the southern, more restive regions, the geographical relationship to the front appears to have been less important as a determining factor than land-hunger and crop failure. However in the north it appears to have been quite significant: all the northern *gubernii* listed above, and therefore close to the front, experienced levels of unrest higher than the norm for the northern area as a whole.

The role played by agitators from the front in helping to spread unrest across the countryside[51] forms part of the process of infection that is so important in the development of unrest of any sort. The implementation of daring or extreme acts on the part of peasants in one area, news of which could be transmitted easily by word of mouth over the short distances separating many peasant communities, frequently provided the stimulus for new outbursts of unrest in neighbouring regions. The most graphic example of this was the spread of violence and destruction from Koslov *uezd* Tambov *guberniia* in September. On 7 September a land-owner wounded two peasants from the village of Sychevki. That evening a large crowd of peasants gathered, killed the land-owner and sacked his estate. This acted as a signal for peasants in neighbouring *uezdy*, who rose up and sacked virtually all landed estates in the vicinity. This wave of *pogrom* and destruction spilled over the boundaries into the neighbouring *gubernii*. In the words of the Riazan *guberniia* commissar in mid-September:

There is a heightened mood in Kasimov and Egor'ev *uezdy*, in connection with the threat of hunger, and in Dankov, Riazh and Ranenburg under the influence of the Tambov events.

Similar *pogrom* activities broke out in other *gubernii* surrounding Tambov soon after the Tambov events—Penza, Orel, Kursk and Nizhegorod[52]—apparently sparked off by the wave of destruction embracing Tambov. Although on a much smaller scale than the

Tambov-centred developments, similar instances of infection appear to have occurred widely throughout the Russian countryside during 1917.

A number of other factors were significant in individual areas in determining the course, nature and extent of unrest. However accurate determination of which areas were affected by which factors is impossible because precise detail on the courses of development in all localities does not exist. The first of these factors was the mood of the local garrison. If the troops remained loyal to the government and placed that loyalty above any feelings of kinship with the peasants, they could be used, at least early in the year, in an attempt to keep unrest within bounds. The suppression of unrest in Vitebsk in August is an example of the successful use of troops by the government. In contrast, if the troops either were affected by revolutionary sentiment or felt strong links with the peasants, they tended to heighten unrest rather than to depress it, as in Tambov in September when soldiers sent to bar the peasants' path stepped aside and allowed them to sack the estate.[53]

Individual personalities also were significant in the development of unrest. The role of peasant leaders in encouraging and stimulating extreme action has been noted previously. The personality of the local land-owners and their reaction to peasant antagonism frequently played an important part in determining the course of events in the local areas. Extreme violence and killing on the part of the peasants often was touched off by action taken by the land-owner to defend his property in the face of peasant depredations. The Tambov events referred to above provide an example of this. In those instances when land-owners and their staff fled, leaving their property to the peasants, violence was rare; when they stayed to fight, violence and increased levels of unrest were the inevitable result.

However these factors, the mood of the garrisons and the individual personalities of the main actors in the localities, and even the effect of the front, were all secondary in determining the distribution of rural unrest. The most important factors were traditional considerations of land-hunger and crop failure. Where these coincided, as in the Central Agricultural and Middle Volga Regions, unrest reached a high level and was extremely violent and destructive; where they did not coincide, the level of unrest was lower and the violent, destructive theme generally was less evident. Traditional considerations were the prime-movers of rural unrest.

As well as the broad distribution of unrest outlined above, regional patterns of disturbances in the countryside can be discerned. Although the entries in the militia reports for many *gubernii* are too few to enable the accurate reconstruction of the patterns of unrest in those *gubernii*, patterns can be seen in most of the regions into which European Russia has been divided.[54] The pattern of rural unrest was basically similar throughout European Russia, although regional variations did occur. Such variations consisted in the relative significance of different strands of unrest in the regional patterns as a whole.

In the most restive part of the country, the Central Agricultural region, the direct seizure of land was the most important form of unrest, followed closely by actions involving the destruction of private and state property. Reflecting frustration and disappointment at the harvest failure, sharp land-hunger, and bitter feelings toward the land-owners from whom they were renting land and the separators who were challenging the dominant repartitional commune, the peasants launched a wave of destruction so great that this was the only region in which such action was a dominant strand of rural unrest. The seizure of timber also was a significant element, reflecting the long-standing pressure on the farmer of the region to put as much land under the plough as possible thereby creating widespread timber shortages. The seizure of privately-owned crops was not a major aspect of unrest in this region, possibly because the severity of the peasants' plight encouraged them to seize land and crop together instead of the latter alone and because the extent of privately-owned arable land on lease to the peasants severely limited the amount of sown land remaining outside peasant control.

In the Middle Volga, Little Russia and the Southwest, and Central Industrial regions the seizure of timber was the single most important form of unrest after the direct seizure of privately-owned land. The first two regions both suffered from the same sorts of pressures causing the peasants to plough under much woodland, thereby creating major shortages of timber, which operated in the Central Agricultural region. In the Central Industrial region forest land was more widespread and the Moscow market very demanding, with the result that the opportunities for, and the effects of, the peasant seizure of timber were more extensive. The seizure of crops also was important in these three regions, reflecting the harvest failure that struck wide areas of the Middle Volga region, the chronic food shortage in the consuming Central Industrial region, and the extensive commercially-oriented private farming sector in Little Russia and the Southwest. The proximity of the front and its need for food may also have been significant in the level of crop seizure in Little Russia and the Southwest, while the influence of deserters from the Rumanian front may be reflected in the levels of personal violence and, less importantly, of destructive activity characteristic of this region. The levels of destructive activity and personal violence in the Central Industrial region may in part reflect proximity to Moscow, the presence of agitators from that city, and the urban migration to the countryside that occurred in 1917.

In Byelorussia and Lithuania and the Lakes regions the direct seizure of land was surpassed as the most significant strand of unrest by the seizure of timber. In both regions, and most particularly the Lakes, the lumber industry was a major form of economic activity and there was therefore more opportunity for, and more effect to be gained from, the peasant seizure of timber on a wide scale than in many other regions of the country. The seizure of crops also was important in these regions, reflecting the consuming nature of these areas within the national grain market. Undertones of personal violence and the destruction of private property were present in both areas. Militia reports suggest that, particularly in Byelorussia and Lithuania, incidents of this type were often caused by soldiers from the front.

In the New Russia region the seizure of privately-owned land was clearly the most important strand of rural unrest. Acts of personal violence were also of major concern in this region, once again reflecting the close proximity to the front and the disruptive effect of hungry and discontented soliders in the countryside. In this overwhelmingly agricultural region, the seizure of crops was a major form of peasant action while the seizure of timber was less significant here than in any of the other regions for which the pattern of rural unrest can be discerned.

The Lower Volga region was characterised by a very high incidence of the seizure of privately-owned land, while the seizure of crops and timber also were significant. Other forms of unrest were less important, although the destruction of private property was common in parts of Samara. In the Urals region the seizure of privately-owned land comprised almost half of all instances of unrest occurring between the two revolutions. The seizure of timber and incidents involving personal violence also were significant strands of unrest, perhaps reflecting respectively the prominence of lumbering in the region and the proximity of radical metal-workers in the industrial centres. The absence of the widespread cultivation of major food grains explains the low level of crop seizure.

It is clear from this brief regional survey that the contours of unrest were not precisely the same in all areas of the country. Variations occurred as a result of the differing effects of those factors outlined in the discussion of the distribution of rural unrest as a whole. However despite these variations, the importance of the seizure of land is clear. In all regions with the exception of Byelorussia and Lithuania and the Lakes, the direct and open seizure of land was the single most important strand of rural unrest. Furthermore in all regions of the country this method of land seizure was far more significant than seizure through 'surreptitious' methods, the removal of labour power and the fixing/abolition of rent. One generalisation concerning land seizure should be made: in the grain-producing southern part of the country seizures focused primarily on arable land, while in the consuming north where the production of cereal grains was less widespread, the seizure of meadow and pasture land was more common. The seizure of timber was significant in all regions except New Russia, while the seizure of crops was of central importance everywhere except for the Central Agricultural and Urals regions. Finally the destruction of private property was of major significance only in the Central Agricultural region and personal violence only in New Russia and the Urals. Precise explanation of these differences awaits the emergence of far greater information on the socio-economic situation and the exact sequence of events in the individual regions. The factors alluded to above as having regional importance can only be tentative suggestions until such information becomes available.

Although the immediate causes of the specific courses of development of unrest in the individual regions remain unclear, the traditional nature of the broad sweep of peasant disturbances is not in doubt. Peasant discontent was rooted in traditional grievances, manifested in traditional forms, and mediated through traditionally-based organisations. The peasants' horizon was limited to the bounds of their traditional economic market-place. It was the government's failure to solve their traditional economic problems and to put right their long-standing feelings of injustice that were at the heart of peasant opposition to the government rather than any political opposition based on ideological grounds. It was this traditionalist upsurge from the countryside which sapped the strength of the government and so weakened it that the bolsheviks were able easily to push it from power. The October revolution owed more to traditional forces than Lenin cared to admit.

5 City and Countryside in Revolution

During 1917 the established pattern of authority relationships, land-holding and social hierarchy in the countryside were completely overturned by peasant direct action. The tsarist administrative system collapsed and the organs developed by the Provisional Government failed to take root in the countryside. Throughout the villages peasants turned to their traditionally-based institutions for guidance, rejecting all forms of external interference in village life. The formal state structure characterised by the dominance of an urban-based government over the rural areas was ruptured as villages and *volosti* became, in effect, independent enclaves; the territorial integrity of the state evaporated. The government was left as a head without a body. This development was accompanied by the elimination of the traditionally-dominant group in the countryside, the private land-owners. Although not all non-peasant-owned land was seized between the two revolutions, the peasants took over sufficient to smash the established land tenure pattern and to cripple the private land-owners as a political force in the country. By the autumn, the non-peasant land-owner was little more than a memory in many areas of the countryside, his lands seized, his home frequently destroyed, and his traditional dominance broken. The peasants turned on their traditional exploiters and eradicated their influence in the rural areas. This was only the most obvious aspect of the social revolution that the peasants' actions wrought in the countryside, a revolution which cut back all of those whose positions were not rooted in the local traditional peasant land tenure system.

The vast changes occurring in the rural areas had important ramifications for the fate of the Provisional Government. The rejection of governmental authority in the rural areas, exemplified by the failure of local government organs to become established widely in the countryside, meant that governmental authority did not extend into the villages. Without this authority and the means of implementing its decisions, measures announced by the government remained little more than empty pronouncements. The peasants were unresponsive to government exhortations and the government lacked the ability to enforce peasant obedience. This situation was exacerbated by the plight of the private land-owners. The elimination of this group as a major political force not only removed from the countryside a body of people who could have been expected to exercise a moderate, pro-government influence in the rural areas, but it also created an issue upon which the government's position was clearly at odds with the peasants' desires, thereby contributing to the growth of the popular disillusionment with the government that was a feature of 1917. The failure of local government to become firmly established in the countryside and the elimination of the private land-owners rendered the government impotent and virtually friendless in the rural areas. When the bolsheviks made their push for power, the government remained isolated; it had neither force nor popular support in the countryside upon which it could call because the only possible sources of assistance from this region had been rendered helpless by peasant revolt.[1] In the rural areas the government was bereft of power and support.

The upsurge of peasant unrest which so undermined the government's position outside the capital was traditional in all respects. The traditional nature of the matters which concerned the peasants, of the organisations they turned to, of the types of actions undertaken by them, and of the sources and timetable of those actions has already been outlined. Their vision was restricted to the established horizons of peasant life. Their world remained the world of village and custom. In their actions they rarely seem to have ventured beyond the immediate region of which their village was a part, the area which traditionally was the arena of their primary concern. They appear to have had little conception of belonging to a wider social grouping within the Russian state; they lacked any sense of that class consciousness which could span distances and unite the peasants *qua* peasants in all areas of the country. Their primary loyalty was to the traditional village, or at most *volost*, community, not to any broader notion of 'the peasantry' as a whole.[2] Actions rarely were coordinated between villages, often resulting in clashes between communities, while instances of peasants in one region refusing to supply grain to hungry peasants in neighbouring areas abound. The peasants' concerns were immediate and local, with everything outside the traditional, limited horizons of peasant interest of secondary importance.

The restricted nature of peasant horizons is reflected in the hazy perceptions that they had of developments in the capital. In many areas links existed with Petrograd and the nearest metropolitan centres through agitators coming to the villages and through local peasants who had sought employment in the cities. However these links had little effect in widening the peasants' awareness from their traditional, localised concerns. The peasants in the villages had little knowledge or understanding of developments in the capital. Petrograd traditionally was seen as the ultimate source of authority, but the vision the peasants had of it was undifferentiated, especially after the fall of the tsar whose person had given a focus and a unity to the peasants' view of the formal seat of power. They had little accurate knowledge of the numerous organisations that sprouted in Petrograd, and their understanding of the ebb and flow of political debate in the capital was very limited. The politics of the elite groups was largely outside the scope of awareness of the peasants. However this does not mean that the peasants were completely lacking in political consciousness. Political consciousness, or awareness, can be defined in terms of understanding the way in which the political process operates, including the role one plays in it.[3] One indication of the possession of a minimum level of awareness is willingness to blame the political system and those in dominant positions in it for personal misfortune instead of directing such blame onto mystic and impersonal forces beyond human control, a practice characteristic of the complete absence of political awareness. The peasants were politically aware to the extent that they blamed the established structure of land-holding and power relations for their plight and they realised that it was within the power of the government in Petrograd to grant them the land they wanted, and yet it was refusing to do so. Furthermore they possessed at least a minimum level of understanding of the local power structure, realising that by destroying the power exercised by that structure in the countryside, personified by the local land-owners, by local government organs, and by the power exercised by the towns over the countryside, their demands could be satisfied. The level of political awareness required for this was not high; there was no need for knowledge of the intricacies of party politics in Petrograd or of the precise details of governmental administration in the rural areas. All that was needed was the knowledge that Petrograd was not going to accede to their demands and an awareness that those demands could be met by smashing the established power structure in the rural areas. The peasants possessed this level of awareness, a level which was consistent with the traditional nature of their lives.

The peasants sought to satisfy their demands primarily through direct action at the local level rather than by attempting to influence the political actors in Petrograd to change the law. However the peasants' actions did have a significant, if unintended, effect on developments in Petrograd. The local orientation of the peasants' actions, which realised its ultimate expression in the turning inward of peasant communities and the rejection of everyone outside those communities, was an important part of a wider phenomenon which was of fundamental significance in 1917, the breakdown in the normal symbiotic relationship between the cities and the country-side. This relationship between metropolis and hinterland was placed under enormous strains in all parts of Russia, but nowhere was this as politically-significant as in the capital. Petrograd was the main theatre of elite politics in Russia, where the manoeuvres and shifting alignments of elite groups and segments within elites created a fluid and unstable political environment. A key feature in the instability of the elite political process was the uncertain position of the Provisional Government. It had no formal standing in Russian constitutional law[4] and could build up no tradition of popular acceptance which, over time, could cloak with legitimacy institutions which initially enjoyed no such status. Stepping into the power vacuum created by the fall of the tsar, the Provisional Government had to rely almost completely on popular support for its base. In this respect the support of the peasants, because of their role in food supply, and the soldiers at the front, whose possession of arms potentially made them the ultimate arbiters of direct conflicts between major power groups in the society, was essential for the government's survival. However in an immediate sense it was the population of Petrograd, both the workers and the soldiers of the garrison, who held the fate of the government in its hands. If the government were to lose the support of mass opinion in the capital, it would be left isolated and vulnerable to attack by any elite group that could summon the resolve and the force to do so.

In the half century prior to the outbreak of the war, Russia had experienced extensive, although erratic, industrial development.

Centres of industry grew up in many areas of the empire, including the capital where metallurgy, textiles, and chemical industries developed in the suburbs surrounding the city centre, the heart of privileged Russia. However this rapid industrialisation brought with it social strains of immense magnitude. The influx of peasants seeking work in the capital and the other industrial centres completely changed the political physiognomy of those areas. Poor living conditions, rising prices, low wages, long hours, and little job security or satisfaction were reflected in rising discontent on the part of the proletariat. This was particularly evident on the eve of the war.[5] This situation was exacerbated during the war. In Petrograd the number of industrial workers increased from a figure of 242,600 at the beginning of 1914 to approximately 400,000 by February 1917. In addition there were about 160,000 soldiers quartered in the capital.[6] The increase in population in the capital placed immense strains on the economic infrastructure of the city, particularly since the industrial structure of the capital was geared at this time primarily to the war effort; the production of articles that had no immediate military utility was a very low priority. Thus with increased pressure on the resources of the city, with the industrial structure of Petrograd unable to meet the demands made upon it, and with most foreign sources of imports closed by the war, the capital became even more reliant on imports from the remainder of Russia than it had been in pre-war times. However at this time of heightened dependency, the links between the capital and the hinterland broke down.

Two elements of the rupturing of relations between city and countryside were highly significant in 1917, the breakdown of the food supply and the dislocation of the supply of fuel and raw materials to the capital. Throughout 1917 Petrograd suffered a chronic food shortage. Between the two revolutions Petrograd received by rail only 43.9 per cent of the grain it had received in 1913, while according to one calculation Petrograd *guberniia* suffered a shortage of 25,600,000 *pudi* of food grains in 1917.[7] Although an accurate assessment of the changing food situation per month which would allow comparison by month could not be made from the sources available, the following account conveys an idea of the magnitude of the problem facing the capital.

The food crisis that had acted as a catalyst for the downfall of the tsar appears to have been eased temporarily by the surge of grain into the reception points in the early post-February revolution days.[8] However the situation remained grave; on 15 March there was only one or two days' stores of the staple rye meal and ten days' of wheat meal available in Petrograd.[9] In late March and early April there was a country-wide fall in deliveries of grain to the reception points: 20 to 27 March 15 million *pudi*, 27 March to 3 April 12 million *pudi*, and 3 to 10 April 5·4 million *pudi*. According to a future Food Minister, A. V. Peshekhonov, during April Petrograd was living on a day-to-day basis.[10] Little relief was forthcoming in the early summer; in the May–July period the monthly delivery of grain to the capital fell, with the monthly totals for 1917 substantially below those for 1916 (in numbers of wagons):

	1917		1916	
	By rail	*By water*	*By rail*	*By water*
May	7149	–	9768	–
June	5695	–	8664	2887
July	5195	1863	7784	5889[11]

According to an official survey, on 4 July Petrograd had sufficient grain to last about twenty days, buckwheat until the end of August, and milk supplies for about twenty days. Only about 3 per cent of the city's forage needs had been received, and both vegetables and eggs were in short supply. Flour deliveries for the month by rail amounted to 596,000 *pudi* compared with a norm of 1,200,000. During August grain deliveries to the capital increased. According to one source deliveries of grain by rail amounted to 1,051,000 *pudi*, almost achieving the norm, while another asserts that during the last weeks of August 75 per cent of the needed wagons were arriving; in early September this norm was exceeded. However this apparent improvement was not long-lived, and by October the capital's food supply was once again at a low level. During October 792,000 *pudi* of grain were delivered by rail, constituting about 68 per cent of the city's norm. According to Food Minister Prokopovich, on 14 October an average of 20–22 wagons of grain were arriving per day compared with a daily requirement of 40 wagons, while supplies were sufficient for only three to four days.[12] Throughout the year Petrograd was never far from famine.

The source of Petrograd's food shortage lay in three factors. The first was the size and distribution of the 1917 harvest. The gross yield of the six major grains (rye, wheat, oats, barley, millet, and buckwheat) throughout Russia in 1917 was substantially less than the average for the immediate pre-war period, but only marginally lower than that for 1916:

1909–13	1916	1917
4,045,000,000 *pudi*	3,597,000,000 *pudi*	3,503,000,000 *pudi*[13]

To the 1917 yield must be added the grain that remained on hand in the country from the previous harvests, and the total thereby gained compared with the country's requirements. One source has calculated the situation as follows (in millions of *pudi*):

Resources		*Requirements*	
Major grains (gross harvest)	3503	Army	501
Minor grains (gross harvest)	306	City population	263
		Rural population	1472
From previous harvests	669	Livestock	1001
		Field work	685
Total grain resources	4478	Total	3922
Surplus	556 *pudi*[14]		

Thus although the 1917 harvest was lower than that for 1916, there was still sufficient grain in the country to satisfy all needs. However the surplus produced in the country as a whole did not occur in European Russia where the crop failure in part of the traditional growing area created a major shortage of grain. Production in European Russia in 1917 was 12.8 per cent less than that of the previous year:

1909–13	1916	1917
3,406,000,000 *pudi*	3,036,000,000 *pudi*	2,646,000,000 *pudi*

The crop failure in the Middle Volga and part of the Central Agricultural regions could not be compensated by increased production in the New Russia – Little Russia and the Southwest, and the northern Caucasus and western Siberian growing areas; central and nothern European Russia suffered a grain shortage of approximately 200,000,000 *pudi* in 1917.[15]

The distribution of the harvest, with surpluses found in areas far from the capital, placed a premium on an efficient transportation system. However this was sadly lacking in Russia in 1917. The road network was of little use as a major means of transport; few roads had metalled surfaces, mechanised transport outside army control was limited, and few horses could be spared from the demands of field-work and the front.[16] The internal water transport system, traditionally a major means of shifting grain from the southern producing areas to the northern consuming areas, also was of only limited use in the critical months of 1917. Frequent industrial disputes, the over-use of old equipment and the inadequacy of repair facilities made this mode of transport unreliable. Moreover this was a very slow means of transporting goods, and therefore highly vulnerable to interdiction, and was impractical for large parts of the year because of weather conditions.

The main mode of transport was the railways, but here too capacity was far below that necessary to satisfy the demands made upon it. The outbreak of war placed a heavy burden on the railways. However this led to the rapid deterioration of the rolling stock, a process which increased the longer the war dragged on as a result of the inadequate repair facilities following the fall of Warsaw to the Germans, and the shortage of replacement parts.[17] This situation proceeded apace during 1917. In the revolutionary year the Russian railway had more rolling stock than it had possessed during 1916: at the time of the February revolution there were 20,600 engines and 569,223 wagons, compared with 19,506 and 514,216 at the same time a year earlier. However during 1917 there was also a higher proportion of rolling stock out of operation than there had been in 1916; in April 1916 there had been 15,936 engines in action, compared with 15,690 one year later. By the beginning of July 24.2 per cent of engines were out of action, a figure which represents a substantial increase not only over the 16.5 per cent at the start of the year, but also over the 18 per cent of July 1916. By early August 25.3 per cent of engines were in a state of disrepair, with the result that there were 1427 less engines in action than there had been twelve months earlier. By October 26.1 per cent of engines were undergoing repair. Between April and September an average of 200–400 engines left service per month. A similar tale of deterioration applies to railway wagons. At the start of the year 4.5 per cent had been off the tracks. By July this had climbed to 8 per cent (compared with 4.7 per cent in 1916), August 9 per cent, September 7.9 per cent (19,000 more under repair than in 1916), and October 6.8 per cent. Although the accuracy of these figures must be accepted only with caution, they do show the deterioration in the railway system in 1917. Russian industry could not make good these losses: the number of engines produced in the factories was an average of 33 per month in 1917 compared with 50 in 1916 and 75 in 1915.[18]

However, as well as the deterioration of the rolling stock, the railways also had to contend with a grave shortage of fuel. This was part of the more general fuel crisis discussed below. It has been calculated that to sustain the existing level of activity on the railway network early in 1917, 55 million *pudi* of coal per month were required. However according to a report from early October, railway reserves of coal throughout the year were as follows (in millions of *pudi*):

March	57	July	51
April	44	August	48
May	53	September	35
June	54		

By the beginning of September reserves were almost three times less than at the same time in 1916, causing the railways to eat into fuel ear-marked for industry; by 1 October reserves totalled only 22 million *pudi*.[19] Between the two revolutions the railways were constantly faced with the problem of insufficient supplies of hard mineral fuel to continue working at the required capacity. Furthermore this shortfall could not be made up by using wood as a substitute. The opposition of the peasants to the widespread felling of timber for commercial purposes has already been noted. This greatly hindered the railways in their attempt to use wood as a fuel; according to a report in early October, only about 66 per cent of the railways' requirements for wood had been procured.[20] Thus throughout 1917 the railways suffered from a fuel shortage of major dimensions.

The final factor in the disorganisation of the railways was the state of the work-force. In the period between 1900 and the February revolution the size of the work-force on the railways had expanded significantly. However after the 1905 revolution, the socio-economic position of the railwaymen in the labour hierarchy had declined; their perception of themselves as the elite of the work-force took a buffeting as their wages increasingly fell behind prices and a narrowing of differentials obscured the distinction between skilled and unskilled labour. Progressive demoralisation provided fertile soil for the growth of revolutionary sentiments during 1917, a development which was not conducive to the efficient operation of the railway system. Strikes were common on the various lines from early summer, while railway workshops frequently were disrupted by labour disputes. The productivity of the railway workers declined, exacerbating the difficulties the system already faced.[21]

The deterioration of the railway system is reflected in the low level of operations undertaken in 1917. In May 1916 the average distance travelled in twenty-four hours by an engine was 76 *versta* and by a freight car 71 *versta*; by April 1917 both had fallen to 55 *versta*. Furthermore in June 1916 an average of 91,541 wagons was moved daily; by January 1917 this had declined to 70,118, and by October to about 43,000. During the first half of 1917 700,000 less wagon-loads were carried than in a similar period in 1916; by the beginning of September this short-fall had increased to 1,300,000 and by October to 1,500,000. The movement of goods by rail into the capital had declined so much that in late August the section of the Petrograd railway junction handling Russian railways was working at only 73 per cent capacity while that dealing with Finnish railways was even lower, at 52 per cent.[22] Transport dislocation was a major factor in Petrograd's food shortage.

The third element central to the capital's plight was the interdiction of food supplies at their source and in transit. Peasant refusal to market their grain has already been noted. This had a major effect on the government's ability to obtain the grain needed to feed the population. In all months except one between the February and October revolutions, the state purchase of grain fell below the monthly target (per cent of monthly norm):

March	98.2%	July	56.7%
April	38.3%	August	16.9%
May	87.8%	September	31.3%
June	111.6%	October	19.0%

It has been calculated that for the whole period, state purchases achieved only about 48 per cent of the target.[23] The government was unable either to force or to persuade many peasants to give up their grain. In some areas peasants were willing to surrender their grain for the army at the front, but they refused to give it up if it was to be shipped to the cities.[24] Furthermore when the government was able to extract grain from the producers, frequently that grain was seized in transit by hungry peasants seeking to satisfy their own needs. Thus the actions of the grain producers in withholding their grain from the market and of peasant consumers in many parts of the country in seizing grain in transit contributed significantly to the capital's food crisis.

As well as suffering an acute food shortage, the capital was also confronted by a breakdown in the supply of fuel and raw materials. The most important aspect of this was the drastic fall in the delivery of hard mineral fuel to Petrograd. This is reflected in the decline in the average monthly delivery of this type of fuel to the capital over the years: 1915 9 million *pudi*, 1916 8 million *pudi*, and 1917 3.3 million *pudi*. In October the total was even lower, falling to 1.5 million *pudi*.[25] The situation for many industrial enterprises appears to have been worse than these figures indicate. According to one source, 145 enterprises in Petrograd received 17,495,400 *pudi* of Donets coal in 1917, compared with 48,807,300 *pudi* in 1916, a decrease of 280 per cent.[26] During 1917 Petrograd was faced with a shortage of fuel and raw materials of major dimensions.

An important factor in the decline in the delivery of fuel and raw materials to Petrograd was the reduction in the level of coal production in 1917. The war had isolated Russia from her major sources of supply abroad and forced her to rely overwhelmingly on her internal resources. The main production centre for coal was the Donets Basin, which experienced a major decline in output during 1917 (in millions of *pudi*):[27]

	1916	1917		1916	1917
January	150.0	154.1	June	147.2	127.0
February	149.0	143.4	July	144.0	119.0
March	164.2	150.0	August	137.0	112.0
April	95.0	121.0	September	149.0	110.0
May	140.0	127.5	October	157.0	110.0
			Total	1432.4	1274.0

Production in the January–October period was 158.4 million *pudi*, or 11 per cent, down on that for 1916, while production in October was 23 per cent lower than that in February and 30 per cent lower than in October 1916. This resulted in a sharp decrease in the export of Donets coal to consumers: over the whole of 1917 22.4 per cent less coal was delivered than in 1916, while shipments to Petrograd in the first half of 1917 were less than half what they had been in 1916. In the July–September period, the delivery of coal averaged 90 million *pudi* per month while the 'hunger norm' was 125 million *pudi*; in October only 67.8 million *pudi* were delivered.[28]

Two further factors exacerbated the effect of the decline in coal production. Firstly, the state of the transport system greatly complicated the question of delivery to the consumer of the coal available for supply. The transport network was unreliable, both in terms of its ability to shift the amount of fuel on hand at any one time efficiently to the place of need, and in its practice of using fuel specifically designated for industry for its own use as its stocks ran low. There was no reliable means of moving the available fuel from the pit-head to the customer. Secondly, the deficit in coal production could not be compensated by the increased use of wood as a fuel because of the widespread peasant opposition to tree-felling. By rejecting commercial exploitation of timber resources in their region, many peasants not only choked off traditional sources of fuel supply, but also made it impossible to use timber as a surrogate for coal and thus overcome the shortages of that fuel in major consumption areas. Certainly in many regions peasant refusal to market the wood was not total; peasants in some areas made substantial financial gains by selling wood to the fuel-hungry towns and transport network. Nevertheless the establishment of peasant control over the timber resources of the country was one element in the fuel shortage experienced throughout many of the cities of Russia in 1917.

Thus during 1917 Petrograd was afflicted by serious shortages of food, fuel and raw materials, shortages which played an important part in developments in the capital between the two revolutions. The food shortage and the government's attempt to overcome it through the operation of a ration system made queues outside distribution points a common occurrence in Petrograd. However standing in queues for long periods of time was not always a guarantee of obtaining adequate supplies. On many occasions supplies ran out before everyone was satisfied and, almost inevitably, when people did obtain supplies, they received less than they needed and had anticipated. In such situations popular patience frequently snapped; tired from working in the factories during the day and standing in queues for four to five hours after finishing work, the weariness and frustration of the Petrograd workers turned into anger. Hunger riots, the raiding of food stores and attacks on officials connected with the food question were popular reactions to the exhaustion of supplies in many instances. Troops were needed on some occasions to protect supplies from the hungry populace.[29] Hunger sharpened popular discontent, the necessity to queue provided an environment receptive to the outbreak of disturbances, and the ration system focused that discontent on the government.

Food shortages also resulted in a significant rise in the price of foodstuffs in the capital. The price rises of four major grains for the region of which Petrograd was a part have been estimated as follows (with 100 the average for 1909–13):[30]

	Rye	Winter wheat	Oats	Barley
Spring 1917	336.0	351.6	409.1	368.0
Autumn 1917	1354.4	1431.5	1361.4	1325.2

The price rises indicated by these figures were reflected in a steep increase in costs in factory canteens: over the July–October period in a factory in the Shlissel'burg region the cost of a meal with meat increased from 15 to 58 *kopecks*, without meat from eight to 42, a portion of porridge from ten to 32, and vegetable dishes increased three to four times.[31] Although the workers' nominal wages continued to rise, their real purchasing power fell. According to one study, wages moved as follows (in roubles):[32]

	Nominal monthly wage	Real wages (in roubles of pre-war buying power)
First half 1917	70.5	19.3
Second half 1917	135.0	13.8

On the eve of the February revolution the internal purchasing power of the rouble stood at 27 pre-war *kopecks*; by October it was down to six or seven *kopecks*. It has been calculated that in October the real wage of an unskilled labourer was worth only 43 per cent of its value in January.[33] Although all of these figures can be accepted only as rough indications of the actual situation, they do highlight clearly one essential fact of 1917: inflation was rampant and out of control. There was no way that the industrial workers could escape the rising food prices and the declining value of the rouble.[34] They were faced with a situation in which either they obtained no food at all or they received small amounts of food at exorbitant prices.

In this situation of shortage and high prices there was a thriving black market. It has been estimated that at the time of the doubling of the fixed price of grain in late August, the market price of grain was 75 per cent higher than the fixed price.[35] Speculation and the illicit purchase of grain occurred in Petrograd, but only wealthy individuals or business concerns could profit from this situation; it has been estimated that by October workers had to get 66 per cent of their food needs on the black market at exorbitant cost.[36] This situation heightened feelings of resentment and gave birth to rumours of profligate living on the part of all of those groups who, in the mythology of a deprived and anxious working class, live purely on the labour of others, the Jews, the bourgeoisie, and the intellectuals. Such rumours frequently were fanned by reports in the radical press of the export of grain overseas at the expense of the Russian people, a practice reputed to bring in very large profits.[37] Class hatred thrived on such rumours.

However popular ire was not focused on these groups alone. The government could not avoid shouldering much of the blame for the food crisis in the eyes of the workers of the capital. Food shortages naturally channelled resentment toward the government because the establishment of the grain monopoly and of grain rationing formalised governmental responsibility for the supply of grain to consumers. Hunger meant that the government was failing in this task. The Petrograd Central Food Committee had introduced grain rationing on 24 March, with the ration set at one *funt* per day for those not engaged in physical labour and a 50 per cent supplement for those thus occupied. A little over a month later the ration level was reduced to three-quarters and one *funt* respectively.[38] However with the establishment of rationing on a nation-wide scale on 29 April, the norm established for all urban areas became 30 *funti* of flour and three of buckwheat per month, with those engaged in heavy physical labour receiving a 50 per cent supplement. Petrograd thus reverted to its original ration levels. On 26 June these amounts were reduced to 25 and 37½ *funti*, respectively and on 20 September the nation-wide ration for those engaged in heavy physical labour was reduced to 36 *funti*.[39] However the serious position within which Petrograd found itself forced the local authorities to be responsive to fluctuations in the market, with the result that the national ration levels frequently were modified in the capital. On some occasions this meant that the ration level applying in the city was lower than that nominally in operation over the country at large; for three weeks from late August, and therefore including the period which witnessed the Kornilov affair and the attainment of a bolshevik majority in the Petrograd Soviet, the ration for those engaged in heavy physical labour stood at one *funt* per day, while on 21 October, four days before the bolshevik *coup*, ration levels were reduced even further, those undertaking heavy physical labour receiving three-quarters of a *funt* per day and those not thus engaged half a *funt*.[40] Not only were ration levels popularly considered to be excessively low, but there was no guarantee that even these levels would be met when food was available; the government had declared that these levels were maxima rather than minima and that the establishment of a ration amount involved no obligation on the part of food organs to ensure that individuals received that amount. In most cases amounts received appear to have been less than the declared ration.[41] When people were hungry responsibility was laid at the foot of the government.

The government also had to take the popular blame for the price increases throughout the year. By increasing the established grain price by 60 per cent in March and by doubling it in August, the government was directly responsible for substantial increases in grain prices to the consumer; these government-induced rises were not absorbed by food organs but were passed on to consumers through the rationing system. But prices rose not only as a result of these decisions. Increases in freight rates and government taxes led to further increases in food prices throughout the year; between August and October prices for food goods rationed for those engaged in physical labour rose 150 per cent.[42] Governmental responsibility was clear, at least in the peoples' minds. The existence of hunger and of escalating food prices in Petrograd signified the government's failure in this most basic field of human concern, the provision of sustenance.[43]

The decline in the supply of fuel and raw materials to Petrograd also had significant effects on life in the capital. Productivity in the industrial sector of the economy declined throughout Russia during 1917: 25 per cent less iron and steel was produced than in 1916, textile production fell by 33 per cent, metal-working and machine construction by 32 per cent, chemicals by 40 per cent, tanning by 20 per cent and tobacco by 24 per cent. Gross factory production in 1917 fell by 36.4 per cent compared with 1916, while that of Petrograd declined by 35 per cent.[44] This decline in production was accompanied by the widespread restriction of work and the closure of enterprises, leading to increased levels of unemployment. From March to the end of July 568 enterprises employing 104,372 workers closed their doors throughout the country, while in August and September a further 231 enterprises involving 61,000 workers ceased operations.[45] Accurate figures for the number of unemployed are impossible to obtain: the trade unions had 6000 to 8000 registered as unemployed in Petrograd in mid-October, while Ministry of Labour figures for mid-September placed the number at 40,000.[46] Some of those thrown onto the streets were able to find employment elsewhere, but this was neither a quick nor a simple process. Moreover as the year wore on and more enterprises closed, increased numbers found themselves without work. Many fled back to the villages, but this did not stop the army of the urban unemployed from growing and dissatisfaction from mounting.[47]

The closure of enterprises resulted in large measure from shortages of fuel and raw materials. According to one newspaper survey, 66 per cent of those enterprises closing between March and July were forced to shut their doors because of lack of raw materials and fuel.[48] The decreased productivity of the work-force resulting from the breakdown in traditional factory discipline, and the resultant decline in profitability, was another factor forcing enterprise owners to cease operations. However in many instances closures resulting from purely economic factors were branded as 'sabotage' by the workers, a claim heartily reiterated by the bolsheviks. Enterprise owners were accused of using the excuse that there was insufficient fuel and raw materials to continue operations in order to justify a closure that was motivated by a desire to suppress the revolution and dampen down the extremes of the workers' passions. This period undoubtedly saw a decrease in the desire of many enterprise owners to continue operations. In the words of one newspaper sympathetic to the cause of private enterprise:

On the part of enterprise owners one notices a significant weakening of interest in their affairs, for ensuring the materials, fuel and everything necessary for the enterprises. All of this constitutes grounds for the further closure of enterprises.[49]

Some enterprise owners may have attempted to use the closure of the plant to stifle revolutionary enthusiasm, or at least to bring the workers and their demands into line; the political and economic situation made for conflict between capital and labour, and under such conditions lock-outs and closures were as valid a method of struggle as strikes. It was this aspect of the closures that was popularly emphasised, with the result that the resentment and frustration resulting from the hardship workers and their families suffered owing to the closure of their place of work were very heavily tinged with class antagonism.

The breakdown in the traditional symbiotic relationship between countryside and city thus produced widespread hardship among the population of the capital. The constant threat of hunger, continually rising prices for all items of need, and either the threat or reality of the loss of their source of income produced frustration, resentment and anger among the workers of the capital. This anger was directed against 'privileged Russia' for profiting from their hardship through speculation, for being in part protected from hardship by their wealth, and for helping to cause their suffering through enterprise closures, and against the government for failing to ensure the adequate supply of goods needed in the city. As their economic situation deteriorated, the population of the capital became increasingly disenchanted with the government and its failure not only to satisfy their exaggerated expectations,[50] but also to provide them with the necessities of life. It was this deterioration in the economic position of the population of the capital that provided the basic motor force for the radicalisation of the popular mood, which left the government isolated and vulnerable.[51] Lacking the support of the garrison troops and the working class of the capital, the government had no immediate power to bring to bear against the bolsheviks when the latter were finally able to pull themselves together sufficiently to launch an attack on the government. The government's inability to maintain the traditional symbiotic relationship between city and countryside and the resulting collapse of the urban economy and the alienation this created in their immediate power base in the capital was a significant factor in its fall.

Thus the single most important reason for the fall of the Provisional Government was the government's failure to retain the support of the mass of the population, thereby rendering it vulnerable to bolshevik attack. The government was left behind by the radicalisation of the popular mood between the two revolutions, a process of radicalisation affecting both countryside and town and stemming primarily from inadequacies in the government itself. Its refusal to attempt to satisfy the peasants' traditional grievances and its inability to alleviate their immediate problems alienated the peasants and led to a process of revolution in the countryside which, in the name of traditional values, destroyed completely the established patterns of power, property, and hierarchy. The peasants turned inward, rejecting all authority that was not rooted in the traditional milieu of the village. In so doing they made a substantial contribution to the breakdown in the normal relationship between town and countryside, a breakdown which caused the significant deterioration of the economic position of the urban dwellers, thereby providing a major motor force in the radicalisation of urban opinion. Unable to halt this urban economic deterioration and unwilling to satisfy the demands stemming from the villages, the government lost support in both regions. Combined with the war-weariness of the soldiers, the disillusionment of rural and urban dwellers left the government defenceless. The Provisional Government was easily pushed from power with few lamenting its fall and even fewer rushing to its defence.

Appendix I

Regions and Gubernii

Central Agricultural

Kursk   Orel
Tula   Riazan
Tambov   Voronezh

Middle Volga

Simbirsk   Penza
Kazan   Saratov
Nizhegorod

Lower Volga

Samara   Astrakhan
Orenburg

New Russia

Bessarabia   Kherson
Taurida   Don oblast'
Ekaterinoslav

Little Russia and the Southwest

Kiev   Volynsk
Podolsk   Chernigov
Kharkov   Poltava

Baltic

Lifland   Estland
Kurland

Byelorussia and Lithuania

Mogilev   Minsk
Vitebsk   Smolensk
Vilensk   Kovno
Grodno

Central Industrial

Vladimir   Kaluga
Yaroslav   Moscow
Kostroma   Tver

Urals

Perm   Ufa
Viatka

Lakes

Pskov   Petrograd
Olonets   Novgorod

Northern

Vologda   Arkhangel

Appendix II

Levels of rural unrest between the February and October revolutions (in terms of proportion of total period).

March	April	May	June	July	Aug.	Sept.	Oct.
1.9	7.1	11.6	16.6	17.1	13.1	16.0	16.6

Types of peasant action against landed property per month

	March	April	May	June	July	Aug.	Sept.	Oct.
Open land seizure	2.6	24.9	34.3	37.0	34.5	35.8	23.6	18.2
Destruction	51.3	8.0	6.7	3.6	4.3	10.0	19.7	23.4
Personal violence	7.7	12.7	10.6	9.1	7.1	11.2	12.3	7.5
Crop seizure	7.7	1.9	2.6	7.8	23.7	22.2	11.9	11.3
Seizure of timber	25.6	20.2	19.9	17.9	10.9	11.0	26.7	32.6
Seizure of inventory	–	4.7	8.6	10.1	9.6	6.0	3.9	5.1
Establish rental rates	2.5	5.6	3.8	1.0	0.8	0.7	0.2	0.2
Remove labour	2.6	22.1	13.4	13.5	9.1	3.2	1.6	0.2

Source: Kotel'nikov and Meller: see Ch. 2, n 47.

Appendix III

(a) Types of unrest by region

	Land seizure	Pogrom/destn	Personal violence	Seizure of: crop	timber	Inventory	Remove Labour/est. rent
Cent. Agric.	20.3	40.9	15.1	16.9	17.2	26.4	34.9
Middle Volga	18.8	15.2	13.6	17.3	17.2	30.0	20.2
Lit. Russia and the Southwest	12.9	10.5	16.4	13.5	15.3	7.1	18.5
Byel. and Lith.	14.7	10.5	12.8	21.5	24.0	7.5	6.5
Cent. Indust.	5.1	5.5	7.4	8.7	6.4	4.6	4.3
New Russia	7.6	3.0	10.0	5.5	1.7	4.6	7.4
Lakes	3.4	1.9	4.1	5.9	9.5	2.9	2.0
Lower Volga	8.2	4.2	3.3	6.1	3.6	7.5	4.0
Urals	6.0	2.7	7.9	1.1	4.1	1.4	0.9
Baltic	1.4	4.9	6.4	1.5	0.5	4.6	–
Northern	0.2	0.2	–	0.4	0.2	–	0.3

(b) Regional unrest by type

	Land seizure	Pogrom/destn	Personal violence	Seizure of: crop	timber	Inventory	Remove Labour/est. rent
Cent. Agric.	26.3	21.1	6.4	8.1	15.7	8.1	13.3
Middle Volga	30.5	9.8	7.2	12.4	18.9	11.4	9.7
Lit. Russia and the Southwest	28.1	9.1	11.7	13.0	22.6	3.6	11.8
Byel. and Lith.	27.9	8.0	8.0	18.0	31.0	3.3	3.7
Cent. Indust.	25.2	10.7	11.9	19.0	21.5	5.4	6.2
New Russia	40.3	6.2	17.2	12.8	6.2	5.7	11.5
Lakes	21.7	4.8	8.5	16.3	40.7	4.2	3.7
Lower Volga	43.2	8.8	5.7	14.1	12.8	9.2	6.1
Urals	44.4	8.0	19.1	3.7	20.4	2.5	1.8
Baltic	18.9	25.5	27.8	8.9	4.4	14.4	–
Northern	25.0	12.5	–	25.0	25.0	–	12.5

The figures in (b) for the Baltic and Northern regions are too small to provide an accurate indication of the regional patterns.

Source: Kotel'nikov and Meller: Ch. 2, n 47.

Appendix IV

Kazan	5.4	Simbirsk	2.5	Petrograd	1.4
Penza	5.0	Ekaterinoslav	2.2	Orenburg	1.2
Orel	4.9	Kiev	2.1	Estland	1.2
Riazan	4.4	Vitebsk	2.1	Vladimir	1.1
Minsk	4.2	Kaluga	2.0	Nizhegorod	1.1
Podolsk	3.7	Novgorod	1.9	Taurida	1.0
Mogilev	3.5	Poltava	1.9	Vilensk	1.0
Kursk	3.4	Kherson	1.8	Kostroma	0.9
Tula	3.2	Chernigov	1.8	Don Oblast'	0.7
Tambov	3.1	Kharkov	1.8	Viatka	0.7
Samara	3.1	Perm	1.7	Astrakhan	0.6
Volynsk	3.1	Lifland	1.7	Vologda	0.3
Voronezh	2.9	Bessarabia	1.6	Yaroslav	0.2
Smolensk	2.8	Ufa	1.6	Olonets	0.1
Pskov	2.7	Moscow	1.6	Arkhangel	0.1
Saratov	2.6	Tver	1.6		

The level of recorded unrest was negligible in Grodno, Kovno and Kurland. Almost the entire area of each of these *gubernii* was under German occupation.

(b) *Unrest provided by each region*

Central Agricultural	21.8	Lakes	6.2
Middle Volga	16.6	Lower Volga	4.9
Little Russia and the Southwest	14.3	Urals	4.1
Byelorussia and Lithuania	13.9	Baltic	3.0
Central Industrial	7.4	Northern	0.5
New Russia	7.3		

Source: Kotel'nikov and Meller: see Ch. 2, n 47.

Appendix V

Peasant land ownership 1917

	Per cent of all land owned by peasants	Av. des. of exploitable land per person		Per cent of all land owned by peasants	Av. des. of exploitable land per person
Viatka	98.7	1.7	Kaluga	72.4	1.3
Astrakhan	93.6	2.4	Poltava	72.2	0.8
Ufa	96.6	2.5	Penza	72.1	1.0
Don oblast'	94.0	1.8	Yaroslav	71.9	1.6
Vologda	93.3	1.1	Tambov	70.5	1.0
Orenburg	93.2	4.3	Ekaterinoslav	69.7	0.8
Arkhangel	92.5	0.9	Mogilev	69.4	1.3
Vladimir	82.9	1.5	Tula	68.3	1.0
Riazan	80.7	1.0	Orel	67.1	1.0
Samara	80.0	1.8	Olonets	66.1	3.3
Nizhegorod	78.6	1.2	Kostroma	64.6	2.0
Simbirsk	77.9	1.1	Kazan	61.7	1.1
Chernigov	77.7	1.1	Kiev	58.9	0.6
Novgorod	75.8	2.9	Moscow	55.1	0.7
Kursk	75.3	0.9	Vitebsk	54.9	1.5
Kharkov	74.8	0.8	Petrograd	52.7	1.9
Saratov	74.3	1.5			
Tver	72.5	1.9			

Average des. of exploitable land per person by region

Little Russia and the Southwest	0.8	Central Industrial	1.5
Central Agricultural	0.9	Urals	2.3
Northern	1.1	Lower Volga	2.5
Middle Volga	1.2	Lakes	2.7
Byelorussia and Lithuania	1.2	All Russia	1.3
New Russia	1.3		

Source: Tsentral'noe . . . Perepisi

Notes

1. No attempt is made to give a comprehensive outline either of the traditional peasant life-style or of the course of socio-economic development in the countryside during the latter half of the nineteenth century. For summaries of these in English *see*, on life-style, Shanin, Ch. 2, and Vucinich, and on socio-economic development, Robinson.

2. Robinson, Ch. V, discusses this legislation. See also Liashchenko (1949), p. 376–402.

3. The peasants' attitude to land-ownership is discussed in Ch. 4.

4. Robinson, p. 88. Market value of land is for the period 1863–72.

5. Liashchenko (1949), p. 312, has estimated that the average allotment per person under *barshchina* was rarely above 2.5–3 *dessiatiny*, while under *obrok* it was 4–5 *dessiatiny* or more.

6. Robinson, p. 87–8, and Willetts (1972), p. 117.

7. Pavlovsky, p. 90, has estimated that anything less than 5 *dessiatiny* was generally insufficient to support a peasant household, while Favstov, p. 126, has shown how on some estates in Orel, Riazan and Tula, peasant plots averaged only 2.1 *dessiatiny*. It has been estimated that under the agricultural system used by the Russian peasants the area of meadows and pastures needed to be approximately equal to that of arable. Pavlovsky, p. 84.

8. Robinson, p. 120.

9. Even in the Ukraine where private ownership was well-advanced, 86.2 per cent of all peasant agricultural land was in strips at the start of the century. Gorbatiuk and Ionkina, p. 111.

10. Robinson, p. 72–77, discusses the various permutations to these procedures that were possible.

11. The peasants were entitled to some representation in these bodies, although this was minimal. The *guberniia* governor was to appoint peasant representatives from candidates elected by the peasants. In 1906 this power was abolished and peasants were able to elect members directly to the *zemstvo* assembly. Polner, Ch. 1, and Robinson, p. 209.

12. Although villages and communes did not always coincide, a recent study concluded that most communes seem to have corresponded to villages or small peasant settlements in a common locality. Shanin, p. 34.

13. Stepniak, p. 36.

14. This question is discussed in Robinson, p. 104–5.

193

15. Robinson, p. 101.
16. Vucinich, p. 150.
17. Rubach, p. 46. Figures for land-holding in 1905 will be found in Ezhegodnik, p. xxv-xxvi and xxviii-xxx.
18. These figures will be found in Robinson, p. 291, fn 42. Corresponding figures for the later part of the period do not exist, although figures cited by Robinson, p. 306 and 270, suggest that a similar situation existed: between 1896 and 1914 the population increased by 36 per cent, while between 1905 and 1914 the land area under peasant control grew by 6 per cent.
19. For a stimulating discussion of the economics of the peasant household, *see* Shanin. These figures, cited by Liashchenko (1928), p. 56, also include the decrease occurring at the time of emancipation. Citing Statisticheskiia svedeniia po zemel'nomu voprosu v Evropeiskoi Rossii. (St. Petersburg, 1906), p. 20-33, Vucinich, p. 149, reproduces the following figures for the same years: 5.1 and 2.7. According to Robinson, p. 94, from 1877-1905 the average size of household allotments fell from 13.2 to 10.4 *dessiatiny*.
20. Robinson, p. 99-100. Both the low level of technology and the fact that most leases were for short periods, which encouraged attempts to maximise production without concern for the long-term consequences to the land, inhibited the improvement of peasant farming and the placing of peasant agriculture on a firmer foundation.
21. Cited in Willetts, p. 120.
22. Robinson, p. 96. *See* figures published in Favstov, p. 131. That it was the peasants in particular who suffered from these handicaps is clear from the fact that between 1871 and 1875 *zemstvo* and state levies on the land and person of peasants were ten times greater than on the land of private owners. Robinson, p. 95.
23. Dubrovskii (1925), p. 68-9.
24. There is still no adequate, comprehensive survey of the Stolypin reforms and their effects. *See* Dubrovskii (1963), Pershin (1922), and Robinson, Ch. XI. Only the barest outlines of the legislation are presented here.
25. *See* an excellent discussion of the statistics in Atkinson. According to Pershin (1922), p. 8, 10.5 per cent of all peasant households had become enclosed holdings between 1905 and 1917. O zemle, App. II, cites a figure of 10.9 per cent, Atkinson, p. 785-6, 15.4 per cent, and Robinson, p. 225, about 10 per cent. A larger proportion—Willetts, p. 133, cites a figure of 24 per cent—obtained individual proprietorship of their land, but not all of these had their strips consolidated into one unit.
26. Robinson, p. 229.
27. Robinson, p. 230-1. Much of the land they did not own was forest and waste land.
28. Tsentral'noe . . . Perepisi and Antsiferov, p. 116-7.
29. Shestakov (Ocherki), p. 80-3, discusses this point and cites some figures on the use of prisoners-of-war and refugees. Also *Ekonomicheskoe polozhenie . . .* III, p. 61.
30. Liashchenko (1928), p. 40. According to Antsiferov, p. 128, imports of agricultural machinery from the west declined as follows (in thousands of *pudi*): 1909-13 (annual average) 8454, 1914 6239, 1915 199, 1916 540, 1917 1796.
31. Kir'ianov, p. 230.

32. According to the 1916 census, the peasants had in their hands 85.8 per cent of the sown area in the 50 *gubernii* of European Russia, while the 1917 census accorded to them 77.8 per cent of the exploitable land in 34 *gubernii* and *oblasti* of the region. Respectively Shestakov (Ocherki), p. 79, and Tsentral'noe . . . Perepisi. Shanin, p. 20, has argued that by 1914 only about 10 per cent of the sown land in Russia belonged to the estates.

33. Shestakov (Ocherki), p. 67, cites this figure as a minimum. Compare with Antsiferov, p. 149, who quotes a figure of 8.2 per cent over the 1914–16 period and Liashchenko (1928), p. 41, who cites 8.4 per cent over 1913–16.

34. Shestakov (Ocherki), p. 80.

35. Antsiferov, p. 118.

36. Liashchenko (1928), p. 39. Antsiferov, p. 125–7, asserts that there remained ample animal labour power in European Russia because of the pre-war surplus of working animals. In any case, many peasant households did not own working animals.

37. This is illustrated by the increased deposits in cooperative banks and decreased loans made by these institutions. Kohn and Meyendorff, p. 171. Liashchenko (1928), p. 46, attacks such theories of the enrichment of the countryside, but his argument is not convincing. *See* a discussion of this in Keep (1976), p. 29–30.

38. This is reflected in the figure cited by Antsiferov, p. 278, of a decline of 3.2 per cent in peasant land in 1917 compared with 1916.

39. Inflation is discussed in Stone, Ch. 9. Increases in food prices are cited in Shestakov (Ocherki), p. 63, and in Struve, p. 269–78.

CHAPTER 2 THE SPRING HONEYMOON

1. Mart-Mai, p. 33–4.

2. Mart-Mai, p. 35; Iakovlev (1967), p. 103.

3. It matters little that satisfaction of the basic demand for the seizure of landowners' land would have made only a marginal difference to most peasants' land-holdings. According to one report, the seizure of landed estates resulted in individual farmers in most *gubernii* receiving less than half a *dessiatina* each. *O zemle*, p. 29. Some regional figures are cited in Keep (1976), p. 414–5.

4. Gaponenko (1957), p. 669 and 383. According to an official report, to the extent that the peasants differentiated between the government and the soviet, it was to the government that they directed their loyalty. Mart-Mai, p. 36.

5. Gaponenko (1957), p. 693–4.

6. Gaponenko (1958), p. 281–2.

7. Mart-Mai, p. 50. *See* an example in *Delo Naroda*, No. 38, 2/5/17, p. 4. *See* Ch. 5. The desire to disrupt production as little as possible is also evident in the forms of land seizure prominent in the spring.

8. Gaponenko (1957), p. 674.

9. Agrarnoe dvizhenie . . . p. 205–15; Mart-Mai, p. 49.

10. *Vestnik*, No. 2, 7/3/17, p. 1.

11. Respectively Browder and Kerensky, p. 434–5 and *Vestnik*, No. 63, 26/5/17, p. 2.

12. *Vestnik*, No. 13, 23/3/17, p. 2. The post of *zemskii nachl'nik* was suspended on 20

March and officially abolished on 30 June, when the powers of that post were divided between the administrative courts and the *uezd* commissars. *Vestnik*, No. 149, 8/9/17, p. 1.

13. Gaponenko (1957), p. 422. On 12 April commissars were advised that peasant leaders who were unreceptive to the government or not enjoying popular confidence should be removed. *Sbornik' tsirkularov'* . . . p. 9.

14. Gaponenko (1957), p. 440. *See* an instruction of 26 March to *guberniia* commissars on the establishment of *guberniia* committees in *Sbornik' tsirkularov'* . . . p. 6.

15. References to rural unrest, peasant unrest, and disruptive action are used interchangeably throughout this work to refer to a wide range of specific actions undertaken by peasants in 1917. These actions can be classed in a number of different categories. Firstly, on the land question: the seizure of land through direct occupation, the establishment of rental rates, the removal of hired or indentured labour, the seizure of agricultural implements, and the seizure of timber and of crops (both cut and standing). The destruction of private property and the execution of acts involving personal violence often accompanied measures on the land question, although they were also frequent occurrences separate from the land issue. The other most common sphere of action concerned food matters and involved the refusal to surrender grain to the state, the seizure of grain in transit to consumers, and the use of violence against those attempting to implement the government's food policy. The open defiance of the government on other matters, most particularly those of local administration, also were important. Most incidents in the countryside were a composite of a number of these different types of individual actions.

16. Gaponenko (1957), p. 431.

17. Browder and Kerensky, p. 218.

18. Gaponenko (1958), p. 306. This was reaffirmed on 24 April. Kotel'nikov and Meller, p. 407.

19. *Vestnik*, No. 35, 20/4/17, p. 1. The circular was dated 17/4/17.

20. *Vestnik*, No. 38, 23/4/17, p. 2.

21. For example, Gapönenko (1957), p. 670.

22. Gaponenko (1957), p. 678–9. *See also* Mart-Mai, p. 40.

23. Gaponenko (1958), p. 581.

24. *Vestnik*, No. 23, 5/4/17, p. 3.

25. Gaponenko (1957), p. 675.

26. For example, Gaponenko (1957), p. 668–9.

27. An official discussion of the elections will be found in Mart-Mai, p. 41–2 and 45.

28. Gaponenko (1958), p. 593.

29. Shestakov (1929 Chast II), p. 13.

30. Mart-Mai, p. 37.

31. Mart-Mai, p. 43.

32. Mart-Mai, p. 43 and 54; Chugaev (mae-iiune), p. 413–4; Chugaev (okt.) p. 447.

33. Cited in Vermenichev, p. 186.

34. Kotel'nikov and Meller, p. 3, *see* n. 47 below.

35. The richest source of such decisions and resolutions easily available in the west is the series of documents edited by Gaponenko and by Chugaev. Not all

resolutions and decisions conformed to this pattern. In very general terms, it seems to have been less common later in the year as peasant rejection of those from outside the villages became more widespread.

36. Gaponenko (1957), p. 669.
37. Gaponenko (1958), p. 599.
38. Krasnov, p. 122.
39. Mart-Mai, p. 42.
40. The effect of this was far less marked at the *uezd* level and above where the 'intelligentsia' retained their influence to a far greater extent than in the villages. *See* next chapter.
41. Discussions of committee membership will be found in Mart-mai, p. 41–3, Iakovlev (1967), p. 56, and Kravchuk, p. 98.
42. *Agrarnoe dvizhenie* . . . p. 186.
43. Shestakov (1928) p. 106, discusses both the size of the village committees and the range of their authority.
44. The size of these committees varied greatly. Most appear to have had less than twenty members, but there were some with as many as sixty-two. The larger *volost* committees normally elected executive committees or special commissions to handle the affairs of the *volost* while the committee was not meeting. Shestakov (1929 Chast I), p. 62.
45. Gaponenko (1958), p. 613.
46. Respectively, Kravchuk, p. 96, *Vestnik*, No. 86, 22/6/17, p. 4 and Pershin (1966), p. 353.
47. These are reprinted in Kotel'nikov and Meller. Appendix II outlines the varying levels of unrest over the year and the different types of actions prominent at different times of the year. The figures found in the appendices and cited throughout this work for levels of rural unrest are based on personal study of the published reports sent to the Chief Department of the Militia, not on the table published on p. 364–99 of Kotel'nikov and Meller and criticised so trenchantly, if somewhat unfairly, by Mel'gunov (1953), p. 137–42. All reports which do not fit into the typology of unrest given in fn. 15, such as that on p. 353, reporting the enactment of a prohibition on the playing of billiards by the Oranienbaum volost committee, have been omitted from the analysis.

All statistics relating to rural unrest must be considered only as approximations of the situation in the countryside in 1917. The degree of accuracy implied by taking the figures to one decimal point is an accurate reflection of the pattern of the reports in Kotel'nikov and Meller, but the precise degree to which those reports reflect the actual situation throughout Russia cannot be known. This is without doubt an imperfect source: the chaotic situation in the rural areas hampered the collection of accurate information, the sources of information were not impartial observers of the rural scene, reporting was unstructured with limited guidance given from the centre as to what should be reported and what should not, and the published collection has been edited without any clear indication of the criteria used by the editors. Nevertheless if used with care, this collection can be accepted as a reliable source for the analysis of rural unrest. By focusing on percentages rather than total figures, the fact that not every instance of unrest was recorded does not matter. The question of consistency, both across the country and throughout the year, becomes of prime importance. There is no evidence to suggest that the collection is lacking in either of these respects. Comparison of the results of the analysis of the Milita figures with those of the Chief Land Committee (in *Agrarnoe dvizhenie* . . .) and with those cited by Soviet historians based on local archival material (for example, Kravchuk) shows a broad similarity. Until the Militia figures are shown to be grossly deficient in some respect, they should be accepted as a reliable, if rough, guide to what was happening in the countryside in 1917. Keep (1976), p. 187–9, draws a similar conclusion.

48. Gaponenko (1957), p. 683.
49. Iakovlev (1928), p. 83; Owen (1963), p. 139.
50. Gaponenko (1957), p. 689. In many instances rentals were not established in absolute terms but as a proportion of the rental paid in the previous year. *Agrarnoe dvizhenie* . . . p. 193 and 219 and Shestakov (1929 Chast I), p. 51, provide instances of rent fixing.
51. Kotel'nikov and Meller, p. 13.
52. Kotel'nikov and Meller, p. 15 and 47 and Mart-mai, p. 46.
53. Kotel'nikov and Meller, p. 19.
54. Gaponenko (1957), p. 672.
55. Gaponenko (1957), p. 691–2.
56. Gaponenko (1957), p. 672–3.
57. The pattern of rural life and farm-work used in this analysis refers specifically to a village situated just north of Moscow. Regional variations on this pattern existed, but they do not substantially affect the analysis.
58. According to the commissar in Ranenburg *uezd*, Riazan *guberniia*, the peasants in some areas took labour power, animals and tools from the land-owners only when they were deficient in those resources themselves. *Agrarnoe dvizhenie* . . . p. 189.
59. *Vestnik*, No. 1, 5/3/17, p. 2–3. The standards of the requisition were published in *Vestnik*, No. 8, 14/3/17, p. 2.
60. *Vestnik*, No. 7, 12/3/17, p. 1.
61. Membership was expanded a month later. *Vestnik*, No. 27, 9/4/17, p. 2. In this amended membership, the reference to representatives of the Soviet of Peasants' Deputies has been replaced by representatives from the All-Russian Peasants' Union. It is probably this latter body that was meant in the first place since moves had not yet begun to convene the All-Russian Soviet of Peasants' Deputies.
62. *Vestnik*, No. 6, 11/3/17, p. 1.
63. *Vestnik*, No. 20, 30/3/17, p. 1–3.
64. Lists of the prices were published in *Vestnik*, No. 20, 30/3/17, p. 2, No. 25, 7/4/17, p. 1, and No. 30, 13/4/17, p. 2. The fixed prices, which differed from area to area, were about 60 per cent higher than those prevailing in 1916. Lozinskii (1927), p. 137.
65. It is evidence of the haste with which the food legislation was drawn up that the power to take-over and use a land-owner's unused equipment, accorded to the food committees in the law transferring grain to the state, was not included in the formal array of their powers outlined in the temporary statute bringing them into existence discussed below. The granting of this right to the local committees provided an obvious cover for the 'surreptitious' seizure of land by the peasants. *See* above.
66. *Vestnik*, No. 50, 7/5/17, p. 1. *See* below.

67. *Vestnik*, No. 87, 23/6/17, p. 1.
68. Mart-Mai, p. 51.
69. *Vestnik*, No. 44, 30/4/17, p. 4.
70. *Vestnik*, No. 65, 25/5/17, p. 1.
71. The *zemstvo* board was to appoint representatives to fill these positions on both the *guberniia* and *uezd* food committees until the *zemstvo* was 'democratised'.
72. Not all food committees were oblivious to government directives early in the year. Many seem to have tried to implement government policy in the areas under their control. Gaponenko (1958), p. 218 and 367, cites some examples. Early government recognition of this problem appears to be reflected in the despatch to the countryside in late April of special emissaries armed with the authority of *guberniia* food committees to try to improve supply and to counteract some of the negative effects of many of the food committees. They do not appear to have had much success. Lozinskii (1927), p. 127.
73. *Vestnik*, No. 31, 14/4/17, p. 1.
74. *Vestnik*, No. 45, 2/5/17, p. 1.
75. *Vestnik*, No. 39, 25/4/17, p. 1–2.
76. *Vestnik*, No. 38, 23/4/17, p. 3, where the Petrograd Soviet acknowledges this problem.
77. *Vestnik*, No. 38, 23/4/17, p.1–2.
78. *Vestnik*, No. 50, 7/5/17, p. 1.
79. *Vestnik*, No. 45, 2/5/17, p. 1–2.
80. *Vestnik*, No. 44, 30/4/17, p. 2.
81. Browder and Kerensky, p. 523–4.
82. *Vestnik*, No. 14, 21/3/17, p. 1. The first declaration of the new government dated 7 March made no mention of the land question. *Vestnik*, No. 2, 7/3/17, p. 1.
83. *Vestnik*, No. 10; 16/3/17, p. 1; No. 11, 17/3/17, p. 2; No. 21, 31/3/17, p. 1; and No. 29, 12/4/17, p. 1.
84. *Vestnik*, No. 19, 29/3/17, p.1.
85. *Vestnik*, No. 38, 23/4/17, p. 1–2.
86. Twenty-four commissions were established within the Ministry of Agriculture throughout the year to work on this question. Tsereteli, p. 220. Chernov (1936), P. 236.
87. For example, the legislation of 21 April accorded to the land committees responsibility for land relations and the prevention of actions leading to the depreciation of the value of the land. However the 11 April legislation gave responsibilities to the food committees which impinged upon these areas. Food committees were enabled to take over unworked land and to transfer it to those willing to work it, thereby bringing about a change in land relations, and they were to prevent the depreciation of the land caused by popular unrest or a failure to work it by the owner. There was thus a direct conflict of responsibility.
88. Most of the appointees were Kadets. Chernov (1936), p. 187 and 233.
89. PSR, Popular Socialists, SD (Bolsheviks), SD (Mensheviks), Trudoviks, Kadets, Progressive, Octobrist, Centre Group, Nationalist, and Independent Rightist.
90. On the party nature of the membership of the executive committee, *see* Pershin (I, 1966), p. 295. On the distorting effect that the ideological convictions

shared by most SRs had on their perceptions of the peasants and on their responsiveness to peasant demands, *see* Radkey (1958).

CHAPTER 3 THE SUMMER UPHEAVAL

1. However, there was disagreement over the precise terms under which members of the Soviet would enter the government. Despite opposition from the Kadets, the members of the Soviet entered as formal representatives of that body and were subject to recall by it.
2. *Vestnik*, No. 49, 6/5/17, p. 1.
3. *Vestnik*, No. 51, 9/5/17, p. 2.; Lozinskii (1929), p. 127.
4. *Vestnik*, No. 49, 6/5/17, p. 1.; No. 89, 25/6/17, p. 2.
5. *Vestnik*, No. 72, 6/6/17, p. 1.; No. 77, 11/6/17, p. 2; No. 138, 24/8/17, p. 2. According to the initial decision (*Vestnik*, No. 49, 6/5/17, p. 1) the administration of food supply was to remain under Shingarev's control in the Ministry of Finance until 1 June to enable it to complete the organisation of the grain monopoly. Keep (1976), p. 498, *fn* 12, suggests that this was done to keep it out of Chernov's hands.
6. *Vestnik*, No. 61, 24/5/17, p. 3.
7. Respectively *Vestnik*, No. 61, 24/5/17, p. 3. and Browder and Kerensky, p. 633–6.
8. *Vestnik*, No. 73, 7/6/17, p. 2.
9. *Vestnik*, No. 78, 13/6/17, p. 2. The introduction of rationing encountered problems in many areas. For example, Delo Naroda, No. 65. 3/6/17, p. 3. and No. 106, 21/7/17, p. 3.
10. *Vestnik*, No. 91, 28/6/17, p. 2.
11. *Vestnik*, No. 90, 27/6/17, p. 1. The former body replaced the Council for the Development of the Productive Forces of the Country, an organisation established on 5 May but which appears to have been moribund from the start. Both bodies frequently were ignored in decision-making, while the Economic Council was stripped of much of its formal power during the course of the year. Volobuev, p. 135–46; Lozinskii (1929), p. 56, and Browder and Kerensky, p. 643, discuss these points.
12. *Vestnik*, No. 146, 5/9/17, p. 2–3.
13. *Vestnik*, No. 114, 26/7/17, p. 1.
14. Fixed prices were established on metals and metal goods on 19 July and attempts were made to streamline the supply of agricultural equipment and some textiles to producers. Meat was the most important foodstuff to have fixed prices placed upon it at this time. Browder and Kerensky. p. 687–8 and 698., *Vestnik*, No. 118, 30/7/17, p. 2–3.; No. 135, 20/8/17, p. 2.; and No. 139, 25/8/17, p. 1.
15. *Vestnik*, No. 110, 21/7/17, p. 3. and No. 169, 5/10/17, p. 1.
16. *Vestnik*, No. 120, 2/8/17, p. 1. and No. 124, 6/8/17, p. 4.
17. *Vestnik*, No. 123, 5/8/17, p.1.
18. *Vestnik*, No. 133, 18/8/17, p. 4.; No. 137, 23/8/17, p. 2.; and No. 141, 27/8/17, p. 1. The decision to create the special appointment for the region of the theatre of war was taken in the wake of a decision by Stavka to requisition grain and forage in the *gubernii* bordering on the South-western and the

Rumanian fronts. Ekonomicheskoe polozhenie . . . II, p. 285. This decision was reaffirmed in mid-September, *Vestnik*, No. 153, 14/9/17, p. 1.

19. *Vestnik*, No. 150, 10/9/17, p. 1. For the explanation of this decision to double the price *see* Chugaev (avguste), p. 136–8.

20. The government also appears to have hoped to induce those who had concealed grain to surrender their produce by reducing the penalty for this action from a reduction of 50 per cent in the established price to one of 30 per cent.

21. According to one report, the new price was only the equivalent of 33 per cent of production costs, while another despatch reported that the increase in price had made articles of prime necessity more difficult to obtain. Respectively Ekonomicheskoe polozhenie . . . II. p. 340 and 324. Also *see* Lozinskii (1929), p. 136–8.

22. Ekonomicheskoe polozhenie . . . III, p. 200 and 202.

23. *Delo Naroda*, No. 160, 21/9/17, p. 4.; Kotel'nilov and Meller, p. 335. Some areas, such as Nizhegorod, reported that there was no increase in delivery. Ekonomicheskoe polozhenie . . . II, p. 319. The doubling of the price placed great burdens on the government treasury and forced it to rely even more heavily on the private banks for its continued financial solvency. Many local committees remained unable to pay for the grain that producers delivered to them, with the result that the producers refused to hand over their grain. Ekonomicheskoe polozhenie . . . II, p. 363–4. Many other producers were resentful because they had surrendered their grain prior to the price rise and had thereby missed out on its benefits and forced to suffer its consequences.

24. Lozinskii (1929), p. 136, *Vestnik*, No. 179, 17/10/17, p. 3.

25. *Vestnik*, No. 49, 6/5/17, p. 1.

26. *Vestnik*, No. 100, 9/7/17, p. 1. It was this promise which was a major factor precipitating Prince Lvov's resignation from the government. *See* his letter of resignation in Golder, p. 470–1.

27. Both congresses are discussed in Rosenberg (1974), p. 86–93 and 124–33. The Kadet programme is reprinted in an edited form in Browder and Kerensky, p. 605–8. Rosenberg (1974), p. 85, also asserts that a plenary session of the Kadet Central Committee meeting in Petrograd from 10 to 13 March decided that final solution of the agrarian question should await the end of the war.

28. The SRs were never explicit about exactly how this concept was to work in practice, probably because they were not sure themselves about its precise contours. Some of the problems entailed in the notion of 'land socialisation' are discussed in Radkey (1955). The congress is discussed briefly in Radkey (1958), Ch. VI. The resolution on land was published in *Delo Naroda*, No. 68, 7/6/17, p. 3.

29. For examples of condemnations of arbitrary land seizures by Chernov *see* *Vestnik*, No. 46, 3/5/17, p. 4, and No. 55, 16/5/17, p. 3. On the Constituent Assembly and the land question *see* the interview in *Izvestiia*, No. 61, 22/5/17, cited in Golder, p. 374–5.

30. Respectively *Delo Naroda*, No. 82, 23/6/17, p. 4, and Tsereteli, p. 231–2.

31. The collapse of the first coalition was brought about by the resignation of the Kadet ministers because of what they perceived to be government weakness

in handling Ukrainian demands for greater autonomy. However this was simply the final evidence for the Kadets that the government was not going to be the strong authority which they believed Russia needed. This weakness was blamed in large part on the socialist ministers, and particularly Chernov.

32. *Rech.*, No. 165, 16/7/17, p. 1, cited in Browder and Kerensky, p. 1402–3.

33. Kerensky had a bitter personal dislike for Chernov, blaming the Agriculture Minister for engineering his failure to gain election to the Central Committee of the PSR at the III Congress. This personal antipathy gave a sharp cutting-edge to Kerensky's opposition to Chernov's policies.

34. On the peasants' views *see* Mart-mai, p. 48. and Shestakov (II, 1929). p. 34, 47, and 94. On the opposition to this view and on Lvov's role in the government *see* Tsereteli, p. 231–7 and 226.

35. Pershin (I, 1966), p. 302–3. *Vestnik*, No. 104, 14/7/17, p. 1. According to Tsereteli, Pereverzev's action had been ratified by the socialist ministers prior to its implementation. Tsereteli, p. 227.

36. Respectively *Vestnik*, No. 117, 29/7/17, p. 1.; No. 114, 26/7/17, p. 1., and *Delo Naroda*, No. 104, 19/7/17, p. 2., and Chernov (1936), p. 239.

37. Reports of the sessions were published in *Delo Naroda*, Nos. 54–58, 20/5–26/5/17; Nos. 90–94, 2/7–7/7/17; and Nos. 137–142, 26/8–31/8/17.

38. Semenov Tian-shanskii, p. 291–4.

39. For some of the proposals *see* Pershin (I, 1966), p. 311–325; Chugaev (avguste), p. 181–2.; and Browder and Kerensky, p. 549–554. On government opposition *see Vestnik*, No. 153, 14/9/17, p. 3., and Lozinskii (1929), p. 145–183. Chernov (1936), p. 236–9, gives a summary of the Agriculture Minister's views from hindsight.

40. Semenov Tian-shanskii, p. 292.

41. *See* Chernov's unpublished letter to N. V. Nekrasov in early July. Fleer.

42. Respectively *Vestnik*, No. 45, 5/5/17, p. 1.; No. 52, 11/5/17, p. 2.; No. 124, 26/8/17, p. 2; No. 91, 28/6/17, p. 2; No. 123, 5/8/17, p. 1. This last decision represents the granting to food committees of a power which the legislation establishing the grain monopoly declared they would have but which the legislation bringing them into existence omitted. On labourers *see Vestnik*, No. 74, 8/6/17, p. 1; No. 104, 14/7/17, p. 2; and No. 119, 1/8/17, p. 2. and on institutions to coordinate their activities *Vestnik*, No. 84, 20/6/17, p. 2. and No. 88, 24/6/17, p. 2.

43. The Special Commission was in favour of elections being held on 1 November but it was overruled by the cabinet. The announcements of the election dates will be found in *Vestnik*, No. 80, 15/6/17, p. 1. and Golder, p. 415–6. One view of the Kadets' approach to this problem will be found in Kochan (1967). The major provisions of the electoral law have been printed in Browder and Kerensky, p. 454–64.

44. On 21 May Temporary Rules on the Election of *Guberniia* and *Uezd Zemstvo* Members (the much-heralded 'democratisation') and a Temporary Statute on *Volost Zemstvo* Administration were issued, *Vestnik*, No. 62, 25/5/17, p. 1–2. For election instructions *see Vestnik*, No. 78, 13/6/17, p. 1–2. and No. 122, 4/8/17, p. 1.

45. According to a report in *Delo Naroda*, No. 160, 21/9/17, p. 2, peasants in one area asserted 'We do not want the *zemstvo* because we were already tired of it under the old regime'. For reports of the elections *see* Shestakov (II, 1929),

p. 22; Kotel'nikov and Meller, p. 306; Browder and Kerensky, p. 293–4.

46. The unsatisfactory nature of many of these committees was a common talking point within government ranks. *See* comments by Prince Lvov, cited in Vermenichev, p. 187, and the call by Assistant Minister of Agriculture Rakitnikov for *guberniia* and *uzed* land committees to ensure that *volost* committees assisted the harvest, not hindered it. Ekonomicheskoe polozhenie . . . III, p. 250–1. For the actions cited in the text *see*, respectively, *Delo Naroda*, No. 69, 8/6/17, p. 3; Pershin (I, 1966), p. 383; *Vestnik*, No. 117, 29/7/17, p. 1, and No. 141, 27/8/17, p. 1. In addition, the Ministers of Interior and War were granted powers of administrative arrest of individuals committing criminal actions. Browder and Kerensky, p. 1440–1.

47. *Vestnik*, No. 107, 18/7/17, p. 2. *See also* his circular published four days later in which he repeated the substance of the circular of 17 July and threatened *guberniia* commissars with dismissal and arrest if they countenanced illegal or counter-revolutionary activity. *Vestnik*, No. 111, 22/7/17, p. 2.

48. *Vestnik*, No. 114, 26/7/17, p. 1. *See* above, n 13.

49. Chugaev (iiule), p. 305–9.

50. Gaponenko (1958), p. 327.

51. Kotel'nikov and Meller, p. 410. For a complaint about the lack of guidance *see* Browder and Kerensky, p. 570–1.

52. *Vestnik*, No. 179, 17/10/17, p. 3.

53. For Kornilov's threat, *see* Pershin (I, 1966), p. 381–2, and for his circulars, Kotel'nikov and Meller, p. 416–17. Kornilov's circular of 8 July was issued in his capacity as Commander-in-Chief of the South-western Front, and this was re-issued at the end of the month applying to the area behind the whole front after he became Supreme Commander on 18 July.

54. Kazinkin and Sobolev, p. 21. Shestakov (Ocherki), p. 161, cites a figure of 22 for the Central Agricultural and Middle Volga regions during July and August.

55. For example, Pershin (I, 1966), p. 384–91, and Kravchuk, p. 173–91.

56. Kotel'nikov and Meller, p. 198.

57. This seems to have become less and less frequent the longer the year went on. For an example, *see* Shliapnikov, p. 349.

58. Kotel'nikov and Meller, p. 40. For early reports of armed opposition by peasants to attempts to requisition the grain mentioned below, *see* Mart-mai, p. 52.

59. Kotel'nikov and Meller, p. 49.

60. Grain purchased in this way could cost up to eight times the price fixed by the government. Mart-mai, p. 51.

61. Chugaev (iiule), p. 472–3. Also Agrarnoe dvizhenie . . . p. 218.

62. Kotel'nikov and Meller, p. 236.

63. Chugaev (mae-iiune), p. 437.

64. *Vestnik*, No. 56, 17/5/17, p. 4; No. 57, 18/5/17, p. 4.; No. 131, 15/8/17, p. 3–4.; and Kotel'nikov and Meller, p. 206–60. Among those reporting shortages were Orel, Nizhegorod, Astrakhan, Vladimir, Kaluga, Kostroma, Mogilev, Novgorod, Moscow, Perm, Tver, Smolensk and Vitebsk.

65. Kotel'nikov and Meller, p. 176. The debate over the extent of desertion from the front during 1917 is still continuing. The traditional view of the disintegration of the army, for which Golovine has been the standard-bearer,

has come under trenchant attack in the recent book by Norman Stone. Although Stone completely reverses the balance from the one-sided picture that previously prevailed, his work by no means proves that deserters from the front were not the significant element in the countryside that contemporary reports show them to have been.

66. Respectively Chugaev (iiule), p. 445, and Kotel'nikov and Meller, p. 145.
67. Kotel'nikov and Meller, p. 161. For other reports *see* Iakovlev (1967), p. 36, 47, 64, 80, 95, 112, 146, 148, 149, 227; Chugaev (iiule), p. 482; and Soiuz zemel'nykh . . . p. 103.
68. For example, Pershin (I, 1966), p. 384–91, and Kravchuk, p. 173–91.
69. According to Radkey (1958), p. 328, quoting the SR Bykhovskii, only 17 or 18 members of land committees were arrested and none of them were prosecuted. Pershin (I, 1966), p. 389–90, asserts that punitive expeditions were mounted by government forces in the following *gubernii*: Kazan, Smolensk, Poltava, Chernigov, Voronezh, Tambov, Tula, Riazan, Pskov, Mogilev, Volynsk, Ufa, Penza, Saratov and Kiev.
70. According to figures from the Chief Land Committee, the number of instances of unrest during this period was as follows:

May	Ist half:	175	July	Ist half:	481
May	2nd half:	337	July	2nd half:	286
June	Ist half:	391	August	Ist half:	58
June	2nd half:	464			

Rabochii, No. 2, 8/9/17 (26/8), p. 3.

71. According to Vermenichev, p. 203, 60.4 per cent of all meadow land seized between the two revolutions occurred in June and July. In contrast, the seizure of arable land was far more evenly distributed over the whole period (in terms of monthly proportion of the total):

March	April	May	June	July	August	September	October
0.5	8.8	13.1	17.7	15.6	13.4	12.4	18.5

These figures must be treated with caution.
72. This is discussed at greater length in Ch. 4.
73. Gaponenko (1958), p. 592.
74. *Vestnik*, No. 81, 16/6/17, p. 3. I could find no other record of a '*guberniia* committee of peasants' deputies' or of a 'committee of the united organisations of Voronezh' existing in the *guberniia*.
75. On the role of party ideology obscuring the perceptions of party members of the party which nominally dominated organisations at these levels for much of the year, the SRs, *see* Radkey (1958). For a succinct outline of one aspect of the view of developments in the villages shared by most major political groups at this time, *see* Shanin, p. 1–2. On the role of SRs in these bodies, *see* Lebedev, Antonov-Saratovskii (1924), and Vrachev.
76. Cited in Vermenichev, p. 199.
77. For examples of the weakness of links, *see* Gaponenko (1958), p. 613, Shestakov (II, 1929), p. 32, Agrarnoe dvizhenie . . . p. 209, and Chugaev (iiule), p. 468.

78. For examples of meetings in urban areas stimulating unrest in the country-side, *see* Agrarnoe dvizhenie . . . p. 206 and Chugaev (okt), p. 447.

79. Schemes of the organisational structure of soviets propounded by these bodies will be found in Shestakov (I, 1929), p. 178., Shestakov (Miliutin), p. 109–113, and Shestakov (II, 1929), p. 266–8d.

80. Respectively Shestakov (II, 1929), p. 42–3 and 71; Chugaev (sent), p. 166–7; and Moiseeva, p. 173. Moiseeva gives a *guberniia* breakdown of the numbers of *volost* soviets on p. 173. Keep (1976), p. 228, cities figures on this question. The figures in the text for Vladimir relate to October, and for the other two *gubernii*, to September.

81. For comments on this *see Delo Naroda*, No. 104, 19/7/17, p. 1.; Chugaev (iiule), p. 487; and Shestakov (II, 1929), p. 80.

82. On occasions when this happened, work usually was divided; committees undertook administrative work while soviets concentrated on 'cultural-enlightening' activities. Shestakov (I, 1929), p. 31–2 and 57, cites some instances of the two bodies existing side by side.

83. Kravchuk, p. 101. Shestakov (II, 1929), p. 9, cites higher figures. He asserts that by October 79.9 per cent of peasants in European Russia were organised into *uezd* soviets. Kravchuk's figures are for all of Russia.

84. The figures and organisational details cited in this paragraph come from Shestakov (I, 1929), p. 57–9; Shestakov (II, 1929), p. 28–31; Shestakov (Miliutin), p. 130; and Gaponenko (1957), p. 380 and 383. Many soviet executive committees had similar commissions to those cited in the text.

85. Anweiler (1972), p. 151. Such soviets did occur in some places, for example Tver *uezd*, Kazan *guberniia*, and Smolensk *guberniia*, but the peasants invariably occupied a subordinate position in them. Remezova, p. 26. Moiseeva, p. 87.

86. According to a bolshevik activist in Saratov, the peasants were represented by a section of the soviet of workers' and soldiers' deputies, with the result that peasant questions received little consideration. The soviet did not even adopt a specific resolution on the land question. Antonov-Saratovskii (4, 1924), p. 189 and 199.

87. Shestakov (I, 1929), p. 59. and Shestakov (II, 1929), p. 31.

88. *See* examples of resolutions by peasant bodies in April in Gaponenko (1958), p. 570–1, 584, 586–7, 610–12, 621–3 and 637–9. The proceedings of the congress are reported in *Delo Naroda*, Nos. 41–61, 5/5–30/5/17. The composite instruction and the congress resolutions are reprinted in Shestakov (I, 1929), p. 136–50.

89. *See* a discussion of differences of nuance between the resolution and the composite instruction in Keep (1976), p. 510–11. The individual instructions which comprise the composite instruction have not been published and therefore how accurately the latter reflects the former is unknown.

90. This is discussed in Shestakov (Miliutin), p. 148.

91. Information on these bodies can be found in Shestakov (Miliutin), p. 161–2; Shestakov (II, 1929), Ch. 8; Pershin (I, 1966), p. 344; and Soiuz zemel'nykh . . . p. 100.

92. Shestakov (I, 1929), p. 210.

93. Shestakov (Miliutin), p. 116, and Delo Naroda, No. 38, 2/5/17, p. 4.

94. Shestakov (I, 1929), p. 196.

95. For examples *see Delo Naroda*, No. 76, 16/6/17, p. 4 and No. 87, 29/6/17, p. 3, and Shestakov (I, 1929), p. 187-9.

96. Shestakov (I, 1929), p: 195.

97. According to one study, the number of cooperatives increased throughout Russia as follows:

	Producers	Consumers	Credit
1906	584	1332	3145 (1908)
1912	3500	6609	8533
1916	6500	14,750	13,728

Consumers' cooperatives particularly flourished during the difficult times of the revolution. There were about 20,000 in 1917 and 25,000 in 1918. Kayden and Antsiferov, p. 39, 71, 244, 248, 272 and 356. They were given legal recognition in *Vestnik*, No. 18, 28/3/17, p. 2.

98. Shestakov (I, 1929), p. 126. In the financial assistance which cooperatives gave to soviets at all levels there is no evidence to suggest that they were guided by considerations of a partisan nature. Finance seems to have been given to all groups regardless of political colouration.

99. *See* the views expressed in *Zemlia i Volia*, No. 11, 1/4/17, cited in Shestakov (I, 1929), p. 45-6.

100. Shestakov (II, 1929), p. 13; Sed'maia . . . p. 156; Iakovlev (1967), p. 35; and Khronika (Saratov), p. 76.

101. A report from Samara indicated that most of the inhabitants of a village were nominally SRs but they did not know the party's policy platforms. Iakovlev (1967), p. 221. *See also* Radkey, (1958), p. 234-5.

102. On the state of organisation in the countryside *see* Sed'moi . . . p. 12, and Shestoi . . . p. 41-2. Figures on the distribution of newspapers come from Kravchuk, p. 56.

103. An extensive list of bolshevik organisations is given in Anikeev, p. 132. According to Sverdlov there were only 162 organisations of the party represented at the VI Congress. Of the 63 organisations that completed a questionnaire at the congress, only 15 claimed to carry out any work among the peasants. Shestoi . . . p. 36, 295, and 327-84. According to a party worker in Saratov, new members were coming only from among the workers and soldiers. Lebedev, p. 242.

104. Smirnov, p. 88, and Kravchuk, p. 71.

105. Olonets, Arkhangel, Kostroma, Smolensk, Vladimir, Tver, Novgorod, Pskov, Kaluga, Yaroslav, Riazan and Vitebsk. In October they were joined by representatives from Vilensk, Tula, Voronezh, Viatka, Nizhegorod, Mogilev, Minsk and Penza. Smirnov, p. 105.

CHAPTER 4 THE DÉNOUEMENT

1. The three non-party members were Tereshchenko, Verkhovskii and Verderevskii. Verkhovskii was Commander of the Moscow military district in 1917 and Verderevskii was Commander of the Baltic Fleet.

2. *Vestnik*, No. 147, 6/9/17, p. 2; No. 158, 21/9/17, p. 2; No. 162, 26/9/17, p. 2;.

No. 169, 5/10/17, p. 2; and No. 178, 15/10/17, p. 2.

3. *Vestnik*, No. 168., 4/10/17, p. 1. This was followed ten days later by a call for *volost* committees to stop hindering the collection of grain. *Vestnik*, No. 156, 19/9/17, p. 3–4.

4. *Vestnik*, No. 161, 24/9/17, p. 2. For the previous decision *see* n 18 in Ch. 3.

5. *Vestnik*, No. 182, 20/10/17, p. 1. Prokopovich's speech referred to below is reported in *Vestnik*, No. 179, 17/10/17, p. 3–4.

6. Kazinkin and Sobolev, p. 21.

7. Respectively Bor'ba za zemliu . . . p. 96–7; Chugaev (okt), p. 202–3; and *Vestnik*, No. 184, 22/10/17, p. 1.

8. *Delo Naroda*, No. 183, 18/10/17, p. 4. Lozinskii (1929), p. 164, 174–7. Maslov was in favour of some compensation for private owners whose land was seized, and he was opposed to the principle of free and equal access to the land. Thus he was a long way from the formal PSR programme. However his position did not have complete support within the Ministry of Agriculture; on 20 September his deputy, Assistant Minister of Agriculture Rakitnikov, called on Kerensky to transfer all the land into the hands of the land committees. Ekonomicheskoe polozhenie . . . III, p. 258–9.

9. In the minds of many government ministers the land question was intimately related to that of the war. They feared that if action was taken to resolve the land question by redistributing the land to the peasants, this would encourage mass desertion from the front by soldiers wishing to share in the changes in the villages. This would disrupt the war effort and increase the chaos in the countryside.

10. Chugaev (okt), p. 447.

11. Kotel'nikov and Meller, p. 274.

12. Lutskii, p. 71; Mints (II), p. 840 and 847; and Kotel'nikov and Meller, p. 323 and 334.

13. Kotel'nikov and Meller, p. 323.

14. Volkonskii, p. 239–40.

15. For example, Kotel'nikov and Meller, p. 278, 355 and 356.

16. Kotel'nikov and Meller, p. 261–361; Lositskii, p. 31; Shestakov (10, 1927), p. 94–5; and Ekonomicheskoe polozhenie . . . II, p. 312 and 317.

17. Respectively Kotel'nikov and Meller, p. 263 and 268, 365. *See* Ekonomicheskoe polozhenie . . . II, p. 316–22 for a survey of *gubernii* in which the link between food shortage and violence is clearly shown.

18. Chugaev (okt), p. 430.

19. *Rabochii Put'*, No. 26, 16/9/17 (3/10), p. 2.

20. Kotel'nikov and Meller, p. 175. In May the government had introduced special legislation to deal with drunkenness. *Vestnik*, No. 54, 14/5/17, p. 1.

21. Kotel'nikov and Meller, p. 264.

22. Volkonskii, p. 239–40.

23. Kotel'nikov and Meller, p. 289.

24. Kotel'nikov and Meller, p. 332. The government's ability to deal with rural unrest was probably adversely affected by the Kornilov affair. Not only did Kornilov give the impression of at one minute calling for total obedience to the government and then at the next directly opposing that government, but also with his demise one of the most prominent opponents of arbitrary action in the countryside disappeared.

25. Calculated from figures in Radkey (1950).
26. It does not matter whether these people were actually party-members, 'fellow travellers' or SR opponents trading on the party's name. The important point is that the peasants accepted them as SRs.
27. This view has been prevalent among Soviet scholars since the 1920s, for example, Iakovlev's Introduction to Kotel'nikov and Meller. However it has come under attack in more recent times. *See* Kravchuk, p. 13–14. *See* instances of low level committees retaining an important active role in the autumn in Ekonomicheskoe polozhenie . . . III, p. 227–317.
28. Mart-mai, p. 50. Also see Shestakov (II, 1929), p. 12.
29. According to Pershin (I, 1966), p. 352, only about a quarter of *volost* committees received finance from the government.
30. The resolutions emanating from the meetings of peasant organisations covered a whole range of topics, but four were of major importance. First, the land question. Resolutions usually involved, in one form or another, a demand for peasant control over the land. Many set out the conditions under which land was to be worked: rental rates, the use of equipment and livestock, access to timber and pasture, and the use of hired labour. Second, the grain monopoly, with the vast majority of resolutions opposing that policy. Third, politicial forms in the country. At the local level, resolutions usually involved a call for the abolition of the old structure and its replacement by popularly-elected local self-government. At the national level, many called for the convocation of the Constituent Assembly in order to bring about an early solution to the land question. Calls for a democratic republic also were common. Fourth, peasant resolutions often made reference to the war, with a negative attitude to it appearing to be particularly prominent late in the year. In addition to these major categories, there were also numerous individual demands related specifically to local conditions. Such resolutions are reproduced in many places, for example, the series of volumes edited by Chugaev and Gaponenko.
31. For some examples of *guberniia* bodies out of step with the mood in the villages, see *Delo Naroda*, No. 49, 14/5/17, p. 3; No. 52, 18/5/17, p. 3; No. 64, 2/6/17, p. 3; No. 80, 21/6/17, p. 3.
32. Vermenichev, p. 177. Kravchuk, p. 109, cites figures for the Great Russian *gubernii*: against private land-owners 84.4 per cent, *kulaks* (including separators) 6.3 per cent, authorities 4.1 per cent, priesthood 3.0 per cent, and others 2.2 per cent. In some areas private land-owners' land was not seized until 1918. For example, Iakovlev (1967), p. 209.
33. Gaponenko (1958), p. 610.
34. Gaponenko (1958), p. 582.
35. This traditional principle was also the reason that many land-owners were left, at least early in the year, with what the peasants considered to be enough land to support themselves through their own efforts.
36. Respectively Mart-Mai, p. 46, and Chugaev (okt), p. 450.
37. In the short term land was sometimes divided among those who had little land, the newly-seized estate thus being used to equalise (according to the traditional formula) land-holding in the village. On other occasions the peasants might instal a temporary management on the estate until redistribution. Formally this took place between 1918 and 1920. Methods

differed over the inclusion of peasant allotment land in the redistribution, the division only of non-peasant land for addition to current holdings, or the cutting off of strips to gain parity between rich and poor. Shanin., p. 150–1.

38. Gaponenko (1958), p. 622.

39. *See O zemle*, p. 70ff and 225, and Pershin (1922), p. 39–43.

40. Respectively Carr (1963), p. 87, and Rezunov, p. 6–7.

41. The following tables are in complete form in Appendix IV. A list of the *gubernii* comprising each region is in Appendix I.

42. These figures are in Appendix V. Gaponenko and Kabuzan discuss one aspect of the reliability of the source of these figures.

43. Compare the figures in Appendices IV and V from which the above two tables have been drawn. The two *gubernii* varying most from the pattern outlined in the text, Vologda and Arkhangel, both had very small populations. Oganovskii and Chaianov, p. 6–7.

44. Shestakov (7, 1927), p. 97.

45. Male, p. 38. Of the major agricultural areas of the south, the central black earth region had the fewest households enclosed under the Stolypin legislation. In this area enclosures were completely destroyed in 1917.

46. The impact of food shortages in the northern part of the country may not have been as considerable as one may at first imagine. The peasants of this region were far more accustomed to grain shortages than those in the south, and therefore although their plight in 1917 may have been more difficult than in the immediate past, it was not wholly unexpected. In addition, much unrest may have been siphoned off into the towns and cities where expeditions were sent in search of grain. For an example of this, *see* Prodovol'stvennoe Polozhenie . . . p. 129.

47. All parts of these *gubernii* did not suffer from food shortages. Some areas had sufficient for their own needs but they either did not have a surplus to send to their deficient neighbours or they refused to give it up. Some parts of Saratov, Samara, Penza and Simbirsk could also fall back on stocks from previous years. In Riazan the harvest was said to be between three and five times worse than in 1916. Agrarnoe dvizhenie . . . p. 187. Lositskii, p. 31–5, discusses the level of needs in relation to supplies. Many peasant producers experienced shortages as a result of traditional marketing methods. Many of the poorer peasants would appear on the market in the autumn as sellers of grain, but the pressure of their need for capital to buy what they needed to see them through the winter caused them to oversell, with the result that they reappeared on the market in the spring as buyers of grain. Many more enterprising peasants sought to profit from their grain by planting wheat, for which there was a booming commercial market, instead of the staple rye. They would sell their wheat crop when it was harvested and use part of the proceeds to buy the rye they needed in order to live. When the grain market dried up in 1917, they were left without the grain they needed.

48. Lositskii, p. 12–13, gives details by crop and *guberniia*.

49. Of the sixteen *gubernii*, only Astrakhan, Nizhegorod, Mogilev and Minsk were characterised by grain deficits between 1909 and 1913, and the deficits in the last two were so small that they could be classified as self-sufficient. Antisiferov, p. 97–8, gives the following list of *gubernii* characterised by deficiencies of grain

and potatoes in the 1909–13 period. *Deficiencies*: Moscow, St. Petersburg, Arkhangel, Vladimir, Tver, Olonets, Kostroma, Astrakhan, Lifland, Kaluga, Novgorod, Nizhegorod, Yaroslav, Smolensk, Vologda, Vitebsk, Pskov, Perm, Vilensk, Grodno, Mogilev and Minsk. *Surpluses*: Taurida, Kuban, Kherson, Don Oblast', Samara, Ekaterinoslav, Bessarabia, Saratov, Tambov, Ufa, Poltava, Tula, Voronezh, Orenburg, Penza, Simbirsk, Kursk, Kharkov, Kazan, Kiev, Podolsk, Riazan, Orel, Estland, Viatka, Kurland, Volynsk, Kovno and Chernigov. This list clearly shows the pattern of the Russian grain market: a consuming north and a producing south.

50. The role of crop failure in promoting increased destruction in the Central Agricultural region is evident in the increased share of regional unrest provided by destructive activities in the late summer and autumn when the crop failure became manifest: July 4.1 per cent August 10.5 per cent, September 44.2 per cent and October 50.0 per cent. When these figures are compared with those for European Russia as a whole, the steepness of the regional rise is even clearer: July 4.3 per cent, August 10.0 per cent, September 19.7 per cent and October 23.4 per cent. Figures are calculated from the militia reports in Kotel'nikov and Meller.

51. A similar part was played by agitators from the cities in many particular instances of unrest, but because of the lack of any accurate information on the areas most visited by these agitators it is impossible to reach any firm conclusions on the part they played in determining the geographical distribution of unrest. However it is clear that the most restive *gubernii* fall into no discernible pattern of geographical relationship to major urban centres nor do they share a similar level of urbanisation. Figures for urbanisation will be found in Oganovskii and Chaianov, p. 6–7.

52. For information on the Tambov events *see* Lutskii, and Mints (II), p. 845–6. For contemporary reports *see Delo Naroda*, No. 155, 15/9/17, p. 4; No. 157, 17/9/17, p. 3; and Kotel'nikov and Meller, p. 268.

53. Respectively Kotel'nikov and Meller, p. 245, and Iakovlev (1967). p. 57.

54. *See* Appendix III. Compare with Keep (1976), Ch. 15. There are insufficient entries in the Militia reports to enable an accurate profile of the patterns of rural unrest in the Baltic and Northern regions to be compiled.

CHAPTER 5 CITY AND COUNTRYSIDE IN REVOLUTION

1. The army also remained unresponsive. *See* an analysis of the mood in the army in Ferro (1971).

2. It is this traditional aspect that is more important than any notion of class conflict within the villages in explaining rural unrest. A recent study has produced substantial, although not conclusive, evidence to show that although economic differences existed within the villages, by 1917 these had not hardened into firm class divisions. Certainly there was a general levelling within the villages, but this is better seen in terms of traditional perceptions of land-holding and of community than of sharp class antagonisms. *See* Shanin.

3. This concept of political consciousness is based on the typologies of political

culture outlined in Almond and Verba, p. 16–18. Highly-developed political consciousness is characterised by recognition of the political system as a whole, awareness of the political and administrative structures and processes involved in both policy-making and implementation, and a conception of oneself as an actor in the process.

4. The Provisional Government was created by members of the Temporary Committee of the State Duma, a body having no standing in imperial constitutional law. An attempt was made to give some sense of legitimacy to the new body in Mikhail's rejection of the throne. Browder and Kerensky, p. 116; Nol'de, p. 145.

5. This is discussed by Haimson. Quoting Ministry of Trade and Industry figures, he asserts (1964, p. 627) that the number of strikes increased as follows:

1910	222	1913	2404
1911	466	1914	3534
1912	2032		

6. Precise figures are impossible to obtain. Avrich, p. 163, cites a figure of about 400,000, while Stepanov, p. 26, claims greater precision in citing a figure of 417,000. Pethybridge (1972), p. 183.

7. Respectively Tsentral'noe . . . statisticheskii . . . p. 170. and Lositskii, p. 31.

8. *Revoliutsiia 1917 goda* . . . T. 1, p. 87.

9. *Vestnik*, No. 10, 16/3/17, p. 3.

10. *Torgovo* . . . No. 94, 6/5/17, p. 3. The decline in delivery was due in part to peasant opposition to the grain monopoly, although seasonal factors were probably more important at this stage; the onset of spring sowing, the flooding of the transportation routes, and the effect of Easter holidays all played a part. Peshekhonov's speech is reported in Browder and Kerensky, p. 633–6.

11. *Ekonomicheskoe polozhenie* . . . II, p. 241 and 245.

12. The details on food supply come from the following sources: *Vestnick*, No. 96, 5/7/17, p. 2 and No. 179, 17/10/17, p. 3; Volobuev, p. 465; Stepanov, p. 66; *Ekonomicheskoe polozhenie* . . . II, pp. 309–10 and 651. According to *Rabochii Put'*, No. 39, 31/10/17 (18/10), p. 2, in ten days in October only 40–50 wagons were received in the capital instead of the necessary 400. On 4 October a report declared that there was no oats, buckwheat or hay in Petrograd food shops. *Ekonomicheskoe polozhenie* . . . II, p. 286–7.

13. Lositskii, p. 15. *Ekonomicheskoe polozhenie* . . . III, p. 158–61, gives the following figures: 1909–13 4217M, 1916 3791M, 1917 3657M. Figures also have been cited by Keep (1976), p. 183, 478 and 500.

14. Volobuev, p. 386. According to Lositskii, p. 35, the corrected (for local peculiarities) surplus was 559.4M *pudi*.

15. Lositskii, p. 15, and Volobuev, p. 387. According to Lositskii, p. 36, the surplus produced in European Russia as a whole amounted to 360.5M *pudi*. However if production in the New Russia and Little Russia and the Southwest regions is subtracted, this becomes a deficit of 190.5M *pudi*. Figures for production by *guberniia* are reproduced in Lositskii, p. 80–1, and *Ekonomicheskoe polozhenie* . . . III, p. 158–60 and 451–6.

16. *See* the report by Brigadier-General Sir Alfred Knox despatched in August. Golovine, p. 173–4.

17. The figures for numbers of rolling stock in operation normally cited are as follows:

	Locomotives	Wagons
1913	18,662	378,977
1915	20,731	575,611
1916	16,837	463,419
1917	9,201	174,346

Tsentral'noe . . . statisticheskii . . . p. 143–8. However as the figures cited in the text indicate, these totals for 1917 appear to be considerably lower than actually was the case, at least prior to October.

18. The figures in this paragraph come from Volobuev, p. 206–7; Ekonomicheskoe polozhenie . . . II, p. 242, 246, 252, 259, 260 and 264; and Lozinskii, p. 11.

19. Ekonomicheskoe polozhenie . . . II, p. 266, and Volobuev, p. 293. Lozinskii (1929), p. 12, paints an even worse picture, citing the following figures for declining railway coal reserves (in thousands of *pudi*):

April	23,036	August	20,508
May	25,512	September	20,072
June	24,638	October	18,079
July	23,657		

20. Ekonomicheskoe polozhenie . . . II, p. 267.

21. Ekonomicheskoe polozhenie . . . II, p. 249. For a general discussion of the railwaymen *see* Pethybridge (1972), Ch. 1.

22. Volobuev, p. 210 and 213; Lozinskii (1929), p. 11; and Ekonomicheskoe polozhenie . . . II, p. 256.

23. Volobuev, p. 442–3.

24. The peasants' attitude to the towns was hostile not only because they felt it was the urban-based government which was imposing hardship on them, but also because they believed they were being asked to make major sacrifices for the war and the revolution while the town-dwellers sacrificed nothing. Furthermore by sending grain to the front, they were ensuring that their sons and loved ones called away to the war were provided for. Gaponenko (1958), p. 581; *Vestnik*, No. 61, 24/5/17, p. 3.

25. Lozinskii (1929), p. 13, and Stepanov, p. 113. According to an official report, coal deliveries were down 50 per cent on the previous year. Ekonomicheskoe polozhenie . . . II, p. 245.

26. Volobuev, p. 294–5. For some figures for individual factories *see* Ekonomicheskoe polozhnie . . . II, p. 245.

27. Volobuev, p. 289.

28. In addition to the decline in the output of coal, the production of oil also fell by 14 per cent, compared with 1916. Volobuev, p. 290. The reasons for the decline in coal production are numerous: shortages of supplies and equipment and labour unrest caused by the revolutionary sentiments of the miners were important in this. Labour productivity fell by 28 per cent, compared with 1916. On the situation in the Donbass *see* Ekonomicheskoe polozhenie . . . II, p. 305–8.

29. For example, *Vestnik*, No. 25, 7/4/17, p. 3. For the situation in Moscow *see* Prodovol'stvennoe polozhenie . . . In some instances popular organs took over production facilities to bake bread for the populace, thereby short-circuiting the official distribution system. Wade, p. 231.

30. Struve, p. 269–78. These figures can be accepted only with caution because no source is cited for them nor is their method of calculation specified.

31. Stepanov, p. 57.

32. Lozinskii (1927), p. 148. Stepanov, p. 54–55, argues that real wages were only 14–15 per cent of nominal wages in late 1917.

33. Lozinskii (1927), p. 155, and Stepanov, p. 54–5.

34. Price rises were not restricted to food but affected all the goods and services which the workers of the capital required. All of the main requirements of the urban-dwellers, including clothing, rented accommodation and transport, rose steeply during 1917. Keep (1976), p. 73, cites figures that prices in Petrograd rose by 48 per cent between February and June. Stepanov, p. 59–60. Even government tax rates rose, Volobuev, p. 336.

35. Volobuev, p. 434.

36. Volobuev, p. 459–60, and Stepanov p. 57.

37. Browder and Kerensky, p. 639 and *Pravda*, No. 78, 23/6/17 (10/6), p. 2, for examples. Profits actually appear to have declined in 1917. In terms of gross output the profits of 345 enterprises surveyed amounted to 9.52 per cent in 1917, compared with 17.58 per cent in 1916. Volobuev, p. 281.

38. *Vestnik*, No. 17, 25/3/17, p. 4, and No. 41, 27/4/17, p. 3.

39. *Vestnik*, No. 45, 2/5/17, p. 1–2; No. 91, 28/6/17, p. 2; and No. 163, 28/9/17, p. 2. Rationing was introduced on a whole range of other food items as well as grain. Volobuev, p. 461.

40. Stepanov, p. 57. Ekonomicheskoe polozhenie . . . II, p. 310.

41. Volobuev, p. 462.

42. Stepanov, p. 56. *Delo Naroda*, No. 101, 15/7/17, p. 2; No. 111, 27/7/17, p. 1, for examples of price rises.

43. The government's attempts to solve the food crisis confronting the capital were not restricted to attempts to regulate supply and consumption in the city. An office was established to coordinate all efforts at the relief of the situation in the city, entry to Petrograd was restricted, attempts were made to improve the distribution network in the capital, and the evacuation of the city was planned. The proposed evacuation also was motivated by fears of a possible German offensive against Petrograd and by a desire to remove disruptive elements from the city. *Vestnik*, No. 143, 1/9/17, p. 1; No. 145, 3/9/17, p. 3; No. 147, 6/9/17; p. 2; and No. 154, 16/9/17, p. 3.

44. Volobuev, p. 289, 292, 293, 295 and 296.

45. *Rabochii Put'*, No. 31, 21/10/17 (8/10), p. 2, and Lozinskii (1929), p. 20. Also Volobuev, p. 295. Stone, p. 201, cites substantially smaller figures: 541 factories involving 37,816 workers closed while 264 factories affecting 21,516 workers opened throughout Russia during 1917.

46. Stepanov, p. 144. According to one report 63 factories involving 4522 workers closed in Petrograd between March and July. Ekonomicheskoe polozhenie . . . II, p. 46.

47. Lozinskii (1929), p. 20, has argued that in the pre-August period most enterprises to close down were in the textile industry, but in August and

September most of the those closing their doors were in metal-working, and it was among these workers that the most ardent bolshevik supporters were to be found.

48. Volobuev, p. 295.
49. *Torgovo* . . . No. 191, 3/9/17, p. 2.
50. For an analysis of these expectations early in the year *see* Ferro (1967), p. 170–84 and Ferro (1969).
51. The move to the left in the popular mood in the capital is not in dispute. It is clear from the vastly improved position enjoyed by the bolsheviks late in the year in those organisations elected directly by the people, the local *dumy*, the soviets, and the factory committees, and by the swelling of bolshevik party membership between the two revolutions. For studies of these *see* Rosenberg (1969), Wade, Avrich, and Rigby, p. 59–63. There may be a closer link between the government decision to double the grain price on 27 August and the achievement of a bolshevik majority in the Petrograd Soviet on 31 August and reaffirmed on 9 September, than has previously been recognised.

Bibliography

I. BOOKS AND ARTICLES

Abramov, P. N., 'Sovetskoe stroitel'stvo na sele v dokombedovskii period (okt. 1917–iiul' 1918g),' *Voprosy Istorii KPSS*, No. 6, (1960).

Agrarnoe dvizhenie v 1917 godu po dokumentam glavnogo zemel'nogo komiteta. *Krasnyi Arkhiv*, T. 14 (1926).

Akademiia Nauk SSSR; *Materialy i issledovaniia po etnografii russkogo naseleniia evropeiskoi chasti SSSR* (Moscow, 1960).

Alavi, H., 'Peasants and Revolution', *Socialist Register* (1965).

Alaev, L. B., 'Problema sel'skoi obshchiny v klassovykh obshchestvakh,' *Voprosy Istorii*, No. 2 (1977).

Almond, G. A. and Verba, S., *'The Civic Culture'* (Boston, 1965).

Andreev, A. M., 'Bor'ba sovetov s kontrrevoliutsiei nakanune velikogo oktiabria', *Voprosy Istorii*, No. 10 (1976).

Anikeev, V. V., 'Svedeniia o bol'shevistskikh organizatsiiakh s marta po dekabr' 1917 goda,' *Voprosy Istorii KPSS*, Nos. 2–3 (1958).

Antonov-Saratovskii, V., 'Oktiabr'skie dni v Saratove,' *Proletarskaia Revoliutsiia*, No. 10 (1922).

Antonov-Saratovskii, V., 'Saratov s fevralia po oktiabr' 1917g' (Iz lichnykh vospominanii), *Proletarskaia Revoliutsiia*, Nos. 2 (25) and 4 (27) (1924).

Antsiferov, A. N., Bilimovich, A. D., Batshev, M. D. and Ivantsov, D. N., *Russian Agriculture During the War* (New Haven, 1930).

Anweiler, O., The Political Ideology of the Leaders of the Petrograd Soviet in the Spring of 1917.' Pipes, R. (ed.).

Revolutionary Russia: A symposium (New York, 1969).

Anweiler, O., *Les Soviets en Russie 1905–1921* (Paris, 1972).

Aprel'skie dni 1917 goda v Petrograde, *Krasnyi Arkhiv*, T. 33 (1929).

Atkinson, D., 'The Statistics on the Russian Land Commune, 1905–1917,' *Slavic Review*, XXXII (1973).

Augustine, W. R., 'Russia's Railwaymen, July–October 1917,' *Slavic Review*, XXIV (1965).

Avrich, P. H., 'Russian Factory Committees in 1917', *Jahrbücher für Geschichte Osteuropas*, XI (1963).

Baevskii, D., 'Iz istorii stroitel'stva bol'shevistskoi partii (okt. 1917 – mart 1919g),' *Istorik Marksist*, No. 2 (1941).

'Baltiiskii flot nakanune Oktiabria (Iz dnevnika I. I. Rengartena)', *Krasnyi Arkhiv*, T. 35 (1929).

Beqiraj, M., *Peasantry in Revolution* (Ithaca, 1966).

Black. C., *The Transformation of Russian Society* (Cambridge (Mass.), 1960).

'Bol'shevizatsiia fronta v pred'iiul'skie dni 1917g,' *Krasnyi Arkhiv*. T. 58 (1933).

'Bor'ba za zemliu v 1917g (po Kazanskoi gub.)', *Krasnyi Arkhiv*, T. 78 (1936).

Bosh, E., 'Oktiabr'skie dni v Kievskoi oblasti', *Proletarskaia Revoliutsiia*, No. 11 (23) (1923).

Browder, R. P., and Kerensky, A. F., *The Russian Provisional Government 1917: Documents*. 3 vols. (Stanford, 1961).

Burov', Ia., *Organizuite derevniu!* (Petrograd, 1918).

Butenko, A. F., and Chugaev, D. A., *Vtoroi Vserossiiskii s'ezd sovetov rabochikh i soldatskikh deputatov: sbornik dokumentov* (Moscow, 1957).

Carr, E. H., 'The Russian Revolution and the Peasant', *Proceedings of the British Academy*, XLIX (1963).

Carr, E. H., '*The Bolshevik Revolution, 1917–1923*', Vol. 1 (London, 1965 (1950)).

Chamberlin, W. H., 'The Russian Revolution, 1917–1921.' Vol. 1 (New York, 1935).

Chernov, V., *Proletariat', trudovoe krest'ianstvo i revoliutsiia* (Petrograd, 1917).

Chernov, V., *The Great Russian Revolution* trans. P. E. Mosely (New Haven, 1936).

Chugaev, D. A., *et al.* (eds.), *Revoliutsionnoe dvizhenie v Rossii v mae-iiune 1917g. Iiun'skaia demonstratsiia. Dokumenty i Materialy* (Moscow, 1959).

Chugaev, D. A., *et al.* (eds.), *Revoliutsionnoe dvizhenie v. Rossii v iiule 1917g. Iiul'skii krizis. Dokumenty i Materialy* (Moscow, 1959).

Chugaev, D. A., *et al.* (eds.), *Revoliutsionnoe dvizhenie v Rossii v avguste 1917g. Razgrom kornilovskogo miatezha. Dokumenty i Materialy* (Moscow, 1959).

Chugaev, D. A., *et al.* (eds.), *Revoliutsionnoe dvizhenie v Rossii v sentiabre*

1917g. Obshchenatsional'nyi krizis. Dokumenty i Materialy. (Moscow, 1961).

Chugaev, D. A., *et al.* (eds.), *Revoliutsionnoe dvizhenie v Rossii nakanune oktiabr'skogo vooruzhennogo vosstaniia 1–24 okt. 1917g. Dokumenty i Materialy* (Moscow, 1962).

Daniels, R. V., *Red October. The Bolshevik Revolution of 1917* (New York, 1967).

'Diplomatiia Vremennogo Pravitel'stva v bor'be s revoliutsiei', *Krasnyi Arkhiv*, T. 20 (1927).

Dmitriev, I., 'Oktiabr' v Orshe, *Proletarskaia Revoliutsiia*, No. 10 (1922).

Drabkina, F. I., 'Vserossiiskoe soveshchanie bol'shevikov v marte 1917 goda,' *Voprosy Istorii*, No. 9 (1956).

Dubrovskii, S., 'Krest'ianskoe dvizhenie v 1905g', *Krasnyi Arkhiv*, No. 9 (1925).

Dubrovskii, S. M., 'Vremennoe pravitel'stvo i krest'ianstvo.' Miliutin, V.P. (ed.), *Agrarnaia revoliutsiia v chetyrekh tomakh. T. 2. Krest'ianskoe dvizhenie v 1917 godu* (Moscow, 1928)

Dubrovskii, S. M., 'K voprosu ob urovne razvitiia kapitalizma v sel'skom khoziaistvo Rossii i kharaktere klassovoi bor'by v derevne v period imperializma (dve sotsial'nye voiny),' Dubrovskii, S. M. (ed.), *Osobennosti agrarnogo stroia Rossii v period imperializma* (Moscow, 1962).

Dubrovskii, S. M., *Stolypinskaia reforma* (Moscow, 1963 (1925)).

Ekonomicheskoe polozhenie rossii nakanune velikoi oktiabr'skoi sotsialisticheskoi revoliutsii, 3 parts (Moscow, 1957).

El'tsin, B., 'Dni oktiabr'skogo perevorota na Iuzhnom Urale i v Ufe', *Proletarskaia Revoliutsiia*, No. 10 (1922).

Evgrafov, V. E., 'Nekotorye voprosy taktiki partii v marte-nachale aprelia 1917 goda', *Voprosy Istorii KPSS*, No. 3 (1962).

Ezhegodnik Rossii. T. 3–4. 1905–6 (St. Petersburg, 1906–7).

Favstov, G. A., 'Iz istorii krest'ianskogo khoziaistva srednechernozemnogo raiona Rossii v poreformennyi period,' *Voprosy Istorii*, No. 8 (1958).

Ferro M., *'La Révolution de 1917. La chute du tsarisme et les origines d'Octobre* (Paris, 1967).

Ferro, M., 'The Aspirations of Russian Society,' Pipes, R. (ed.), *Revolutionary Russia: A symposium.* (New York, 1969).

Ferro, M., 'The Russian Soldier in 1917: Undisciplined, Patriotic, and Revolutionary.' *Slavic Review*, XXX, 3 (1971).

Ferro, M., '1917: La Révolution au village,' *Cahiers du Monde Russe et*

Sovietique, Nos. 1–2, Jan.–June (1973).

'Fevral' skaia revoliutsiia 1917 goda', *Krasnyi Arkhiv*, T. 21–22 (1927).

Fleer, M. V., 'Chernov i iiul'skii dni', *Krasnyi Arkhiv*, T. 5 (1924).

Florinsky, M. T., *The End of the Russian Empire* (New Haven, 1931).

Gaponenko, L. S., *et al.* (eds.), *Revoliutsionnoe dvizhenie v Rossii posle sverzheniia samoderzhaviia. Dokumenty i Materialy* (Moscow, 1957).

Gaponenko, L. S., *et al.* (eds.), *Revoliutsionnoe dvizhenie v Rossii v Aprele 1917g. Aprel'skii krizis. Dokumenty i Materialy*, (Moscow, 1958).

Gaponenko, L. S., and Kabuzan, V. M., 'Materialy sel'sko-khoziaistvennykh perepisei 1916–1917gg. Kak istochnik opredeleniia chislennosti naseleniia Rossii nakanune oktiabr'skoi revoliutsii.' *Istoriia SSSR*, No. 6 (1961).

Gately, M. O., Moote, A., and Wills, J. E., Jr, 'Seventeenth-Century Peasant "Furies": Some Problems of Comparative History,' *Past and Present*, No. 52, May (1971).

Geyer, D., 'The Bolshevik Insurrection in Petrograd,' Pipes, R. (ed.). *Revolutionary Russia: A symposium* (New York, 1969).

Gill, G. J., 'The Failure of Rural Policy in Russia, February–October 1917', *Slavic Review* (June 1978).

Gill, G. J., 'The Mainsprings of Peasant Action in 1917, *Soviet Studies* XXX, 1 (Jan 1978).

Gill, G. J., 'The Role of the Countryside in an Urban Revolution. A Short Note.' *Sbornik*, 2 (1976).

Golder, F. A. (ed.), *Documents of Russian History 1914–1917* (Gloucester (Mass.), 1964).

Golovine, N. N., *The Russian Army in the World War* (New Haven, 1931).

Gorbatiuk, V. T., and Ionkina, T. D., Razvitie kapitalizma v zemledelii i razlozhenie krest'ianstva na ukraine vo vtoroi polovine XIX veka, *Voprosy Istorii*, No. 9 (1956).

Gronsky, P. O., and Astrov, N. J., *The War and the Russian Government* (New Haven, 1929).

Grunt, Ian, 'Oktiabr' v Kolomne', *Proletarskaia Revoliutsiia*, No. 10 (1922).

Gusev, K. V., *Partiia Eserov: ot melko-burzhuaznogo revoliutsionarizma k kontrrevoliutsii* (Moscow, 1975).

Haimson, L., 'The Problem of Social Stability in Urban Russia, 1905–1917', *Slavic Review*, XXIII–XXIV (1964–1965).

Hasegawa, T., 'The Formation of the Militia in the February

Revolution: An Aspect of the Origins of Dual Power,' *Slavic Review*, XXXII (1973).

Iakovlev, Ia. A., 'Krest'ianskaia voina 1917·goda,' Miliutin, V. P. (ed.), *Agrarnaia revoliutsiia v chetyrekh tomakh. T. 2. Krest'ianskoe dvizhenie v 1917 godu* (Moscow, 1928).

Iakovlev, Ia. A. (ed.), *1917 god v derevne (vospominaniia krest'ian)* (Moscow, 1967 (1929)).

'Iiul'skii dni 1917g,' *Krasnyi Arkhiv*, T. 57 (1933).

'Iiul'skie dni v Petrograde,' *Krasnyi Arkhiv*, T. 23–24 (1927).

Il'ina, M. S., 'Demonstratsiia i miting na marsovom pole v Petrograde 4 iiunia 1917 goda,' *Voprosy Istorii*, No. 6 (1957).

'Iz dnevnika gen. V. G. Boldyreva,' *Krasnyi Arkhiv*, T. 23 (1927). *Iz dnevnika generala M. V. Alekseeva* (Prague, 1929).

'Iz ofitserskikh pisem c fronta v 1917g,' *Krasnyi Arkhiv*, T. 50–51 (1932).

'K istorii bor'by krest'ianstva Pravo-berezhnoi Ukrainy protiv Tsentral'noi rady i Vremennogo pravitel'stva v 1917g,' *Krasnyi Arkhiv*, T. 105 (1941).

'K istorii oktiabr'skikh dnei v petrograde (Iz materialov Petrogradskogo Voenno-revoliutsionnogo komiteta),' *Krasnyi Arkhiv*, T. 53 (1932).

Katkov, G., *Russia 1917. The February Revolution* (London, 1967).

Kayden, E. M., and Antsiferov, A. N., *The Cooperative Movement in Russia During the War* (New Haven, 1929).

Kazinkin, I. Ia., and Sobolev, P. N., 'Bor'ba krest'ian za zemliu nakanune oktiabr'skoi revoliutsii,' *Voprosy Istorii*, No. 6 (1957).

Keep, J., 'October in the Provinces,' Pipes, R. (ed.), *Revolutionary Russia: A symposium* (New York, 1969).

Keep, J. L. H., *The Russian Revolution. A Study in Mass Mobilization* (London, 1976).

Kerensky, A., *The Kerensky Memoirs. Russia and History's Turning Point* (London, 1965).

Khriashcheva, A., *Krest'ianstvo v voine i revoliutsii* (Moscow, 1921). *Khronika revoliutsionnykh sobytii v Saratovskom Povolzh'e 1917–1918gg* (Saratov, 1968).

Kibardin, M. A., Shishkin, A. A., and Medvedev, E. I., *Oktiabr' v derevne (Na materialakh Srednego Povolzh'ia)* (Kazan, 1967).

Kir'ianov, Iu. I., 'Krest'ianstvo stepnoi ukrainy v gody pervoi mirovoi voiny (1914–1916gg)', Dubrovskii, S. M. (ed.), *Osobennosti agrarnogo stroia Rossii v period imperializma* (Moscow, 1962).

Klepikov, S., *Sel'skoe khoziaistvo Rossii v tsifrakh. Atlas diagramm i kartogramm* (Moscow, 1924).

Kochan, L., 'Kadet Policy in 1917 and the Constituent Assembly,' *Slavonic and East European Review*, 45 (1967).

Kochan, L., *Russia in Revolution* (London, 1970).

Kohn, S., and Meyendorff, A. F., *The Cost of the War to Russia* (New Haven, 1932).

Kotel'nikov, K. G., and Meller, V. A. (eds.), *Krest'ianskoe dvizhenie v 1917 godu*. (Moscow, 1927).

Krasnov, V., 'Iz' vospominanii o 1917–1920gg,' *Arkhiv' russkoi revoliutsii*, VIII (1923).

Kravchuk, N. A., *Massovoe krest'ianskoe dvizhenie v Rossii nakanune oktiabria* (Moscow, 1971).

Kritsman, L., *Materialy po istorii agrarnoi revoliutsii v Rossii* T. 1–2 (Moscow, 1928–29).

Kuznetsov, I. D., 'Agrarnyi vopros v chuvashii nakanune oktiabria,' Dubrovskii, S. M. (ed.), *Osobennosti agrarnogo stroia Rossii v period imperializma* (Moscow, 1962).

Landsberger, H. A., *The Role of Peasant Movements and Revolts in Development: An Analytical Framework* (New York, 1968).

Lebedev, N., 'Fevral'–oktiabr' v Saratove (Vospominaniia),' *Proletarskaia Revoliutsiia*, No. 10 (1922).

Leiberov, K. P., and Shkataran, O. I., 'K voprosu o sostave petrogradskikh promyshlennikh rabochikh v 1917g,' *Voprosy Istorii*, 1 (1967).

Lelevich, G., 'Iz istorii krest'ianskogo dvizheniia v Mogilevskoi gubernii nakanune oktiabr'skoi revoliutsii,' *Proletarskaia Revoliutsiia*, No. 11 (1922).

Lenin, V. I., *Polnoe Sobranie Sochineniia* (Moscow, 1962).

Liashchenko, P. I., 'Ekonomicheskie predposylki 1917g,' Miliutin, V. P. (ed.), *Agrarnaia revoliutsiia v chetyrekh tomakh. T. 2. Krest'ianskoe dvizhenie v 1917 godu* (Moscow, 1928).

Liashchenko, P. I., *History of the National Economy of Russia to the 1917 Revolution* (New York, 1949).

Liebman, M., *The Russian Revolution* (New York, 1970).

Lositskii, A. E., *Urozhai khlebov' v' Rossi v' 1917 godu* (Moscow, 1918).

Lozinskii, Z., *Vremennoe pravitel'stvo v "bor'be" s promyshlennoi razrukhoi*, *Proletarskaia Revoliutsiia*, No. 10 (69) (1927).

Lozinskii, Z., *Ekonomicheskaia politika vremennogo pravitel'stva* (Leningrad, 1929).

Lutskii, E. A., 'Krest'ianskoe vosstanie v Tambovskoi gubernii v sentiabre 1917g,' *Istoricheskie zapiski*, T. 2 (1938).

Makarov', N., *Krest'ianskoe khoziaistvo i ego interesy* (Moscow, 1917).

Male, D. J., *Russian Peasant Organization Before Collectivization* (Cambridge, 1971).

'Mart-Mai 1917g' *Krasnyi Arkhiv*, T. 15 (1926).

Mavrodin, V. V., Kadgon, I. Z., Sergeeva, N. I., and Rzhanikova, T. P., 'Ob osobennostiakh krest'ianskikh voin v Rossii,' *Voprosy Istorii*, No. 2 (1956).

Maynard, J., *The Russian Peasant and Other Studies* (London, 1943).

Meijer, J. M., 'Town and Country in the Civil War,' Pipes, R. (ed.), *Revolutionary Russia: A symposium* (New York, 1969).

Meller, V. A., and Pankratova, A. M. (eds.), *Rabochee dvizhenie v 1917 godu*. (Moscow, 1926).

Mel'gunov, S., *Kak bol'sheviki zakhvatili vlast': Oktiabr'skii perevorot 1917 goda* (Paris, 1953).

Mel'gunov, S. P., *Vospominaniia i dnevniki*, Vyp. I–II (Paris, 1964).

Mett, I., *Le Paysan Russe dans la révolution et la post-révolution* (Paris, N. D).

Miliukov, P. N., *Istoriia vtoroi russkoi revoliutsii*, T. I. (Sofia, 1921).

Miliutin, V. P., 'Predposylki oktiabr'skoi revoliutsii 1917 goda,' Miliutin, V. P. (ed.), *Agrarnaia revoliutsiia v chetyrekh tomakh. T. 2. Krest'ianskoe dvizhenie v 1917 godu* (Moscow, 1928).

Mints, I. I. (ed.), *Robochii klass i rabochie dvizhenie v Rossii v 1917g* (Moscow, 1964).

Mints, I. I., *Istoriia velikogo oktiabria*, 3 vols. (Moscow, 1968).

Moiseeva, O. I., *Sovety krest'ianskikh deputatov v 1917 godu* (Moscow, 1967).

Monkevitz, N., *La Décomposition de l'armée russe* (Paris, 1919).

Moore Jnr., Barrington, *Social Origins of Dictatorship and Democracy* (London, 1967).

Nabokov. V. D., Vremennoe pravitel'stvo, *Arkhiv' russkoi revoliutsii*, I (1922).

Narkiewicz, O. A., *The Making of the Soviet State Apparatus* (Manchester, 1970).

Nol'de, B. E., *Dalekoe i Blizkoe. Istoricheskie Ocherki* (Paris, 1930).

O zemle, T. I. (Moscow, 1921).

Oganovskii, N. P., and Chaianov, A. V., *Statisticheskii spravochnik' po agrarnomy voprosu* (Moscow, 1917).

'Oktiabr' na fronte,' *Krasnyi Arkhiv*, T. 23–24 (1927).

'Oktiabr'skaia revoliutsiia v baltiiskom flote (Iz dnevnika I. I. Rengartena), *Krasnyi Arkhiv*, T. 25 (1927).

Orlov, N. A., *Prodovol'stevennoe delo v Rossii vo vremia voiny i revoliutsii* (Moscow, 1919).

Osipov, V. A., Gokhlerner, V. M., and Ovrutskaia, S. Sh (eds.), *Istoriia saratovskogo kraia. 1590–1917'* (Saratov, 1964).

Owen, L. A., The Russian Agrarian Revolution of 1917, *Slavonic and East European Review*, 12 (1933).

Owen, L. A., *The Russian Peasant Movement 1906–1917* (New York, 1963 (1937)).

Pares, Sir B., *Russia: Between Reform and Revolution* (New York, 1966 (1907)).

Pavlovsky, G., *Agricultural Russia on the Eve of Revolution* (London, 1930).

Pechat' v dni kerenshchiny, *Krasnyi Arkhiv*, T. 58 (1933).

Pershin, P. N., *Uchastkovoe zemlepol'zovanie v rossii* (Moscow, 1922).

Pershin, P. N., Krest'ianskie zemel'nye komitety v period podgotovki velikoi oktiabr'skoi sotsialisticheskoi revoliutsii, *Voprosy Istorii*, No. 7 (1948).

Pershin, P. N., *Agrarnaia revoliutsiia v Rossii*, 2 vols. (Moscow, 1966).

Pethybridge, R. W., 'The Significance of Communications in 1917,' *Soviet Studies*, XIX (1967).

Pethybridge, R. W., 'The Petrograd Soviet and the Centralist Issue,' *Government and Opposition*, V, 3 (1969–70).

Pethybridge, R. W., *The Spread of the Russian Revolution* (London, 1972).

Pipes, R., *Russia Under the Old Regime* (London, 1974).

'Podgotovka k nastupleniiu na Petrograd,' *Krasnyi Arkhiv*, T. 24 (1927).

Poletaev, V. E., and Tomashevich, Iu. U., 'Shire ispol'zovat' arkhivnye dokumenty pri izychenii istorii oktiabr'skoi revoliutsii,' *Voprosy Istorii*, No. 6 (1957).

Polner, T. J., Obolensky, V. A., and Turin, S. P., *Russian Local Government During the War and the Union of Zemstvos* (New Haven, 1930).

Povolzhskii, V., Pered oktiabrem i v oktiabre (Po kazan i kazanskoi gubernii),' *Proletarskaia Revoliutsiia*, No. 10 (1922).

'Prodovol'stvennoe polozhenie v moskve v marte – iiune 1917 goda (Po doneseniiam komissarov moskovskogo gradonachal'stva),' *Krasnyi Arkhiv*, T. 81 (1937).

Protokoly Tsentral'nogo komiteta RSDRP. Avgust 1917 – fevral' 1918 (Moscow-Leningrad, 1929).

Rabinowitch, A., *Prelude to Revolution. The Petrograd Bolsheviks and the July 1917 Uprising* (Bloomington, 1968).

Rabochee dvizhenie na fabrike Kenil v 1917g, *Krasnyi Arkhiv*, T. 58 (1933).

Radkey, O. H., *The Election to the Russian Constituent Assembly of 1917* (Cambridge (Mass.), 1950).

Radkey, O. H., 'Chernov and Agrarian Socialism Before 1918,' Simmons, E. J. (ed.), *Continuity and Change in Russian and Soviet Thought* (New York, 1955).

Radkey, O. H., *The Agrarian Foes of Bolshevism: Promise and Default of the Russian Socialist Revolutionaries, February–October 1917* (New York, 1958).

Remezova, T. A., Sovety krest'ianskikh deputatov v 1917g. *Istoricheskie zapiski*, T. 32 (1950).

Revoliutsiia 1917 goda. Khronika sobytii, 4 vols. (Moscow, 1923–24).

Revoliutsionnaia bor'ba krest'ian kazanskoi gubernii nakanune oktiabria (Kazan, 1958).

Rezunov, N., *Sel'skie sovety i zemel'nye obshchestva* (Moscow, 1928).

Rigby, T. H., *Communist Party Membership in the USSR. 1917–1967* (Princeton, 1968).

Robinson, G. T., *Rural Russia Under the Old Regime* (New York, 1961 (1932)).

Rosenberg, W. G., Russian Municipal Duma Elections of 1917: A Preliminary Computation of Returns, *Soviet Studies*, XXI (1969).

Rosenberg, W. G., *Liberals in the Russian Revolution. The Constitutional Democratic Party, 1917–1921* (Princeton, 1974).

Rozhkov, N. A., *Gorod i derevnia v russkoi istorii* (Moscow, 1922).

Rubach, M. A., 'Sotsial'naia struktura agrarnykh otnoshenii i klassovoe rassloenie krest'ianstva v ukrainskoi derevne k 1917g,' Dubrovskii, S. M. (ed.), *Osobennosti agrarnogo stroia Rossii v period imperializma* (Moscow, 1962).

Saburova, L. M., and Torzen, M. D., 'Sistemy zemledeliia i sel'skokhoziaistvennye kultury u russkikh krest'ian v seredine XIX – nachale XX, v'. Aleksandrov, V. A., *et al.* (eds.), *Russkie* (Moscow, 1967).

Sbornik tsirkularov' ministerstva vnutrennikh' del' za period Mart'-Iiun 1917 goda (Petrograd, 1917).

Schapiro, L., 'The Political Thought of the First Provisional Government,' Pipes, R. (ed.) *Revolutionary Russia: A symposium* (New York, 1969).

Sed'maia (aprel'skaia) vserossiiskaia konferentsiia RSDRP (bol'shevikov). Petrogradskaia obshchegorodskaia konferentsiia RSDRP (bol'shevikov). *Aprel' 1917 goda*. *Protokoly* (Moscow, 1958).

Sed'moi s'ezd Rossiiskoi Kommunisticheskoi Partii: stenograficheskii otchet. 6–8 marta 1918 goda (Moscow, 1923).

Selivanovskaia, L. A., Ekonomicheskoe polozhenie i sotsial'naia differentsiatsiia orenburgskogo kazachestva v kontse XIX–nachale XX v', Dubrovskii, S. M. (ed.), *Psobennosti agrarnogo stroia Rossii v period imperializma* (Moscow, 1962).

Semenov Tian-shanskii, V. P., 'Glavnyi zemel'nyi komitet', *'Arkhiv' russkoi revoliutsii*, XII (1923).

Shanin, T., *The Awkward Class. Political Sociology of Peasantry in a Developing Society: Russia 1910–1925* (Oxford, 1972).

Shestakov, A., Krest'ianskie organizatsii i pervyi s'ezd sovetov krest'ianskikh deputatov, *Proletarskaia Revoliutsiia*, No. 5 (64) (1927).

Shestakov, A., 'Iiul'skie dni v derevne,' *Proletarskaia Revoliutsiia*, No. 7. (66) (1927).

Shestakov, A., 'Oktiabr' v derevne,' *Proletarskaia Revoliutsiia*, No. 10 (69) (1927).

Shestakov, A. V., *Ocherki po sel'skomu khoziaistvu i krest'ianskomu dvizheniiu v gody voiny i pered oktiabrem 1917g* (Leningrad, 1927).

Shestakov, A. V., 'Krest'ianskie organizatsii v 1917 godu,' Miliutin, V. P. (ed.), *Agrarnaia revoliutsiia v chetyrekh tomakh. T: 2. Krest'ianskoe dvizhenie v 1917 godu* (Moscow, 1928).

Shestakov, A. V. (ed.), *Sovety krest'ianskikh deputatov i drugie krest'ianskie organizatsii*. T. I. Chasty I–II (Moscow, 1929).

Shestoi s'ezd RSDRP (bol'shevikov). Protokoly. Avgust 1917g (Moscow, 1958).

Shliapnikov, A., *Semnadtsatyi god. Kniga tret'ia* (Moscow, 1927).

Smirnov, A. S., Zemliacheskie organizatsii rabochikh i soldat v 1917g. *Istoricheskie zapiski*, T. 60 (1957).

Sobolev, G. L., Lenin o psikhologii revoliutsionnykh mass petrograda v 1917g, Fraiman, A. L. (ed.), *V. I. Lenin v Oktiabre i v pervye gody Sovetskoe vlasti* (Leningrad, 1970).

Soiuz zemel'nykh sobstvennikov v 1917 godu, *Krasnyi Arkhiv*, T. 21 (1927).

Stepanov, Z. V., Voprosy chislennosti i struktury rabochikh petrograda v 1917g, Mints, I. I. (ed.), *Rabochii klass i rabochee dvizhenie v Rossii v 1917g* (Moscow, 1964).

Stepanov, Z. V., *Rabochie petrograda v period podgotovki i provedeniia oktiabr'skogo vooruzhennogo vosstaniia* (Moscow–Leningrad, 1965).

Stepniak., *The Russian Peasantry* (London, 1888).

Stone, N., *The Eastern Front 1914–1917* (London, 1975).

Struve, P. B., Zaitsev, K. I., Dolinsky, N. V., and Demosthenov, S. S., *Food Supply in Russia During the World War* (New Haven, 1930).

Trotsky, L., *The History of the Russian Revolution* (London, 1967 (1932)).

Trukan, G. A., 'O nekotorykh voprosakh rabochego dvizheniia v tsentral'nom promyshlennom raione (fev.–okt. 1917),' Mints, I. I. (ed.), *Rabochii klass i rabochee dvzhenie v Rossii v 1917g* (Moscow, 1964).

'Tsentral'noe statisticheskoe upravleniia,' *Pogubernskie itogi vserossiiskoi sel'sko-khoziaistvennoi i pozemel'noi perepisi 1917 goda po 52 guberniiam i oblastiam* (Moscow, 1921).

'Tsentral'noe statisticheskoe upravleniia,' *Statisticheskii sbornik za 1913–1917 gg*, Vyp. I–II (Moscow, 1921–22).

Tsentrarkhiv, *Tsarskaia Rossiia v mirovoi voine*, T. 1. (Leningrad, 1925).

Tsereteli, I., 'Rossiiskoe krest'ianstvo i V. M. Chernov v 1917 godu, *Novyi Zhurnal*, 29 (1952).

Uldricks, T. J., 'The "Crowd" In the Russian Revolution: Towards Reassessing the Nature of Revolutionary Leadership,' *Politics and Society* (1974).

Velikaia oktiabr'skaia sotsialisticheskaia revoliutsiia. Khronika sobytii. Vols. 1–2 (Moscow, 1957–59).

'Verkhovnoe komandovanie v pervye dni revoliutsii,' *Krasnyi Arkhiv*, T. 5 (1924).

Verkhovskii, A. I., *Rossiia na golgofe. (Iz pokhodnago dnevnika 1914–1918g)* (Petrograd, 1918).

Vermenichev, I., Krest'ianskoe dvizhenie mezhdu fevral'skoi i oktiabr'skoi revoliutsiiami, Miliutin, V. P. (ed.), *Agrarnaia revoliutsiia v chetyrekh tomakh. T. 2. Krest'ianskoe dvizhenie v 1917 godu* (Moscow, 1928).

Volkonskii, S., *Moi vospominaniia. III. Rodina* (Berlin, N. D.).

Volobuev, P. B., *Ekonomicheskaia politika Vremennogo pravitel'stva* (Moscow, 1962).

Vrachev, I., 'Oktiabr'skaia revoliutsiia v Voronezhe (Zametka uchastnika)' *Proletarskaia Revoliutsiia*, No. 10 (33) (1924).

Vucinich, W. (ed.), *The Peasant in Nineteenth Century Russia* (Stanford, 1968).

Wade, R. A., 'The Rajonnye Sovety of Petrograd: The Role of Local Political Bodies in the Russian Revolution,' *Jahrbücher für Geschichte Osteuropas*, XX, 2 (1972).

Willetts, H., Lenin and the Peasants, Schapiro, L. B. and Reddaway, P. (eds.), *Lenin. The Man, the Theorist, the Leader* (London, 1967).

Willetts, H. T., The Agrarian Problem, Katkov, G. et al. (eds.), *Russia Enters the Twentieth Century. 1894–1917* (London, 1971).

Wolfe, E. R., *Peasant Wars of the Twentieth Century* (New York, 1969).

Zagorsky, S. O., *State Control of Industry in Russia During the War* (New Haven, 1928).

Zapiski A. I. Koz'mina (1917), *Krasnyi Arkhiv*, T. 60 (1933).

Zelenin', A. F., *Uchet' i prodovol'stvie* (Moscow, 1917).

2. NEWSPAPERS

Delo Naroda
Pravda
  Listok Pravdy
  Proletarii
  Rabochii
  Rabochii Put'
Torgovo-Promyshlennaia Gazeta
Vestnik Vremennago Pravitel'stva

3. UNPUBLISHED SOURCES

Archives de la Ministère de la Guerre. Vincennes. Missions militaires en Russie. Missions militaires en Roumanie.

Bonine, R. P., *The Russian Peasant and the Failure of Rural Government. March–October 1917*. Unpublished Ph.D. thesis (London University, 1960).

Mel'gunov Archives, Gruppa 2. Karton 1917g, British Library of Political and Economic Science.

Public Record Office, F. O. 371, 2995–3020.

Index